SEXUAL
Authenticity

SEXUAL
Authenticity

An Intimate
Reflection on
Homosexuality
and Catholicism

MELINDA SELMYS

Our Sunday Visitor Publishing Division
Our Sunday Visitor, Inc.
Huntington, Indiana 46750

Our Sunday Visitor Publishing Division
Our Sunday Visitor, Inc.
200 Noll Plaza
Huntington, IN 46750

1-800-348-2440
bookpermissions@osv.com

ISBN: 978-1-59276-493-8 (Inventory No. T732)
LCCN: 2009921231
Cover design by Lindsey Luken
Cover photo © Steve Bonini/Images.com
Interior design by Sherri L. Hoffman

PRINTED IN THE UNITED STATES OF AMERICA

Contents

Apology

I was going to open this book with an introduction, but I decided against it: an apology is much more appropriate.

There are two senses for this word. The first is the modern colloquial sense; to apologize is to say "I'm sorry" and ask forgiveness. The second is the philosophical sense, the sense in which Socrates' last dialog is an "Apology" and the defense of the Catholic Church is "apologetics." This is an apology in both senses.

I have been asked by several people what the thesis of this book is. I briefly considered opening with an essay about how the entire idea of a thesis is a socially constructed artifact of heteropatriarchy, but I decided against it. Too snide, too tongue-in-cheek, too clever. Still, I don't have a thesis. What I have, instead, is a method: this is a series of meditations, an essay in the sense of "an attempt," to try to overcome the general trend towards sterile, cross-purpose dialog between Christians and homosexuals on the subject of sexual morality. My goal is to create some sort of common ground on which a dialog could be had and then start trying to say something meaningful and, God willing, true. The fodder for these meditations is a combination of research, experience, and autobiography. My goal is threefold.

First, to produce a document that will help Christians to understand where homosexuals are coming from, so that they will not, armed with the best of intentions, drive people with same-sex attractions out of the Church.

Second, to explain the Catholic understanding of sexuality and homosexuality in a way that will not immediately alienate a homosexual reader, and that will dispel some of the stereotypes and misunderstandings about Christianity that are currently circulating through the secular world.

Finally, and in many ways most importantly, I am trying to understand this issue: what is it all about, what does it mean, what are its implications? In most cases, I have arrived at answers that I am satisfied with, but this is not always the case. Sometimes, the things that I would have liked to discover (because they would have dovetailed very nicely with my own presuppositions), turned out, as far as I could see, not to be true. This will no doubt earn me some enemies in the "home camp," fellow Christians who would really have liked for me to come out and say that homosexuality is definitely a psychological illness, or that everyone can become a heterosexual if they really try. I have not done this because I am confident that honesty will always, in the end, lead to truth, so I am not willing to deliberately fudge the data along the way.

Too often, Christians writing about homosexuality start their research at the NARTH Web site and end it with the Vatican's *On the Pastoral Care of Homosexual Persons*. They then rummage around at PFLAG trying to fish up some incriminating quotes to demonstrate their points. The result is writing that is extremely convincing to the "choir" and absolutely inaccessible to everyone else.

This has not been my approach. I have been very careful to keep my research balanced: if I have read a book of ex-gay testimonials, I have also a read the testimonials of ex-ex-gays. If I have read a study of conversion therapies, I have also read a study of young people discovering their same-sex identities. If I've looked at research conducted by Christian research collectives, I've also looked at research conducted by homosexual scientists. More importantly, I have looked at all of my sources with both a sympathetic and a critical eye. If I have encountered a source that seems to support my own views, but I think that the authors were hasty in jumping to conclusions, I will not rely on it. If I read an interview with a homosexual whom I do not like, I will not quote it. Every single homosexual researcher, writer, author, poet, or filmmaker whose words or work I reference in this book is someone whom I think I would like if I met them in person. (This was not hard to do — there was actually only one man, an openly proclaimed pederast, whom I met in my readings and disqualified on the basis that he made my skin crawl.) This, I think, is essential: you can't talk meaningfully about someone's ideas and experiences if you believe that they are stupid, ignorant, dishonest, or evil.

The first two sections of the book deal the issues as they appear in modern discourse, in the world, and in theory. Towards the end of the second part, and heading into the third, I will begin to put forward my own beliefs, to take a position instead of merely pointing out the flaws in other people's approaches. It may be tempting to skip to this point, but I would urge you not to: there is an old Buddhist story about a philosopher who came to see a Zen monk, seeking to learn about enlightenment. The monk asked him if he would like some tea, and when the philosopher said "Yes," the monk placed a full cup of tea in front of his guest, picked up the teapot, and proceeded to pour more tea into the already overflowing vessel. The point, of course, was that the philosopher could not learn Zen because his mind was already full of Hegel. In the case of homosexuality, the cup is full, the liquid in the cup is stale, and there have been so many conflicting beverages (false dichotomies, pseudo-dilemmas, miscommunications) poured into it that it is no longer safe to drink. The first two parts of this book are spent on emptying and scrubbing out the cup so that it can hold fresh tea.

The three latter sections, on the Human Person, Faith, and Identity, are the most personal — and with good reason. It is very easy to figure out what people think about homosexuality, and how they talk about it to others. It is simplicity itself to discover what homosexuals want the world to believe of them, or how the Christian right has tried to argue against gay marriage. But to penetrate the human heart is another matter. Real glimpses into the hearts and lives of other people are rare — though some of the interviews and memoirs that I have read certainly do go beyond the superficial elements of the issue and into the lived experience of men and women with same-sex attractions. For the most part, though, I am relying on my own introspective eye, and on very intimate conversations that I have had with close friends — conversations that have shaped my thinking and perspective, but which it is absolutely none of my business to reference or quote.

That said, I do not think that I have realized my goals perfectly. I have not been as sympathetic, or as charitable, or as honest as I should like to have been. For these lapses, I apologize, and I pray that you will be forgiving.

Notes on Language

If you couldn't care less what I call people with homosexual desires —
gays, queers, homos, homosexuals, persons with same-sex attractions,
sexual strugglers, fags, dykes, sodomites, Sapphics, practitioners of the
Grecian mode, androphiles, persons of alternative sexual identity, etc.,
etc., etc. — if it's all the same to you, provided I'm using more or less
intelligible English, you can safely skip this note. Otherwise, this is a
delicate matter that requires some clarification.

There is a tremendous amount of controversy over what to call
people who are attracted to members of their own sex. On both sides of
the left/right divide, there are words that touch a sore spot — and what,
exactly, these words are is intensely personal and subject to constant
revision. Twenty years ago, the word "queer" would have been an insult.
The word "gay" originally referred to prostitutes, "gay girls," and was
applied sneeringly to homosexuals. Who knows, perhaps in another
twenty years the word "fag" will have been reclaimed in much the same
way as the black community has reclaimed "nigger" and Mary Daly
has reclaimed "hag." Already "gay" is back on its way to ignonimity:
its standard use in schoolyard slurs ("That's so gay!") indicates that its
usefulness as a politically correct safe word is probably approaching an
end. No doubt in fifty years, if anyone bothers to pick up this book, they
will choke on the words "gay" and "lesbian" the same way that modern
readers choke on Chesterton's use of "Red Indian" — even though that
was the absolutely correct, nonracist usage at the time.

For some, there is a concern about using any kind of "identity label"
at all — a concern that crops up on both sides of the ideological fence.
Groups like Courage are concerned about using words that define people by their sexuality, while psychologists studying alternative sexual
trajectories are concerned about using words that restrict sexuality or
that isolate people into sexual ghettos. The solution proposed in this
case is to use a very clinical definition: to speak not of homosexuals,
but of homosexual persons or, if that is not sufficiently clear, "persons
with same-sex attractions," "persons with homoerotic inclinations,"
"gay- and lesbian-identified persons," and the like.

I am technically sympathetic to these concerns, but I don't share the
overwhelming desire for linguistic exactitude. When I hear someone

called a "cancer patient," I understand that this means a person suffering from cancer, not someone whose fundamental being is defined by their disease. When I use the word "redhead," I do not mean someone whose ontological dignity is contingent on the redness of their hair. I feel that it is clear enough, from what I say, and from the context of the book, that I do not intend the word "gay" as a fundamental identity category, but as a simple, relatively safe (and mercifully compact!) term for men who are attracted to men.

The real guiding principles behind my word choices in this work are aesthetic: if "person with same-sex attractions" fits well into the meter of a sentence, and is appropriate to the tone of a passage, I'll use it, but I'm not going to scruple about using the word "homosexual" if that's a better fit. After all, in a book of this length, it gets very tedious to be reading the same terminology over and over again, particularly if the terminology is clunky and inelegant. This is also, incidentally, the reason that I use "man" and "mankind" — I know perfectly well that these are andronormative words, but they are often euphonious in a way that "people" and "humankind" are not. I dearly hope that English will eventually develop an elegant solution to this problem, but until it does, I will choose poetic over ideological language in almost every case. I am, after all, a woman who eschewed painkillers the first three times she gave birth because they offended my sense of beauty. The fourth time, I was undone: they had changed the pain medication of choice in Ontario to morphine — a drug redolent with poetic and mythic associations. I was willing to suffer to avoid having something as ugly and prosaic as an epidural, but if you could have relief from pain without compromising aesthetics . . . well, that was a different matter.

For the same reason I generally use "he" in non-gender-specific contexts, because it is not awkward and doesn't draw attention to itself. Where it has seemed possible, however, to use "she" without crippling my sentences, I have done so.

Some words I generally avoid: fag, dyke, sodomite, etc. There are, however, a couple of contexts in which they crop up. If, for example, I am trying to convey the flavor of discourse in the fifteenth century, I may very well use "sodomite" — not because I think it's an accurate term, but because I know it is accurate to the period. Usually these usages are encased in quotation marks, but if they are not, the context should still be obvious. The other place that you may find them is in gay-slang compounds like "fag-hag" or "bulldyke." Here, obviously, they are intended colloquially.

The word "sodomy" demands a particular reference, because the left and the right have radically different understandings of what this word means. I actually had one reader tell me that he had never heard "sodomy" used to refer to consensual sex, and another say that he had never heard it used to imply rape. I would avoid the word altogether, except that when I am talking about sodomy laws or the story of Sodom, it becomes very difficult. Suffice it to say, historically, sodomy was any act of anal or oral sex involving a man and a partner of either gender (lesbian sex may or may not also be included, depending on time and place). In some jurisdictions it continues to hold this meaning as a legal term, used in laws that forbid homosexual acts. In modern usage, sodomy generally refers only to non-consensual anal rape. Generally, where I have had to use the word at all, the meaning should be clear from context.

When dealing with Christians who oppose homosexual sex, I have actually had to struggle with language more than when dealing with homosexuality itself. Here, there just is not any good terminology. If I say "Christians," I am implying that all those who call themselves Christians agree on the morality of same-sex relations, which is just not true. If I say, "Catholics," I have the same problem — plus, then I exclude those Protestants who agree with the Church's position. If I say "orthodox Christians," then people will think I'm talking about the Greek and Russian churches. If I say "right-wingers," I'm implying that everyone who is against gay unions also votes Republican (which is, at best, inaccurate). If I say "homophobes," or "bigots," or "Bible-thumpers," I'm demonizing and giving weight to stereotypes about Christians and Christianity. I even thought about coining a neologism: "pwogs" — people who oppose gay sex — but it sounded too stupid.

So what have I done? I've used all of the above, and as many other circumlocutions as my poor brain could cook up. You'll just have to accept that if I'm using the word "Christians" to refer to people who lobby against same-sex marriages, I mean "Christians who disagree with the morality of homosexual acts." If I use the term "religious right," with all of its negative connotations, it's not because I want to paint religious folks with a black brush but because I didn't have a better term on hand.

The words "left" and "right" often get used in the text to mean "pro-gay" and "anti-gay." This is a matter of convenience. I actually think that the left-to-right political scale is an appallingly weak way of describing people's beliefs, drawn up along the largely arbitrary lines of which special interests ended up in which big tent when political parties were bidding for the loyalties of the people. Consider, for example, a Muslim living in Toronto. She votes Liberal. Why? Because the Liberal party has a more open immigration policy and is less likely to send troops out to help bomb her homeland. Does this mean that she supports gay marriage and publicly-funded abortion? Probably not. Is she on the "left" or on the "right"?

A final matter is the "language of disease." When speaking about psychological theories and psychotherapy, this is almost impossible to avoid. You cannot discuss reparative therapies without using the word "therapy," and you cannot ask whether "cures" for homosexuality work without talking as if it were an illness. When I use these words, it is because I am working within the context of dialog that is drenched in the language of mental health. This language is often in radical contradiction to my own paradigmatic beliefs about the nature of man's interior reality, but it would be hackneyed and irritating if I were to constantly put these words in scare quotes or preface them each time with a contemptuous "so-called."

PART I

Homosexuality in the World

CHAPTER 1

Media

We're going to begin by playing a game. It is one that we all learned when we were children, and we were given a little tract of reading that contained some sort of error which we were supposed to ferret out. The game will go like this: I will tell a story. The story contains one very serious mistake. You get to read it and try to figure out what the mistake is.

Here we go:

It is the first day of Grade 6. A young girl walks into class, swaying childishly as she drags her hands along the rough painted bricks of the two-story building, a tactile habit that she acquired sometime in early childhood and which she will one day pass on, through the miracle of the genetic code, to her eldest daughter. She is dressed in a pioneer dress, believes that a certain tree in her elementary school playground has the capacity to stop time, and thinks of boys primarily as helpmates in the building of elfin forts. She knows nothing about sex except what was taught to her a year ago, in Grade 5, when the public health nurse revealed the mysteries of the human body through the medium of felt and Styrofoam pinned on two cartoonish nudes named Bernie and Bernice. That explanation, a dire prophecy of blood and body hair that was allowed to drop, casually and clinically, in between an exhortation to eat five servings of fruit and vegetables a day and an impassioned diatribe against the evils of coffee, frightened her. Bernie and Bernice are alienating and ugly. In them, the body that God has given to humankind — male and female — seems like a frightful caricature of the childish body that she has always known.

By the end of the year, she will understand how to recognize sexuality in a thousand different places, to understand the ways in which it is exploited and abused in order to make consumer products more appealing. She will know what rape is, and what to do if a stranger approaches her with a handful of candy. She will know that there are some people in the world who are more sexually attracted to their own sex than to the opposite sex, and that the world is crawling with 'homophobes' — backward Muslims and Christians who stone their children and drive them into the streets in irrational fear and hatred. Next year, they will teach her the efficacy rates of condoms, birth control pills, spermicidal jellies, and cervical caps. She will know what a vagina looks like when it has been infected with warts and pustules during an ill-advised bout of "unprotected" sex. The year after that, she will have her first boyfriend and her awkward, uncomfortable first kiss. She will also have her first girlfriend, her first girl-girl kiss, and she will begin the long process of trying to discern, understand, and label her sexuality.

By the time that this young girl enters high school, she is deeply involved in a lesbian relationship, but she is still conflicted. She accepts without the slightest hesitation that every person has a right to know and affirm their sexuality, whether it is heterosexual or homosexual. Still, she doesn't accept that she might be a lesbian. Surely there will be some boy, somewhere, who will eventually arrive and sweep her off into the dazzling realms of high-school normalcy. She will become popular. Ordinary. Accepted.

The pioneer dresses which always marked her as an outsider are gone, replaced by low-cut tops that she wears not because she wants to be a sexual object, but because she has the right to dress the way that she wants to dress. It disturbs her that construction workers whistle at her when she passes, and that creepy old men ogle her out of their car windows, so she joins feminist support groups, takes assertive communications courses, and screams, "Porn is the theory, rape is the practice" at sex-shop customers as she and her sisters "Take Back the Night." She realizes that popularity is for sellouts and losers and stops trying to "fit in." Now, in her mind, conformity is the opiate of the stupid, religion an ignorant excuse for heteropatriarchy. Although she now rejects labels as "confining," she thinks of herself as bisexual, though she doesn't share this information with her family or the boys that she occasionally dates. None of these attempts at heterosexual romance ever blossoms: she enjoys boys for their minds and for their conversation, which is usually more interesting than that of other girls her age, but whenever she dates them, they suddenly expect that the philosophical debate will be followed by necking in the park. She abhors the feeling of their lips on hers, and is terrified by the lurking threat of their sexual organs. The phallus is the ultimate symbol of male oppression. She doesn't want anything to do with it. She starts wondering if maybe she's a lesbian after all.

With God out of the picture, depression sets in. She wanders around in public parks (which serve as a poor substitute for Emily Bronte's brooding moors) and softly whispers John Keats' love poems to melancholia. Her same-sex lover, unable to break through the shell of her emotional imbalances, is forced to sit on the sidelines, frustrated and anxious, while our heroine slides further and further from the waking world. She becomes pale and specter-thin, uninterested in eating, unable to sleep. She takes to wearing black, prancing about in long dark skirts and a black cape, writing aimless works of Gothic fantasy on the banks of swelling springtime creeks. She thinks constantly of death. She doesn't think about her sexual orientation at all.

Summer comes and passes, and melancholy fades. She is older now, more self-possessed and motivated. A fledgling poetic Platonism has been quenched, and she no longer longs to escape her earthly vessel of clay into the wild, resplendent realm of blazing forms. Instead, social questions consume her. She runs presentations to educate bored ninth-grade students about the evils of wife abuse and homophobia, raises money for women's shelters, organizes one of the most successful fund-raising teams in her local AIDS walk. She searches for meaning in Sartre and Kant and becomes utterly scornful of supernatural claims. She is now firmly bisexual, and she and her girlfriend are discussing whether or not they ought to come out of the closet. Finally, in her last year of high school, their relationship is revealed to a select few friends — including this young girl's boyfriend. He knew — because they had agreed to it as two responsible adults — that theirs was an open relationship, but he didn't think that it was *this* open. Faced with the fact that he wanted something more, and with the frustration of feeling that he isn't allowed to object to a same-sex relationship without proving himself "homophobic," he enters into a months-long frenzy of emotional self-torture to which she is oblivious: she doesn't see it as her responsibility. Finally, he explodes, accuses her of emotional immaturity — and for the first time in her life, the word "lesbian" is flung at her as an insult. She considers it, rolls it around on her tongue a couple of times, and looks at the fuming, thwarted, would-be lover. What he says is true: she has never, not even once, done anything with him that she couldn't have done with a girl. The idea of touching him beneath the belt is appalling. It is not, as she has always told herself before, mere prudence — the desire not to get pregnant. Masculinity is repulsive. Lesbian, then, not bisexual. That must be who she is.

Having finally sorted out the mess of identity confusion, she comes out to her family. "Mom, sisters (not Dad), I'm gay." Mom is immediately worried that this means that she's been sexually active with her boyfriend and might be risking pregnancy and STDs. She is utterly confused: why would anyone think that a same-sex sexual identity necessarily implies heterosexual behavior? Nonetheless, Mom is supportive. Mom has seen *Philadelphia* and has friends at church with gay children. Still, sleepovers with the gay girlfriend will no longer be allowed.

"Coming out" is not the cathartic experience that it is supposed to have been. She scruples about whether or not she ought to come out to different groups of people: is she obligated to tell her boss at work that she's gay? She wouldn't tell him about her boyfriend if she had one. Or would she? She is confused again. Sartre has her convinced that authenticity is the hallmark of human freedom, and she doesn't want to be inauthentic. But does being authentic mean that you have to blurt out details of your personal life to everyone that you encounter? The question gets left on the back burner because more important philosophical waves are looming on the horizon. She has just met a young man who not only disapproves of homosexuality (sacrilege!), but also believes in the supernatural and fancies himself a Druid. Ordinarily, this would leave him dismissed and spat upon, placed in the same mental refuse heap as palm-readers and Baptist pastors — but this particular young man, apart from his inexcusable faults, is monumentally intelligent, astonishingly charming, and speaks like he just stepped out of a Shakespearean play. More invidious and terrible: she is unable to squash him in metaphysical debates. He asks her what her religious beliefs are, and she is too intimidated to admit that she is a staunch atheist. She stammers out something about beauty and agnosticism and he hands her a book: Thomas Merton's *Seven Storey Mountain*. She takes it, reads it, and sits in silence, stunned, while the walls of her atheistic tower crumble around her. God is back in the picture. What does this mean for her sexual self?

An epiphany. A revelation. The face of God in the image of Christ. She calls her girlfriend and says that it has to be over. God comes first. She has no idea that sexual orientation can be changed, but it doesn't matter. Chastity in union with the Cross will have to be enough. It doesn't even seem, particularly, like a sacrifice; a small part of her life exchanged for the love of God and life everlasting.

And yet, God intends to give even this little part back. Within less than a year, the impossible has happened: she has fallen deeply, permanently in love with a man. They are married, live in eternal bliss, and she brings forth children like a fruitful vine. Glory and beauty are restored to the world, and the birds sing forever in the cherry trees of life.

The End.

The gay or "straight-ally" reader will find about 750 mistakes in this story, while the Catholic reader is probably scratching her head: "What's wrong with it? It seems to me like a very nice testimonial. I suppose it gets a little sappy and improbable at the end. That must be the problem: she never struggles with her sexuality again. Yes. That's it, the war with temptation is too quickly won."

They're both wrong. There is only one mistake: *spin*.

The difficulty with autobiography is that it's an impossible task. The truth is in there, but to get it out on the page, unblemished, without framing, without choosing an angle, without glossing, airbrushing, editing . . . impossible. Every book ever written, every movie ever made, every personal testimony ever given, is subject to spin. Even a photograph is biased: the photographer must decide what he will leave out, and what he will leave in, and where he will set his F-stop and his focus.

The preceding is my testimony, heavily edited, distilled down until it is the perfect portrait of an ex-gay woman who has finally been saved by the love of Jesus. What follows is, I hope, something a little different. Let's call it a meditation: "On the meaning of sexuality, homosexuality, and love in the modern world."

But before we begin, I would like to take a look at what has been said, and shown, and glossed, and airbrushed, and framed, and focused, and edited together before I dragged my battered little soapbox onto this tired stage. We will begin with the most ubiquitous of charlatans and sham-artists: the media.

Chameleonic Stereotypes

The problem with truth in a media-mad world is that only activists and intellectuals have time for it. The evening news gives no more than five minutes of thought, and thirty seconds of airtime, to any given issue. The strategies, for those who wish to rouse the information-overloaded peasants, are twofold: reduce your message to a thirty-second sound clip, or deliver it to a captive audience. The latter is the more effective strategy, and the favorite audiences of the media-savvy are television viewers (duly bedazzled into a more receptive brain-wave state) and schoolchildren (who are generally disinclined to question the doctrines that are droned down at them day after day).

Whatever the message, it will be most effectively communicated through the use of images. Although people tend to process their immediate circle of acquaintances as rich, complete human beings, when it comes to others, they are more inclined to snatch at archetypal or stereotypical images to fill in the gaps in their knowledge.

Such images are the grist for every media mill, and they have shaped the debate over homosexuality ever since the television almighty began to pour its glory onto the hearts and minds of the American people. The gay community, understandably unimpressed with a plethora of demeaning stereotypes, has sought to find a solid image of itself to present to the public: one which will satisfy the heterosexual majority that "gay is okay," but which will also come close enough to the truth that homosexuals won't feel completely alienated from what straights believe them to be. The result is that "gay" has been repeatedly reinvented over the past decades, with a particular acceleration following the sexual revolution. An exuberant culture of sexual and artistic excess, gender-bending, and brightly colored leisure suits in the '70s turned into a staid nonentity during the conservative resurgence of the '80s. It emerged as a psychologically bloodied victim with holes in his arms and a noose around his neck in the '90s. Now, postmillennially, it is normal almost to the point of banality: the gays are the people in your neighborhood, as straitlaced and ordinary as Mr. Rogers.

Kirk and Madsen, whose book *After the Ball* details many of the strategies that were used to change America's mind about homosexual relations and same-sex-attracted people, wrote in the early '90s that "The Gay Revolution has failed."[1] What they meant was that the revolution of the Stonewall riots and the Village People had produced a short-term fascination with homosexual eccentricity amongst drug-using, sexually liberated youth, but did not lead to lasting tolerance or acceptance.

A new strategy was in order. According to Kirk and Madsen, "Gays must be portrayed as victims in need of protection so that straights will be inclined by reflex to adopt the role of protector."[2] If homosexuals were portrayed as innocent victims of circumstance, as explicit victims of violence and discrimination, as ordinary people living upstanding lives, and as a ubiquitous (*one in ten!*) part of American life, then straights would feel compelled to tolerate, accept, and perhaps even condone homosexual activity. The campaign worked like a charm, in spite of the fact that its orchestrators knew that some of their claims were dubious. *After the Ball* explicitly states that "for all practical purposes, gays should be considered to have been born gay — even though sexual orientation, for most humans, seems to be the product of a complex interaction between innate predispositions and environmental factors during childhood and early adolescence."[3] Simon LeVay, the researcher whose famous studies into the brain-structure of known homosexual cadavers added some weight to the biological interpretation of homosexuality, cites numerous studies that show that actual rates of homosexuality are much closer to the 1-5% range[4] (figures that are usually attributed to "right-wing homophobes" in mainstream discourse), and I have personally encountered a number of homosexuals who frankly advise their "straight allies" that the 10 percent figure is used only because it has media appeal.

Of course, those of us growing up in the shadow of the media campaign had no idea of the "spin" we were hearing. It was not just straight America but also homoerotic, same-sex-attracted, questioning, and confused America that heard the message blaring out of every media outlet we encountered. The message was simple: once gay, always gay. Homosexuality was an inborn, genetic trait that could not be tampered with. A gay or lesbian was a category of person who had, by dint of biological determination, to live out their same-sex sexuality or else deny an inalienable part of him- or herself. To try to be "straight," if "gay" was really who you were, was dishonest and inauthentic. It would lead to grief and heartbreak: you would end up either hating yourself and committing suicide, or divorcing your husband or wife and leaving behind a broken family. Homosexuality was not something that many people "experimented with" in adolescence and then "grew out of" — that was a myth. Ten percent of us were gay, and God help us if we didn't get it figured out before we signed up for a life of self-delusion and internalized homophobia that would eat like a corrosive acid at the foundations of our psyches.

Of course, things are not entirely the same for young people now grappling with same-sex attractions. In his book, *The New Gay Teenager*, researcher and psychologist Ritch Savin-Williams notes enthusiastically:

> Even as an avalanche of scientific reports about suicidal, depressed, HIV-risky, substance-abusing gay teens became ubiquitous, MTV's *Real World, Road Rules*, and *True Life* introduced us to healthy, resilient, attractive gay teens who are shown to have the same basic needs as all adolescents. If modeling affects behavior, there are plenty of models now available to teens. And these models confirm that attractive, athletic, popular, and desirable others can have same-sex attractions. A plurality of images, both real and fictitious, exist with which to match one's persona and desires.[5]

A plurality may exist — though it is the sort of plurality that infects all of modern culture, simply a plurality of types easily targeted by advertisers. This is not to finger the gay media, or to pour particular opprobrium on the heads of the producers of *Queer Eye* and *The L-Word*. The ubiquity of market-ready stereotypes in modern American culture emerged while there was still a relatively homogeneous image of homosexuality, and it would persist if gay-friendly media were stricken from the airwaves.

But it's no wonder that so many of the idealistic "old guard" of the gay movement are outraged by the current slate of available programming. They had hoped that homosexuals had a particular genius that they could bring to the world; that gays and lesbians would lead the charge of a glorious new future. They had hoped that homosexuality would turn out to be something greater than just another marketing niche — but a glance at the media images gives little hope of that.

The L-Word is a marketing executive's dream of lesbianism — every type is covered, and there is exactly one of each. The cast is just as unique, quirky, and varied as the Spice Girls. *Queer as Folk* (at least the American version) is exactly the same, except that the characters spend more screen time *having* sex than sitting in a coffee shop talking about it.

All of this suggests that everything that "backward, right-wing bigots" believe about homosexuality must be true: it is a culture obsessed with sex, lacking any sense of modesty or decency, with nothing to say for itself that isn't roughly pornographic. The problem is, I have never met a single homosexual person who conformed to this idea of homosexuality. It is the stuff of over-sexualized fantasy; it has as little to do with the real lives of gays and lesbians as *Desperate Housewives* has to do with the lives of stay-at-home moms.

The World in Uniform

The situation isn't much better on the Christian/right-wing side of the media fence. At the furthest extreme, there is real homophobia: lesbians who gang up to rape straight girls in school washrooms, or gays lurking in closets and playgrounds, waiting to swoop down and seduce or murder your unsuspecting children. They may look sissy and prissy on the outside, but behind the drag-queen façade lurks a puny, frustrated Emperor Caligula, frothing at the mouth with sexual-sadistic rage. Slightly closer to sanity, you find the cowards and effeminates: fat, milky-white blobules of human sludge splashing around in Roman baths, making eyes at dewy-faced boys while their men are slaughtered in the battlefield beyond. At last, on the cusp of compassion, the vicious gay villain gets replaced with a pitiful, confused teenager who pops pills in a desperate attempt to fill his father-wound, and — at the last moment, when the knife is on the vein — is saved by the love of Jesus and the miraculous intervention of angels.

The problem with all of these portrayals, whether on the right or on the left, is that they are more about making a point than portraying reality. Whether we are watching heterosexuals laugh like gape-mouthed idiots at the come-ons of their homosexual betters on *Queer Eye for the Straight Guy*, or cheering as the Prince's princessy boyfriend is pushed out of the tower window, we are imbibing propaganda. The gay-as-villain portrayals are just as unconvincing as a James Bond baddy; the gay-as-ordinary-Joe icons are bland as unsalted oatmeal; the gay-as-pathetic-victim images are condescending and oversimplistic. But this is what everyone — from the gay-rights advocates to the right-wing preachers to the television executives with their eyes on the bankroll — wants. People are messy, difficult to predict, difficult to direct, difficult to portray. Better to keep it simple; one character, one emotion, one dimension. Put everyone — all the gays, all the lesbians, all the Christians, and all the Muslims — into a couple of convenient, color-coded uniforms. Otherwise, the culture war would become terribly confusing. After all, at the end of the day, the purpose of the media is not to inform or enlighten, but to deliver the appropriate messages to the appropriate camps so that everyone has a clear notion of who the enemy is, and where they are supposed to go to fight.

CHAPTER 2

Politics

There are times when I look at the "culture wars" and wonder how it is that this is what became of the Gospel. I suppose I shouldn't be surprised: it's been this way since Peter pulled out his sword in the garden of Gethsemane and cut the ear off the high priest's servant. Somewhere in the heart of every man is the desire to stand up and fight for what he believes in, and to see the enemies of his ideal mown down like fresh hay on a summer's morning. It is a desire that Christ referred to when He was called to the portico of Pontius Pilate to answer the Roman prelate's inquiries. Pilate, it seems, had one primary concern: he wanted the turbulent political situation in Judea to remain stable, so he wanted to make sure that Jesus of Nazareth wasn't a fiery Judas Maccabeus wannabe who thought that He and His band of followers were going to oust the Roman legions from Jewish soil. Not that Pilate was afraid of some Jewish carpenter from Galilee; but riots are riots, and he didn't want any trouble. Christ, perhaps thinking of Peter with his little sword against the heavily armed servants of Caiaphas, explains to Pilate:

> "My kingship is not of this world; if my kingship were of this
> world, my servants would fight, that I might not be handed over
> to the Jews; but my kingship is not from the world" (cf. Jn. 18).

It is easy to forget this. How many times have I argued with an atheist, a feminist, or a Protestant, when I really just wanted their intellectual scalp as a trophy to hang on my wall? I know well the temptation to use the witty jibe that rises in my thoughts at just the wrong moment, to show off how clever I am, to win the argument instead of winning their soul. It is a serious error. No one wants to bend the knee before Christ when the crusader for the Heavenly Kingdom is robed in self-satisfaction, stroking his own ego with Thomistic proofs, and perching smugly on the summit of the moral high ground.

Christ's kingdom is not here, and it is not now. It cannot be brought about by the Founding Fathers and the Constitution any more than it can be brought about by *Das Kapital* and *The Communist Manifesto.* This is a point that must be understood and accepted before any useful thought about the nature of the conflict can begin.

The Tragedy of Being Gay

The "culture war" mind-set makes enemy combatants of other human beings. How many times have we heard allegedly religious pundits crowing triumphantly over the AIDS crisis? "God's fire finally falls on Sodom! The justice of the Lord is at hand! Hurrah!" Never mind that the knell of AIDS is seen most vividly in the heart of Africa, where it wreaks indiscriminate havoc on the lives of faithful wives and innocent children.

The culture wars also make cannon-fodder of one's own "troops." Kirk and Madsen, in their media manifesto *After the Ball*, ponder the pros and cons of the disease:

> The AIDS epidemic — ever a curse and a boon for the gay movement — provides ample opportunity to emphasize the civil rights/discrimination side of things, but unfortunately it also permits our enemies to draw attention to gay sex habits that provoke public revulsion."[6]

Aw, shucks. Why can't we have a more convenient epidemic that would allow the gay-rights movement to garner sympathy for dying homosexuals without causing public embarrassment?

The issue of AIDS is the most striking example of this sort of inhuman calculus, but the same thing is true of many elements of the lives of the same-sex-attracted. If some homosexual kid, for whatever reason, feels compelled to take his own life, he can be sure that he won't die in vain: the Christian right and the gay left will be there at the graveside playing tug-of-war over his private tragedy. On one side of his tombstone the inscription reads, "Here lies John, his untimely end was hastened because no Straight would be his friend," and on the other, "John: another victim of sin, when Sodomy is sanctioned, nobody wins."

The queer activists and televangelists aren't the only ones with their fingers stuck in the morbid pie of gay suicide. There are also the psychologists and social workers; as Savin-Williams points out, "Well-adjusted gay teens present problems for those applying for problem-focused research grants and for the need, as one critic put it, to 'manufacture victims for the psychology industry.'"[7] A quick glance at the payroll of a modern high school is sufficient to show a tremendous increase, over the past twenty years, in the number of professional counselors and social workers employed by schools. They are justified by the notion that youth is in crisis — and no youth more than gay youth.

There is nothing wrong with counselors. The difficulty arises when there is an underlying belief that all suffering and evil is the result of social forces, and thus preventable by social means. Counselors and youth workers will then multiply, not to fit the needs of youth but to fit the desire of the social engineers to see this or that evil erased from public life. Outside of this worldview, on the terrifying borders of reality, is the specter of free will; the possibility that some young people drop out of school because they *choose* to drop out, or that suicidal children might *decide* not to seek the help offered in antidepressant ads. The refusal to acknowledge this radical implication of human volition is an eternal, unavoidable frustration within organizations that seek to eradicate child poverty, wife abuse, economic injustice, violence, or any of the other evils that have plagued society since Cain struck down his brother. So long as there is a single annual gun death in Toronto, there must be a need for more restrictive gun laws. If a single child is killed by her parents, it must be because the system wasn't watching vigilantly enough. Underneath all of this is the delusion that if only we had enough social workers, human evil would be eradicated.

When this ideology is applied to the question of suicide, and of gay suicide in particular, its consequences are terrifying. Young people with same-sex attractions cease to be responsible for choosing to embrace and live their lives. If they are suicidal, it is not because of their choices, but because of the homophobia of their surrounding society. They are just hapless victims tossed on the waves of a social tempest.

The greatest losers in this scenario are those who are supposed to be the beneficiaries: same-sex-attracted youth. Savin-Williams notes that those who are "out," proud, and self-identified as gay or lesbian are the most likely to be suicidal, to abuse drugs, and so forth than their "non-identifying" or "closeted" compatriots.[8] I think at least part of the reason for this is that there is a script for gay suicide among youth, which those who identify as gay are likely to encounter with greater frequency and to choose to incorporate into their personal narrative. I know that when I was young, depressed, and contemplating self-slaughter, the "suicide prevention" lectures were certainly no help. From them, I learned the correct way of slitting my wrists, and that my only hope was to traipse off to the guidance office, bare the recesses of my soul to a flaky, middle-aged woman like the one hosting the series, and put myself on happy pills. I recall sitting in the back of the auditorium, with my black skirts swirling around me like a pool, ruminating on the cluelessness of the people who had arranged the lecture series. Their understanding of *my* psychology, I concluded, was utterly puerile.

I also learned — dangerous realization — that suicidal impulses are *normal* among young people, and that youth who commit suicide are not to blame. Hamlet's moral twisting and turnings were not to be the rubric for our feelings of depression, our unwillingness to "suffer the slings and arrows of outrageous fortune." We were being groomed, with all the best intentions, into a mournful herd of senseless, blameless Ophelias: tragic victims of a tragic end who, by our own hands, would execute society's witless slaughter of the innocents.

It is because of this that I am exceedingly wary of attempts to put the onus for gay suicide on "heterosexist" culture. There are difficulties in proving that there are elevated gay suicides in the first place,[9] but it really doesn't matter whether there are, or not. What matters is that it is not in the interest of any teen-ager — gay, straight, transsexual, or non-sexually-identifying — to be told that suicide is a natural reaction to their reality. I have struggled with depression and suicidal temptations since youth; the removal of moral culpability has never been a help and a comfort when I am working through feelings of inadequacy and self-hatred. On the contrary, more than once, the only thing that kept me from taking my own life was a feeling that I was profoundly culpable, that I was responsible to the people who would suffer for my decision. To be able to say, "It's not my fault, I had no choice, too much was expected of me, society made me do it" has only ever helped make it easier to entertain thoughts of self-annihilation.

Coming Out in the Trenches

Being a teenager is difficult — so much so that most societies have never asked this of their children. The long (and ever-lengthening) years of existential confusion, the smorgasbord of perplexing and largely unappealing life options, the awakening of sexual impulses whose proper use will be postponed for at least ten years, the pressure to succeed in becoming "educated" — in the narrow sense of doing well in mind-numbingly boring classes — the frustrated feeling of never being allowed to make decisions more relevant than whether to declare fealty to Coke or to Pepsi . . . these are products of a society that has done away with its rites of initiation. If a child belongs to an old-world religion, or has a cultural background that their parents trundled along into this Brave New World like a broken suitcase, then there will be some sort of ceremony: a bar mitzvah or a confirmation. But the idea that these represent any genuine change, much less that they are the threshold of adult life, is utterly absurd in our present culture. Life after the ritual goes on exactly the same as before; for most young people, the experience is just another excuse to get presents and eat cake with the relatives.

In such a vacuum, young people must invent their own "coming of age" rituals, or else flounder along in an eternal twilight between childhood and adult life. Many spend years meandering through different courses in universities, toying with different life goals, running through the same "high-school relationship" rubric over and over, until they are well into their twenties or thirties. If we consider the self-fulfilling prophecies of television, we can expect this to intensify: the characters in *Friends, Seinfeld, Will and Grace,* and other sitcoms continue in this perpetual adolescence until they develop bald spots.

The gay community, with perfect intuition, has realized that it must provide its members with the opportunity to seize adulthood and claim the right to self-determination if they are going to carry adolescent homosexual longings forward into a fully realized homosexual identity and homoerotic life. (I am not implying any machinations here; this is not done to artificially cement homosexuality in the lives of young people. Past generations remember being young, confused, and adrift in a "heterosexual world" and are trying to pass on what they have learned.) The entrance ritual into gay adulthood is the rite of Coming Out.

When a young person "comes out of the closet," she sets herself up as the arbiter of her own destiny. By openly declaring her homosexuality, she becomes disentangled from the silent expectations of her parents and the multitude of contradictory pressures that come into her life from outside. Mom and Dad no longer understand what is best for her and are no longer authorized to make decisions in her stead; what is good and right for a heterosexual child is not necessarily right for her.

This, I think, is why "coming out" is such a cathartic and pivotal experience in the lives of some same-sex-attracted individuals and such a spectacular nonevent in the lives of others. Jack Malebranche (a homosexual writer who despises "gays," instead styling himself as an "androphile") writes:

> Coming out wasn't a trying, emotionally cathartic pivotal point in my life that freed me to be who I really was; if anything, I remember feeling inconvenienced by having to address it as if it were some "big deal."[10]

I also found it a slightly irritating imposition. My girlfriend, when she went off to University, wanted to claim her own status as a bisexual woman. It was hardly going to be believable if she did so solo. We had been sharing the same bed every weekend for years, and there were no other significant candidates for the role of same-sex lover in her life. If she came out, I was coming out too.

I had already made my bid on adulthood — I did it at thirteen. I was supposed to get confirmed in the Anglican church. My mother had explained to me that after Confirmation, I would be an adult in my faith life; I would be responsible for my Christianity, for whether I went to church on Sunday, and for defining my beliefs. As a burgeoning young atheist, I found it absurd that I had to begin my adult intellectual life by declaring, as my first truly responsible adult promise, that I believed in God the Father almighty, and in Jesus Christ, His only Son, our Lord. So while my peers were listening to lectures about the gifts of the Spirit, I was fighting a battle with my mother about whether I had to get confirmed at all. The engagements took place every Sunday, at ten o'clock, when the family was piling into the van to go to church. Some weeks I won and got to stay home without adult supervision. Some weeks I lost and was dragged off to sit in a pew and amuse myself with that age-old juvenile atheist pastime of trying to read sexual innuendos into the words of the hymnal. The war lasted for a year, at the end of which I was victorious. I still had to accompany the family to church for the usual holidays, but otherwise I was free to believe what I chose and to act on those beliefs in whatever way I thought best.

Having gained my intellectual adulthood, I didn't see any reason why I needed to separately claim a sexual label: bisexual, lesbian, whatever I was. Time and time again I was told that I ought to come out of the closet, that it would be a liberating experience, and I would be able to join the great, triumphal march of gaydom. I even participated in preaching this gospel to others: I was one of those staunch feminist warrior-girls who march onto high-school stages in September to terrorize the newly arrived freshmen into accepting liberal orthodoxy. We paraded around the gym in the uniform of the battered wife (it was always, unfortunately, necessary to get another girl to play the monstrous and semi-deformed "abusive husband" — for some reason the boys just weren't interested in the part); we cannonaded the younger classes with statistics about rape and violence against women; and, inevitably, we made the occasional foray onto the battlefields of abortion rights and gay issues. I had all the stripes of a veteran of the "coming-out" wars, but I had never actually stepped into the fray. I was still sitting comfortably in the closet, sending out radio broadcasts to other young homosexuals, encouraging them to take up the standard and march stolidly forward into the front lines of the war.

Perhaps if the threat had seemed more grave, I would have taken up arms sooner. The problem was that the enemy never quite seemed to appear. We sent volleys off into the darkness, and shouted down the demons of patriarchy and homophobia, and beat our braless chests, and touched up our never-tested-on-animals war paint — then stood, defiant against the legions of social conservativism and religious tyranny, waiting for a battle that never commenced. The only glimpse of the enemy we ever got was their Red Cross brigades bringing us prayers and medical supplies in case someone was wounded by friendly fire in the long, breathless hours of the night. Occasionally there was a casualty — it would be whispered that someone had been sexually assaulted, or a girl would fall in the lines as a result of anorexia — but on the whole, we found ourselves with no one to fight.

I am not alone in feeling this. Savin-Williams notes that the lives of the young same-sex-attracted individuals that he interviewed are relatively normal and free from homophobic harassment.[11] A friend of mine, who was much more closely involved with the gay support-group political scene when he was a teenager, described a rift between "old guard" gays and the younger generation. Most of the young people who had flocked to the local chapter of the Lesbian-Gay-Bisexual-Transgendered Coalition were just there to make friends and pick up: they were no longer interested in snapping up their rainbow flags and marching out to die for the cause.

Malebranche caustically describes the "true product of The Gay Advocacy Industry" as "the illusion of oppression and victimization." According to him:

> The Gay Advocacy Industry's biggest enemy is not the wicked Religious Right, it is the possibility that same-sex-oriented people don't really need them for anything. If homos don't feel victimized or oppressed, they'll stop writing all those checks.[12]

This, I think, is uncharitable. Certainly people who have made their life and livelihood as crusaders for some cause — whether gay rights, feminism, socialism, or the protection of urban pigeons — will find it difficult to relinquish their salary once the war has been won. They may also have motives beyond the merely pecuniary: they may enjoy the fight, or they may have invested themselves so deeply they can't imagine life beyond victory. In most cases, though, I think they continue to fight because the war *they* are fighting has not been won.

The dead horse of heteropatriarchy is still being flogged because the people flogging it believe that its death will bring about a brave new world — and as the brave new world is not here, the horse must not be dead. They want to eliminate gender, or establish the Holy Orders of sex throughout the world, or form a neo-Grecian paradise in which women can be utterly ignored by "lovers of men." This is what causes the conservative, pro-family types to take up arms: they see that there are homosexuals everywhere, and they assume that most gays want to see the womb replaced by reproductive machines and sex with boys made legal. There is, however, always a divide between the activist and the people on whose behalf they agitate; most women do not desire radical feminism, and gay activists do not accurately represent the thinking of most homosexuals. Most homosexuals would like to see some changes in society, but mostly they want certain basic rights in common with everyone else: the right to housing, jobs, protection from abuse, privacy, and so forth. Most lesbians that I have spoken to would like to see a feminizing of political systems as well — women and men represented in equal numbers, working together in a political culture that is equally advantageous to both sexes.

These are the priorities of most gays and lesbians; this is the reason that the new generation of same-sex-attracted young people are less interested in marching, screaming, protesting, lobbying, parading, and sending checks to gay-rights organizations. The next major battle is for gay marriage, but, as Savin-Williams notes:

> Gay people both detest and long for marriage . . . [On the one hand] Getting married is selling out to heterosexuality. Others want marriage because it represents true equality.[13]

In any case, many feel that the important battles have already been fought and won. They can hold hands with their same-sex lovers and no one will come along and lynch them in the park; they can safely tell everyone at work whom they are living with; they can move into an apartment together, go out for supper at a respectable restaurant, and talk about their sex lives in coffee shops without fear of being put out on the street or locked up in the local jail. They're sick of the Democrats and Republicans sitting around the foot of their cross throwing dice to see which party gets dibs on their torn and bloodied coat. They no longer want to see their suicides and their diseases dragged like a sad black balloon across the headlines of the local newspapers. They want to be left alone, to live their own lives, just like everybody else.

CHAPTER 3

History

Those who do not know their history are doomed to repeat it. I don't know who said this first, but every child is taught this idea (in various words) by the same social science teachers who fail to teach them history. Whether the repetitiveness of human experience could be held at bay by bulwarks of good historical catechesis, I do not know. If the experiment is going to be tried, it will not be tried by my generation. Most of us cannot find modern-day Iraq on a map, or say exactly what caused George Bush, Sr., to march into that country a decade and a half ago. Ask us how we feel the rise and fall of civilizations in ancient Mesopotamia affects the current situation in the Middle East and we will sink back into an iPod-induced catatonia. Mesopotamia? Sounds like a Japanese hippopotamus soup. Never heard of it.

The Myth of Sexual Progress

At the heart of the modern young person's understanding of history is a vague, fluffy feeling that everything is getting better over time. Oh, it's difficult, certainly. People have had to fight to get anti-Semitism, male privilege, racism, and homophobia stricken from the human record, but it has been done. Nowadays everyone believes that homosexuality is a tolerable, if not laudable, form of human sexual desire — everyone except for a few old white men who will soon be dead and forgotten. Everyone else is pro-gay. Well, everyone who counts.

There are always the Muslims. But the Muslims are backward in general, and we only need to ship a few more thousand troops to the Middle East to shut down Islamofascist terrorist cells and get rid of oppressive religious regimes. Hand out a bit of free contraception, send the chicks to school, and build a couple of McDonald's restaurants in Baghdad. They'll come around.

Oh, but then, there are also the Chinese. The official position of the Chinese Communist party is that homosexuality does not exist in China because it is a consequence of Capitalist excess, and therefore nonexistent in the People's Republic.[14] Fortunately, the Chinese are becoming a more modern and open society. I heard somewhere that they've got the Internet now and that their economy is booming since they opened up trade. They're quickly becoming capitalists. Within a couple of years, they'll have a real democracy as well; besides, a lot of Chinese people really liked *Brokeback Mountain*.

And then, there's India. In India, the old British Law Codes are still largely in force, and the average Indian looks on homosexuality as an unnatural vice . . . and most Latinos still think that passive homosexual sex deprives you of your masculinity[15] . . . and same-sex-attracted African-Americans are more likely to go "on the Down Low" than to embrace an openly gay identity.[16]

Okay. So only the Great White West really believes that homosexuality is equal to heterosexuality, but eventually all of those backward savages are going to catch up with us. It's practically inevitable.

Putting aside my sarcastic disdain for the presumption that modern Western culture is "more developed" than all of the other cultures of the world, let's examine this idea that there is a natural historical progression away from "homophobia" towards toleration and acceptance. It might surprise the average reader to discover that Mahatma Gandhi (who was opposed to homosexuality) felt that this "unnatural vice" was encouraged by the Mughal Muslim rulers who ruled India from the sixteenth to the eighteenth century:

> In Islamic Sufi literature homosexual eroticism was used as a metaphorical expression of the spiritual relationship between God and man, and much Persian poetry and fiction used homosexual relationships as examples of moral love. Although the Quran and early religious writings display mildly negative attitudes towards homosexuality, Muslim cultures seemed to treat homosexuality with indifference, if not admiration.[17]

So those "backwards" Muslims were celebrating homoeroticism in verse, and practicing it at court, while the West was still burning homosexuals at the stake. Once upon a time, Chinese Emperors openly kept harems of boys as well as of wives. The first modern sexological institute, and the world's first vigorous "gay rights" movement, were formed in Germany just decades before the Nazis started shipping homosexuals off to concentration camps. Anyone who actually believes Stephen Colbert's quip that "Reality has a well-known liberal bias" is either hopelessly deluded or has not read history.

There is not one jot of evidence to support the idea that, over time, there is a general trend towards the acceptance of homosexuality. The theory, occasionally put forth by ill-educated homosexual activists — that man is evolving from apelike hatred of anything different towards an enlightened inclusivity — is utter balderdash. History does not support the theory that we are progressing towards a golden dawn, crawling up out of the primeval slime of cave-dwelling violence towards some future day when, under the aegis of the great goddess Progress, all will join hands, sing in harmony, and heal the world. There are places in India where people today are peeing into the river, but 5,000 years ago they had sophisticated sewer systems. There are wonders in the ancient world — the Great Pyramid comes to mind — that we do not know how they built. Rome had piston-powered water pumps for fighting fires — a technology that vanished from Europe for over 1,000 years, until it was reinvented in the eighteenth and nineteenth centuries. "Primitive" peoples in ancient Peru made massive mounded designs on the ground that can only be properly viewed by aircraft. The list could be multiplied to fill several volumes, but I will stop here. The point is, Hegel was wrong.

There is another theory: that culturally advanced civilizations in any time will accept homosexuality, while those that are less advanced will despise it. Again, the evidence is lacking. Rome, one of the most advanced ancient cultures, had, perhaps the most primitive (in the sense of being "like primates") understanding of homosexuality: it was acceptable for Roman noblemen to make use of their male slaves and inferiors, just as it is acceptable for the alpha male of a gorilla tribe to establish his dominance by forcing himself on lesser males — but passive homosexuality was seen as a devirilizing humiliation. While the rest of the West had slipped into the dark ages, Byzantine civilization flourished — but its famous "Code of Justinian" showed unprecedented harshness towards practicing homosexuals. On the other hand, anthropologists have found evidence of homosexuality (particularly homosexual sex used as an element of religious worship) in cultures that are comparatively primitive. Some of the New World peoples who lived simple, subsistence-style lives in the forests of North America had a concept of the "two-spirited" — certain people were considered to have both a male and a female spirit, and were often married to someone of the same sex. There are Sambian tribes that believe that a boy cannot become a man unless he drinks "the milk of manhood" from an older male.[18] So, the state of technological, legal, artistic, philosophical, architectural, and religious advancement shown by a culture does not determine its attitudes towards same-sex liaisons.

The Rise and Decline of Sodom and Gomorrah

A further theory, often put forward by opponents of homosexuality, is the theory of "decadence." Societies on the verge of collapse first sink into a mire of unmitigated and disgusting vice, of which, naturally, homosexuality is an essential component. Such a theory dovetails very nicely with the interpretation of the Sodom and Gomorrah story generally circulated by the "Religious Right." Societies rise to decadence, start practicing the "abominable vice of sodomy," and then are burnt to cinders by the Lord God of Israel. A very neat tale.

This, too, is historically problematic. Societies rise, decline, depress, get up again, wane, wax, totter, and eventually fall — not necessarily in that order, though obviously, the rising happens at the beginning, and the falling at the end. We like to think that the abandonment of sexual morality heralds the end, largely because such an interpretation allows us to sit on the mountain outside of Babylon, like Jonah under his leaf, twiddling our thumbs in anticipation as we wait for fire and brimstone to fall from heaven and destroy the infidels. But unless you are reading a historian who assumes the decadence theory from the outset, the trend is far from clear.

Did the Goths succeed in sacking Rome because the citizens had become lax and self-indulgent, or because they were overtaxed, or because the resources of the Empire had been transferred to Constantinople? Did writers at that time see a spike in homoeroticism and sexual excesses, unlike any seen in the glory days of Rome? Given the record of Tiberius and Caligula, it hardly seems likely. Or did certain writers at that time blame the sack of Rome on the abandonment of Roman morals, in much the same way as certain commentators have likened the fall of the Two Towers to the collapse of the Tower of Babel?

This is not to say that I do not believe that societies suffer for their sins, or even that they do not suffer for their sexual sins. It is merely that I think that other matters can be weightier than homosexuality in determining the fate of nations. Warmongering, excess of greed, abandonment of orphans and widows, cowardice under tyranny, and a generalized willingness to place one's own gain before the good of society, are all excellent starting places for the downfall of a civilization. It is pride, not lust, which goeth before the fall (cf. Prov. 16:18).

Doctrinally orthodox Christians constantly whine that liberal Christians are obsessed with social justice and ignore personal virtue — which is largely true. It is equally true that orthodox Christians often turn up their noses at social justice issues just because they don't want to stand toe-to-toe with the bloody liberals. There is a kind of childishness here: "I'm not going to give money to your Wells for Nigeria fund-raiser because you waved around a stupid-looking piece of blue gauze during the liturgy, and you're probably sleeping with your boyfriend out of wedlock." Both sides are equally stuck in a debate that can have no winner — trying to assert that *your* sins are abominable and going to bring about the end of the world, while *my* sins are small and easily forgiven. The reality is that we are both wrong: the sins of the world and the sins of the flesh are both sins, and God's forgiveness is for everyone. We might reflect, though, that Christ probably finds it as easy to forgive the homosexual as the prostitute and the publican, while the Pharisee and the Scribe always bore the most withering criticisms from His lips.

The Sins of Christendom

I would like to be able to say, in unison with other Christian commentators, that homosexuals need Catholicism to protect them from the caprices of the secular world. The argument is nice in theory. It runs like this: "Christians will love homosexual *people* even if homosexuality ceases to be popularly accepted. Those who accept homosexual people only because they accept homosexuality will quickly start lighting funeral pyres again when homosexuality falls out of vogue." Sadly, there is no historical evidence to support this idea. Christians (and particularly, Catholics) have not proven particularly effective in championing the rights of their same-sex-attracted neighbors against tyrants who stone them outside the gates or treat them with nerve gas. This must be admitted, and we must — if we wish our protestations of charity to be taken seriously by the gay community — apologize for it.

The history of the Church is muddied, especially during the Middle Ages, because it is also the history of Christendom. These two things are nearly inextricable, but they are fundamentally different entities. The Church is the living legacy which Christ left behind to carry on His work; Christendom was a political system which men created in the hopes that, despite His precautions that His kingdom was not of this world, they would be able to establish a lasting Christian kingdom on Earth. I am not saying that Christendom was fundamentally evil, or that Christ would have spit it out of His mouth. It was a good idea; flawed, never perfectly realized, subject to abuse, and always at risk of descending into tyranny — which, like all political systems, it did many times.

Christendom was naturally inclined to legislate Christian morality. All too often, this was done without recourse to Christian charity, and with a certain myopia towards the sins that were most common among the ruling classes: avarice, ambition, violence, and so forth. Homosexuality often proved a useful political excuse for seizing the goods of more or less harmless citizens, or for eliminating political opponents. The Emperor Justinian, according to the *Secret History* of his court historian, Procopius, used dubious allegations of sodomy as an excuse to castrate "those reputed to be Greens* or to be possessed of great wealth or those who in some other way chanced to have offended the rulers."[19] During the Inquisition, those who judged or accused a

---

* The Greens were one of the political parties, named for their allegiance to the colors of certain chariot-racing teams, that existed in Byzantium at the time. Apparently, Justinian was ill-disposed towards the Greens.

heretic or sodomite would often become entitled to the property of the convicted, providing a powerful financial incentive for the unscrupulous to bear false witness against their neighbors. Philip IV of France used such laws to the fullest possible advantage when he accused the Templar Knights, to whom he owed a great deal of money, of both heresy and sodomy. Under torture, many of the Knights confessed, but these confessions tended to be retracted the moment the burning coals were no longer on the feet.[20]

Accusations of sodomy were exceedingly difficult to disprove, and never failed to inspire a certain kind of sanctimonious disgust amongst the pious. Add to this the fears that constantly plague societies, and the powerful Sodom and Gomorrah rhetoric that cast homosexuals as the enemy living in the midst of good men and women, threatening their cities with destruction and ruin, and you had a fairly potent recipe for tortures and pilloryings.

The Specter of Guilt

There is a temptation to imagine that the world has grown out of these childish phobias. Only the backward hick-prophets of the religious right are supposed to still fester in such ignorance. This is an ill-supported assumption. Fear is still capable of inducing rational individuals to accept the paranoid delusion that the enemy is here, circulating amongst us, and that if they are not caught, confined in secret prison camps, waterboarded, and executed, then civilization is going to end.

Contrary to the secular atheistic prattle that such fears are more common in "primitive" settings where every going out of the door and coming back in is accompanied by a host of terrors and uncertainties, the evidence suggests that it is the rich, powerful, comfortable, sedentary society that is most easily paralyzed by anxieties. Phobias, anxiety disorders, and depression are rampant in "developed" countries, and relatively unheard of where people face death, persecution, starvation, and war on a daily basis. People who have nothing have nothing to lose; they're therefore not constantly plagued by the fear that they might lose it. People who have seen death, hunger, and sickness, and have survived it, know that they are capable of pulling through. It is the person who does not ordinarily have to face any crisis more startling than an empty beer fridge or a bounced check who suspects that he might not have the inner fortitude and moral character necessary to endure a biological weapon or a world food shortage.

This is why the Coliseum was filled with martyrs while the *pax Romanum* brooded over most of the known world. This is why the *autos de fe* burned with special ferocity in the same years as Columbus was discovering the New World, and Cortes shipping its riches back to Spain. I suspect that there is a great deal of exteriorized guilt here. A society that knows that its heart is plagued with greed, that it is perpetrating catastrophic evils under the guise of some righteous cause, and that the scythe of Divine Wrath is bound, sooner or later, to come cutting down its rotten sheaves, will seek for some way of purging itself of evil without having to repent of its excesses. This, I believe, is the reason that Jews, Muslims, early Christians, French and Spanish Protestants, English Catholics, and, yes, homosexuals as well, so often met with death at the hands of the State.

All too often, religious rhetoric about homosexuality conveys a fundamentally selfish outlook. What comes across is that "we are fighting to keep those 'dirty sodomites' out of *our* schools, *our* apartment buildings, and *our* places of work so they can't corrupt *our* children and spread disease." Homosexuals become the lepers that we stone at the gates to keep our cities ritually clean. Time and time again throughout history, Christians have employed the rhetorical example of Sodom and Gomorrah, working ourselves up into a frenzy of condemnation — as if to assert that, by engaging in genital sex with the wrong gender, homosexuals are placing at risk the very safety of our civilization. This, then, seems to become a thoroughgoing justification for stamping out this unholy vice by any means necessary; historically, "any means necessary" has meant everything from testicular transplant, to castration, to electroshock "therapy," to pillorying and burning at the stake. At some point in history, the "sodomite" became a specter every bit as catastrophic and terrifying as the "terrorist" is today, and it became acceptable to deprive people of the most basic dignities in order to pluck this worm from the breast of civilization.

Sodom Revisited

In order to clear the smoke from several thousand years of fiery executions, let's take an honest look at the story of Sodom and Gomorrah. This story, from chapters 18 and 19 of Genesis, actually offers a vision of divine retribution against a people, and of the means by which it can be prevented. It is not the story of a people obsessed with perverse sexual practices, or of a largely healthy civilization plagued by a cancer of homosexual lust. It is the story of a community that lacked nine righteous men.

Abraham, standing on his mountain, overlooking these cities, does not call on God to send down fire and consume them. Instead, he pleads for divine mercy: he begs God *not* to destroy these people, in spite of their obviously despicable manners. "What," Abraham asks, "if there are fifty righteous men living in these cities?" God, of course, says that He will not destroy the cities for the sake of the fifty, and there is a long conversation in which Abraham eventually haggles Him down to ten. For the sake of ten righteous men, Sodom and Gomorrah will not be destroyed (cf. Gen. 18). As it turns out, there is only one righteous man living there, and so the one righteous man, Lot, is told to flee, and the cities are treated to a brimstone shower that has fueled fiery religious rhetoric ever since.

Abraham understood God's mercy, and he invoked it for a people whose practices were so abominable that it is scarcely conceivable — the vice of Sodom was not "sodomy," in the sense of consensual anal intercourse, but "sodomy" in the sense that a woman left murdered by the roadside is said to have been "sodomized" by her attacker. Sodom was, apparently, ill-inclined to accept strangers in her midst; indeed, she was so adamant in her resolve to discourage visitors that if any happened by, they could expect to be summoned out to the streets and gang-raped by the male members of the community.* Perhaps Christians would do

---

* I am not intending, here, to give my support to the "inhospitality" theory of the Sodom story — at least insofar as such a theory is used to imply that the sin of Sodom was not "sodomy." There is no doubt that the sexual acts which the men of Sodom proposed to enact against Lot's visitors are relevant to the story, but there is equally little doubt that Lot is thinking, at least to some extent, in terms of his obligations as a host, to the point that he is willing to offer his daughters rather than have this disgrace fall on guests who "have come under the shelter of [his] roof." Still, there is a great deal of subtext here that has

well to consider the mercy that Abraham was willing to extend even to this community when they stand by the roadside waving "turn or burn" signs at relatively innocuous drag-queens and leathermen.

At the heart of the story there is a very serious message, equally applicable in any time: the means by which to stem the tide of divine wrath is by personal morality, righteousness, vigilance, charity, and hospitality. Had there been nine more like Lot in Sodom and Gomorrah, the cities would not have been destroyed. If anyone is afraid that divine retribution is going to fall on himself and his family, he has but to reform his own life. The world is not to be saved by protest marches, lynch mobs, or people gathering together in the street to warm their fingers in the glow of the burning heretics and sodomites. It is to be saved by the blood of Christ — by the willingness of Christians to suffer with those who are suffering, and to suffer for those who are dead in sin. Mother Teresa did not applaud the acceptance of homosexuality in the West, but her Sisters of Charity still stand vigil at the bedsides of men dying from homosexually contracted AIDS.

---

very little to do with homosexuality per se. The position of Lot in Sodom is certainly an issue; when he rebukes the men who have assembled at his door, they cry out, "This fellow came to sojourn, and he would play the judge!" (Gen. 19:9). Lot is a stranger; his kinsman, Abraham, is camped on a nearby hill. In a war that took place some years earlier, Abraham had freed slaves and goods captured from Sodom by Chedorlaomer, an enemy king. This might, one can reasonably suppose, have stood both Abraham and Lot in good stead with the King of Sodom, but the text strongly suggests that there is a certain tension between the two: Abraham refuses the king of Sodom's offer to keep the goods that were recaptured, saying "I have sworn to the LORD God Most High, maker of heaven and earth, that I would not take a thread or a sandal-thong or anything that is yours, lest you should say, 'I have made Abram rich'" (Gen. 14:22-23). In other words, Abraham did not trust the king of Sodom or lay much stock in his apparently charitable intentions. In any case, all of the politics here provides the underpinning of the story, and strongly suggests that there is more going on here than meets the eye in a casual reading. Indeed, the simplistic explanation — that this is a story of homosexual lust — is in many ways the most improbable. It is possible to imagine an entire city mobilized against Lot's visitors if they were taken to be spies sent by Abraham, or even if they were simply trying to drive off the foreigners, to say, in effect, "All right, Lot, we've tolerated you, but don't you dare think that you're moving any more of your friends into our country." It is impossible to imagine that "the men of the city, the men of Sodom, both young and old, all the people to the last man" (Gen. 19:4) insisted on raping the strangers because they were all simultaneously overtaken by intense homoerotic desire. As soon as you try to imagine the scene as something that could actually have happened, it becomes clear that the atmosphere is not of an orgy but of a lynch mob.

This is the great lesson history has for the Church. Wherever She has been consumed with Pharisaical self-righteousness, She has been pruned away. Christ, who was always merciful with sexual sinners, corrupt minor officials, and ignorant fishermen from the sticks, had no use for the supercilious and sanctimonious. He still has no use for them today. Christians who wish to do His will must stop picking at the splinters in their neighbors' eyes. Stop. Take one good look in the mirror. It won't take long. A log is hard to miss.

PART II

Homosexuality in Theory

CHAPTER 4

Psychology

Once Gay, Always Gay?

The great question that plagues the debate about homosexuality is that of mutability. Can a gay person be made straight? Jesuit psychotherapist John J. McNeill comments:

> The claim of certain groups to be able to change homosexuals into heterosexuals has been shown to be spurious and frequently based on homophobia (cf. Ralph Blair's pamphlet *Ex-Gay* [HCCC Inc., 1982]). The usual technique used to bring about this pseudo-change involves helping gay persons internalize self-hatred, an approach that frequently causes great psychological harm and suffering. The Christian communities that make use of this sort of ministry usually do so to avoid any challenge to their traditional attitude and to avoid any dialog with self-accepting gays and truly professional psychotherapists (The psychotherapists whom these churches frequently cite are generally very conservative and homophobic in their orientation.).[21]

McNeill reflects the current consensus of the American Psychological Association,* the position taken by most Western media outlets and pro-homosexual groups in general.

Obviously, it suits the gay-rights movement exceedingly well for orientation-change therapies to be discredited and black-marked. The

---

* Discussions of the politics of the APA decision to de-pathologize homosexuality are long, convoluted, and tedious. As with any politically charged situation, it is impossible to find documentation that is not thoroughly saturated with bias and spin. Politics and pressure groups were definitely involved; however, I suspect that a large number of the professionals who voted for the change were genuinely concerned for their patients, and believed, based on their experience, that homosexual orientation is intractable. I have no doubt that this experience was genuine. I have equally little doubt that other psychologists, most likely a minority, have had equally genuine experiences of success in treating unwanted homosexuality.

protest that gay activists have consistently shown towards ex-gays is completely understandable: it is not just that the alleged immutability of homosexuality is a linchpin of the case for gay rights, it is also that most homosexuals — and especially those who are the most vocal about LGBT issues — have a tremendous amount of personal stake in the question. Many of these are people who made the change attempt, formally or informally, at least once during their lives. For those who have struggled to overcome homosexual tendencies and found it impossible, the evidence — often whitewashed and rubbed in their faces by their harshest political opponents — of others who have succeeded is intolerable.

Ex-gays are, in some cases, a little too eager to parade their normalcy, and perhaps even to crow over their victory against homosexual urges. Add to this a right-wing pastor who gets up and introduces them like a veteran breeder presenting his prizewinning peacock at the fair, and you can understand why it rubs the homosexual observer the wrong way. This is not to say that people who have left behind a homosexual lifestyle ought not to speak, but that it is necessary to speak honestly, particularly about the fact that chastity is not a once-and-for-always affair. We, too, are human, and are struggling. We are not success stories who made it past the post. We are simply human beings unwilling to confine ourselves to the straitjacket of a gay identity, who insist on our right to own our sexuality instead of being owned by it.

The ordinary person confronted with homosexual attractions that they do not want is done a great disservice in this political wrangling. It is the right of every individual to choose their religious beliefs, ideological convictions, and manner of living. Gay and lesbian activists have long decried the interference of the "religious right" in their ability to live the sort of lives that they would like. In the process they have, perhaps unthinkingly, created an analogous situation in which psychologists are called to enforce a gay-affirming lifestyle on those who will not have it. The punishment for refusal is often a withdrawal of psychological care; it is presumed that homosexuality is intractable, and that other psychological problems cannot be addressed unless a patient is willing to embrace a homosexual identity.

Is such a situation warranted by the data? Jones and Yarhouse, in their book *Ex-Gays?*, studied the change process used by participants in Exodus, a nondenominational Christian ministry to homosexuals. They analyzed the studies that have been done in the past, and concluded that:

> . . . the dozens of studies that have been published to date all indicate that change from homosexual orientation to full or substantial heterosexual orientation is attainable by some individuals by a variety of means. There is no indication that such change is easy (in fact there are numerous indications that the change process is challenging and substantial), or that a high percentage of individuals attain this change.[22]

So it has allegedly been "shown" that all attempts at sexual orientation change are spurious, and it has also been found that all studies show them to have a modest degree of success. Why the discrepancy?

The quotation with which I began this chapter gives away its biases fairly easily. The presumption that only gay-affirming psychotherapists are "truly professional," and that having an alternative view of homosexuality brands one as "very conservative and homophobic," jumps off the page without a particularly careful reading. Jones and Yarhouse are right: the literature suggests that various therapeutic options for sexual orientation change do have some, albeit limited, success. These successes are dismissed by opponents of reorientation therapies on the assumption that they are false: that the people undergoing therapy had powerful psychological or legal (many therapies were tested on prison populations incarcerated for sodomy) reasons for "faking" a cure.

What the anti-ex-gay movement highlights is the experience of people who have tried, and failed, to change; the profound frustrations and self-hatreds that arise when someone construes a heterosexual orientation to be the *summum bonum* of human existence, and finds him- or herself unable to attain it.

The biggest difficulty is that most of the work done on the subject confines itself to anecdotal evidence. The homosexual lobby can always dig up a steady supply of people who have tried some sort of reparative psychotherapy or support group, who feel they wasted a great deal of time and money, and who report being scarred by the experience. Right-wing pressure groups, on the other hand, can ferret out dozens of converts who have renounced their homosexuality and — often through the same psychotherapies and support groups — have come to a resplendent, fruitful heterosexuality devoid of the problems and struggles of a homosexual lifestyle. Jones and Yarhouse ask why the negative anecdotes — "I was a participant in that research project (or I underwent precisely that therapeutic technique) and my apparent success disappeared over time" — are given credence, while the positive anecdotes — "I made the change attempt and it worked" — are not.[23]

True, a certain kind of Christian observer will do exactly the opposite — credit the positive anecdotes and discount the negative ones. The ex-gays who speak about the healing power of Jesus are given absolute and unmitigated belief, while the anti-ex-gays who claim that they were hurt, scalped, or deceived by ex-gay ministries are pooh-poohed as being contumacious sinners, liars, and saboteurs, planted by the gay-rights movement to undermine the good work of Christian therapists. On both sides, it is the classic situation of the scientist running down his row of experiments, plucking out the ones that don't support his hypothesis, and concluding that he must have made some mistake on these instances. The report, thus doctored, is hardly what anyone would be inclined to call "objective."

A Harmful Cure?

Many of the arguments against therapies for gays and lesbians hinge on the appeal to past abuses — gay men, particularly, were subjected to testicular transplants, hormone injections, electric shock therapies, drug-induced revulsion therapies, childhood behavioral engineering experiments, etc, etc. Many suffered terrible physical or psychological harm from these ill-founded "treatments." It is hardly surprising, then, that the homosexual community is wary of anyone who claims to be able to "cure homosexuality" or "change sexual orientation." Too many times, the drastic nature of the "cure" was simply not commensurate with the severity of the disease: better to live with homosexual temptations and a complete frontal lobe than to drool your way through life in an imbecilic asexuality.[24]

Judging from these experiences, many homosexuals conclude that it is harmful and dangerous for a person to try to change their sexual orientation. This is perfectly understandable, but the conclusion doesn't follow: if I tried to resolve my marital struggles by exchanging my husband's testicles with those of the next door neighbor, putting batteries in his bathwater, and subjecting him to bizarre Pavlovian conditioning experiments à la *A Clockwork Orange*, this would obviously cause tremendous harm both to him and to my marriage. However, we need not necessarily conclude that *reasonable* attempts to work out our nuptial woes will inevitably be harmful.

So how do reasonable means of overcoming homosexual urges fare, if we clear away the detritus of mad scientists and loony-bin laboratories?

According to Jones and Yarhouse:

> Those claiming that . . . interventions [to change "sexual orientation"] cause harm also have failed to follow [professional recommendations] on how to determine if a therapy helps or harms clients. Those claiming harm have never followed actual persons attempting to change to measure the impact of the change attempt; they have produced no scientific evidence justifying their claim.[25]

The study which these authors produced, following Exodus participants over several years, suggests that the anti-ex-gay rhetoric is overblown. Participation in spiritual support groups for homosexuals who wish to change their orientation does not seem to cause measurable psycho-emotional harm. For most, it causes some lessening of an already distressed state. For the remainder, it is generally neutral.

I'm sure some participants do, over time, come to see their participation in a group such as Exodus as a particularly noxious, self-delusional period in their lives. One of the strange quirks of the human brain is that we are always capable of re-editing the footage that fills our memory banks — providing it with a fresh soundtrack, altering the lighting, modifying the color scheme, and selecting which scenes will be included in the final cut of our personal history. For a long time, I looked back on my lesbian relationship with particular revulsion. It seemed to be a time when I was swimming in contradictions, my interior life was a shambles, my emotional life was buried six feet under, and my intellectual life was a crumbling façade concealing the rotting remnants of my soul. It has taken a long time to gain a more realistic perspective, to come to some sort of peace with the fact that the girl in all of those old mnemonic film reels really is *me*.

Unfortunately, the sort of evidence applied to "change" therapies often comes from those who are angry — perhaps because they were lied to, wasted a lot of money, or feel that they failed. Someone who was not particularly agitated while participating in an Exodus-style group might later reassess their experience in the light of disillusionment and cast it as unspeakably horrible and devastating. The private business of coming to terms with embarrassing or disappointing elements of the past is a universal human experience, but it is not a basis for good scientific study.

Therapy is not harmful — or helpful — except as an individual experience. If someone feels trapped by a compulsive pattern of behavior, whether it is sexual, nonsexual, heterosexual, or homosexual, they ought to be able to seek help to regain control of their lives. That help ought not to include an insistence that they reorder their sense of self to fit the therapist's goals and prejudices — a two-edged sword: it applies equally to those who would force a gay identity onto Christians struggling with unwanted same-sex attractions, and also to reparative therapists who would coerce their same-sex-attracted clients into believing that homosexuality is a psychological illness; an explanation which may, or may not, make sense for any given individual.

By the Light of the Inner Eye

With homosexuality, as with every quirk of human existence, it is difficult to address the effect without understanding the cause. If the root of homosexuality is spiritual, then Exodus ought to be successful. If it is psychological, psychotherapy should be able to develop an adequate treatment. If it is genetic, forget it — at least until we come up with those science fiction gene-manipulation rays that allow mad scientists to turn innocent girls into bird-women.

Everyone seems obsessed with the idea that there must be *a* cause, or, at the very outside, three or four causes that could be observed and tested in a rational scientific manner. This is exceedingly problematic.

First, there is the question of precisely what sexual orientation is. Social scientists, psychologists, and researchers on both sides of the fence have spilled gallons of ink on the question, but with every word written, the issue becomes muddier. This is unsurprising for anyone who has put the question to herself from an interior point of view.

I had to confront this when I was involved in the endless, and seemingly obligatory, game of self-labeling after I had put aside lesbianism for the sake of my religious obligations. At first, the situation was simple enough: I did not think that my romantic feelings, sexual attractions, or capacity to respond sexually to men or women had changed. I had done the long and difficult soul-searching, I had finally decided that I was a lesbian, and that was how it was. The fact that I had made a contract with God that demanded I forgo the physical realization of my attractions didn't figure into it: a celibate could remain celibate and still be able to describe his sexuality as heterosexual. I could simply style myself as a nonpracticing lesbian and be done with it — an arduous task in terms of lived experience, but ideologically simple. And I was always the sort to prefer practical complications to ideological ones.

The problem arose afresh when I realized that I was falling in love with Chris, my male best friend. For a while, I was able to excuse the relationship — just as I had excused my relationship with Michelle during its early phases — as merely a deep and intimate friendship. The writing was, however, on the wall, and almost everyone around me could see it except me.

It was shortly after I converted to Catholicism, winter was just beginning, and I was visiting Chris — as I regularly did — in the small city of Waterloo, where he was going to university. I lived some 400 kilometers away, in a dormitory at Queen's University in Kingston. Apart from Michelle, with whom I was still friends in spite of our breakup, my friends were few. Queen's was a university that valued a certain kind of conformity: the usual university wackiness was encouraged, provided it confined itself to preordained locales and times. During frosh-week the engineers were expected to dye themselves purple, spike their hair with egg-whites, and climb a greased pole in the middle of a swamp filled with feces and pickled organs stolen from biology labs. That was a tradition, lovingly crafted by generations of Queen's students, in force since my father's years in Queen's Engineering. But aside from these sanctioned lapses, the atmosphere was, to my tastes, stiflingly stuffy. It was the sort of the place where you would be looked at askance if you failed to purchase the $300 leather jacket — and also where, if you dared to wear said jacket before the appointed day, you could expect to have it stripped from your person and to see its $300 leather arms torn off in front of you. I did have friends from high school who had also come to Queen's, but they were in demanding, specialized programs, so I rarely saw them.

Thus the regular — as the year wore on, almost constant — bus trips across Ontario to visit House of Jer: the modest two-story rooming house where Chris was living, along with David (a recovering Druidic sorcerer who was finding Christ the long way around, via Sri Rama Krishna), and Jeremy (after whom the house was named because it belonged to his grandmother). At House of Jer, I could wear my home-made robes with impunity. I could lounge on the sofa, drink cheap sherry, and listen to Dave's sermons on the evils of woman-and-gold before retiring to play games of computer Risk under the auspices of various handcrafted marzipan marshals (obviously, the cost of losing was to be torn limb from candied limb and then gobbled down by the victor). Schoolwork was easily managed; I did my assignments, e-mailed them back to Kingston, and got Michelle to hand them in for me. It seemed a very satisfactory arrangement.

The only difficulty was that Chris was always reluctant for me to return and would attempt any devious ploy to encourage me to stay. He once rented the first half of *Twin Peaks*, and then asked me how I could — without knowing who killed Laura Palmer — possibly return to Kingston. Who could argue with logic like that?

And so, one night in frigid November, I had finally wormed my way out of the house and down the street to the bus station, and was going through the obligatory motions of saying good-bye, when he grabbed my head and kissed me. I was so astonished — and, to my intense surprise, so grateful — that I didn't have any emotional capacity left for eroticism.

My entire sense of self, my long-won sexual identity, and my determination to accept the burden of life as a chaste, Catholic lesbian, were suddenly thrown into jeopardy, and it was going to take either a great deal of confusion and self-inflicted suffering, or else a great deal of humility, to figure out why he had kissed me, what it meant, and what I felt about it. Naturally, I opted for the drawn-out anxiety. I didn't ask, bring it up again, or risk kissing him back. I also didn't catch my bus.

The dilemma that I was plunged into was one that I was well familiar with. I was being inexorably sucked back into a dialog with myself that had been going on for years, and which has continued, intermittently, to the present day. Am I a lesbian? Am I attracted to women? Am I attracted to men? What precisely does it mean to have a sexual orientation? And does it have anything to do with identity?

These were questions that I had been struggling with since the day Michelle first kissed me. At that time, I was able to fob off my physical involvement as a kind of play — the natural extension of a mutually explored fantasy life that followed from an unwillingness to abandon the childhood world of the imagination now that we were on the cusp of adulthood. As I grew, and learned that sexual fantasy and role-play continued to be a part of many couples' romantic lives well into the gray-haired years, I felt that the pressure was off. Michelle and I could play our games without fear that this was abnormal, or that it would prevent us from having the sort of intimate emotional friendship that we had formed during the first days of our acquaintance. Yet, naturally, the questions of sexual attraction and identity arose, particularly when I noticed that other girls seemed to take an interest in boys as boys. They would muse to each other about which of the New Kids on the Block was the hottest, and chatter about which of the twins in biology class was the cutest, and pin up pictures of male baseball stars on the insides of their lockers. I couldn't have cared less. Jonathan and Jordon were both ugly; boys my age were ungainly creatures with pimples; the baseball heroes looked like my father. The male body held no particular appeal or mystique. I had seen it on several occasions, and had not been impressed with the dangling lump of wrinkly, purplish skin that was supposed to be their proudest organ. The only time I had ever seen an erect penis had been when I happened accidentally upon a pornographic magazine. In this, the male member was the least interesting object of study; it was there, lurking, obscene and vaguely threatening, but the women were what captured my attention. It was not their bodies: as a possessor of a female body, I was more or less aware of what one looked like, and the positions into which they had contorted themselves were disgusting, not titillating. What gathered my attention was their eyes. I had never seen such deep terror and self-abasement lurking in a human being's stare, and the fact that it was paired with such bizarre facial expressions — as though they were desperate to convince me that they were enjoying themselves beyond the bounds of human pleasure — struck a deep, discordant note on the strings of my heart. Whether this had any effect on my feeling that heterosexual sex was threatening and somewhat gross, I don't know; presumably, a great many women have had the same experience without it turning them lesbian, and I was, as I mentioned, unimpressed with physical masculinity to begin with.

It occurred to me that my lack of interest in the bodies of men was not entirely normal, and so I asked myself whether I wasn't, then, attracted to women. Well, women were beautiful. That much was certain. If a particularly beautiful woman walked by, I would notice her, but the feeling didn't correspond very clearly with any of the effects that were supposed to be involved in erotic attraction. My heart did not palpitate, my tongue did not hang out of my mouth, my sexual organs did not tingle, I wasn't drawn into an obsessive stare, unable to pull my eyes away. I was fascinated, but not any more intensely than when I passed a particularly beautiful waterfall, or an awe-inspiring granite formation on a drive through northern Ontario. The experience seemed to be more aesthetic than erotic, but since I was clearly not erotically interested in men, and I was involved in a sexual relationship with another woman, I decided these must be sexual attractions.

There was one occasion during my adolescence on which I had a similar experience of the male body as an object of beauty. It would be very romantic if it had been the first time I saw Chris, the man who would later become my husband, but it was not; the first time I saw him, he was introduced to me as the boyfriend of friend of mine. He was gawky and long-haired, with a bland, pimply face and the wide-eyed zombie stare usually associated with the perpetually stoned (I later found out that it was because he stayed awake all night reading Rabelais and Rudolf Steiner). My initial thought was, "Why on earth would anyone go out with him?" So that particular romantic fairytale will have to be forgone. No, my sole appreciation of the male body came about when I was fifteen, standing in one of those perennially overcrowded museums in Florence. Had the boy in question been of flesh and blood, he might have altered my developmental sexual trajectory forever. David, however, was carved in marble — and I had no difficulty archiving my appreciation as aesthetic.

I've had years now from which to view the problem, and I think I have some insight. It is not, as I sometimes suspected, that I am congenitally frigid. If you show me a sex scene in a movie, I will have a sexual reaction to it — but it doesn't make the slightest difference whether the scene is lesbian or heterosexual. This is not, I discovered, because I am fundamentally lesbian, or fundamentally bisexual, but because this is how *women* generally react to visual erotic stimuli — or at least so the instruments used to measure such things tell us.[26] Still, as my mother once put it, "I can't imagine getting hot and heavy over a picture of a naked man." Nor of a naked woman. This may not be a universal female experience, but it does seem to be a common one: there is a reason why convenience store shelves are not stocked with hundreds of pornography titles catering to women.

I have never found my physiological reactions to erotic film scenes or erotic writing to be particularly pleasant — on the contrary, I prefer to run my body like a military dictatorship, with my will placed firmly on the throne. Plebeian uprisings, whether erotic or emotional, are generally disapproved of, and when I was younger, they were usually ruthlessly stamped out. One of the primary reasons I didn't give much weight to purely sexual/genital reactions was that I couldn't imagine that this was what all the hullabaloo was about. If a girl who felt more tingling sensations in her groin when looking at women than when looking at men was a lesbian, and this was supposed to be the basis for an entire lifestyle and identity, then that was inconceivable idiocy. It was incommensurable with the dignity and intelligence of the people whom I had trusted to teach me about sexuality, and it certainly wasn't worth lobbying the government over. The issue had to be deeper than mere physical "attraction": it had to touch on the higher levels of the human person, or else it was banal and stupid beyond belief.

The Philosopher's Stone of Sexual Identity

Most homosexuals, and most homosexual activists, would agree with this: it is *not* simply a matter of physiological desire, but also of psychological attraction, compatibility, and romantic interest. There are those who pursue homosexual relations because they actually believe that the pursuit of pleasure, in as many varied forms as possible, is the only panacea for the meaninglessness of life. They are generally pan-sexual and don't claim any fundamental homoerotic identity, and they do not represent the majority of same-sex-attracted people. The majority believe in human relationships, in love, in life, and in something higher than the satisfaction of visceral appetites.

This does, however, complicate the issue of defining homosexuality. Researchers struggle with this question constantly: after all, how can you conduct a survey to discover patterns in the lives of homosexual persons if you can't say what a homosexual is? According to lesbian psychologist Susan D. Cochran:

> Sexual orientation is a multidimensional concept including inter-correlated dimensions of sexual attraction, behavior, and fantasies, as well as emotional, social, and lifestyle preference.[27]

Jones and Yarhouse were confronted with tremendous difficulties when trying to frame a study that would demonstrate that movement from a homosexual to heterosexual orientation was possible:

> If there are no tightly defined dichotomous categories of gay and straight, then the reorientation of a person moving from one place to another in a multidimensional space defined by an array of variables related to sexual orientation can always be disputed.[28]

So who is really gay? I have, several times, asked myself, "Am I really a lesbian?" When I was involved in a lesbian relationship; considered human beauty as inhering in the female form; had utterly ambiguous erotic reactions; found my romantic entanglements with men unsatisfactory and often disastrous; reserved my most intimate emotional relationships and attractions for women; preferred traditionally "masculine" ways of thinking and acting; and identified myself as a lesbian, the question seemed simple. Surely the entanglement of these variables produced a clear answer: I was gay.

But which of these things is "sexual orientation"? Where is the philosopher's stone of sexual identity, the chimerical formula to render transparent this muddied muddle of mutable facts? These things, put together, seem to add up to something like an "orientation," and it seemed reasonable, both to me and to the people who counseled me, to let go of the idea that I was bisexual and embrace a lesbian identity wholesale, to assert that I was homosexual. Yet there is not a single thing in the entire pile that is fixed:

a) Relationships end, and the vast majority of same-sex-attracted people have had sexual relationships with members of both sexes.[29] (This is especially true of same-sex-attracted women; hence the increasing multiplication of "sexualities" and sexual labels among women who have sexual attractions to other women.)

b) Disastrous and unsatisfactory relationships are a product of individual relationships. A person who is bad at relating to men doesn't have a deep sexual identity; opposite-sex relationships are difficult to negotiate, and this is an art which many happily married people take years to learn.

c) It is normal for people to have intimate and intense emotional relationships with members of their own sex, and there is evidence to suggest that among homosexuals, emotional intimacy is much closer to what most of us experience in friendship than what most heterosexuals experience in marriage.*

d) The assumption of a masculine self-image is, in most women, a psychological or ideological decision which can be addressed

---

* This was certainly my experience; it seems to be corroborated by others, including David Morrison, Jack Malebranche, some of the homosexuals interviewed by Gay Sunshine, and various gays and lesbians of my acquaintance.

through a change of ideology, a process of accepting femininity as something beautiful and desirable in oneself — or it may simply arise from a too-narrow construct of what constitutes "femininity" in the first place.

e) As for "sexual identity," is it anything more than a label that we adopt in order to make sense of the rest?

The only thing that remains, when all of the factors that are mutable and can be influenced by the action of the will are removed, is raw sexual attraction. The flow of blood to one's sexual organs in response to gender-specific erotic stimulation. If that is all there is, this is a tremendous amount of smoke pouring out of a very insignificant fire.

I do not think, however, that the real issue for most homosexuals is the ability to have sex with the people that they want to have sex with. In almost every case, there is something else on the list that they do not *want* to change. We can argue, of course, about whether or not this is valid — does a woman have the right to cling to a masculine set of gender traits if she so chooses? Do human beings have an obligation to negotiate the dangerous and difficult terrain of heterosexual marriage? — but these arguments, if they are to get anywhere, have to be founded on the recognition that a person is not a "ghost-in-the-machine" or, worse, a "wet-machine" *sans* ghost, but a psychosomatic unity in which the mind and the will have a great deal of power to shape destiny — even the destiny of the body.

The Biodeterministic Crunch

The question of free will is often framed in terms of genetics. If homosexuality were to be proved, beyond a shadow of a doubt, to have a genetic genesis, all bets would be off: it would be unthinkable to tell same-sex-attracted individuals to discontinue their same-sex sexual lifestyles. After all, one thing would follow from the other as naturally as moonlight kisses follow from meandering walks along the riverbank.

It is for this reason that people opposed to the practice of homosexuality have sunk so much time, and often money, into answering the question of genetics in the negative. How many words have been spilled on the infamous "twin studies" arguing back and forth about what they mean? The gay activists say, "There you have it, if one identical twin is gay, the other has a 50% chance of also being gay. This is much higher than the statistical average. It must be genetic." Their opponents riposte: "If it were genetic, there would be a 100% correspondence. If one identical twin is black, is there only a 50% chance that the other will be black? If one is male, is there a significant chance that the other will be female? You see, this genetic nonsense is just a quack."*

What do I say? I say it doesn't matter a single jot. Christianity has always asserted that there is a war on in the human being between the spirit and the flesh. By this we do not mean Cartesian dualism, or Manichaeism: it is not a war between the soul and the body. By the flesh, we mean the feelings of desire, irascibility, and so forth that rise up in contradiction to the intellect and make their effects felt on the body so powerfully that they are difficult to overcome. These feelings are considered to be a consequence of the Fall.

Non-Christians, of course, do not think that man is fallen, but the point is fairly easy to make. Does the body fall prey to diseases? Do cancers grow out of the very cells that make up your physical structure? Of course. Does that mean that illness is a natural part of the body which ought to be loved and encouraged? Absolutely not. When we say that the body is fallen, we mean that it is imperfect, that it falls away from its form, that it confronts the mind and the will with contradictions, that it allows suffering into our lives.

I have very little doubt that as we excavate the genetic matrix underlying the human body, we will discover that many faults and vices have a genetic origin. That violence, perhaps even spousal abuse, is genetically programmed into certain people and not into others. That alcoholism has a genetic basis. Even that innocent personality quirks, like the desire to be constantly chewing on something (a wad of tobacco, a stick of gum, a piece of paper) is coded into the sequence

---

* Is 50% the actual number? It depends on the twin study. The issue is complicated: there have been multiple twin studies, some using convenience samples (i.e., samples garnered by placing ads in gay magazines or gay bars) and one using the Australian Twin Registry. Generally, the more random the sample is, the more the correspondence in homosexuality between identical twins falls off into the nonelevant end of the statistical range.

of amino acids that somehow adds up to you and me. Does this mean that we are therefore to live our lives constantly under the iron boot of genetic dictatorship? Not at all.

St. Paul told us this very specifically:

> For the desires of the flesh are against the Spirit, and the desires of the Spirit are against the flesh; for these are opposed to each other, to prevent you from doing what you would . . . And those who belong to Christ Jesus have crucified the flesh with its passions and desires.
>
> — GAL. 5:17, 24

Christ's crucifixion was a victory over the flesh; Christ, like every human being, had an inborn, genetically determined desire not to be tortured and put to death on a cross. He could have chosen to avoid it: both Caiaphas and Pilate gave Him ample opportunity to deny His divinity, declaim His Kingdom, and save His life. He did not. Why? Because there is something in a human being which is stronger than the genetic code.

Ah! But if it is genetically coded, then God made us that way. In that case, how could it be argued that it was not God's will for gay people to be gay? Thus runs the classic argument. But it's nonsense. This is more difficult to see in modern Western society, where man's unsightly diseases and disfigurations are rarely paraded around the streets. Cosmetic surgeries, wigs, artificial limbs, and prostheses of every sort protect us from the experience of this unpleasant fact of life: when we speak of the body being fallen, we are not talking about some airy-fairy theological point. We are speaking of men born blind, and children born legless; of personality disorders, severe psychoses, autism, incurable depression. To accept the "I'm born that way, God made me that way, therefore it is good" argument is to accept that God also made certain people to be psychopaths, and that this is natural and good for them; that he made others to wring their hands day and night and dream suicide, and that this, too, is a realization of the image and likeness of God. It would make complete nonsense of the idea that

God is good, or that moral categories were a meaningful notion in the first place.

The fact that something is genetic does not mean that it cannot be overcome, nor does it mean that it is therefore somehow good. A moral commandment — an "ought" — cannot be derived from a descriptive statement — what "is." Morality is not an instruction manual on how to follow your inborn impulses. It is a call to overcome the artifacts of fallen nature within oneself, to become better than an animal, to become a complete, self-possessed human being.

Where do we arrive, then? What is homosexuality? What causes it?

I don't know. Frankly, I don't think anyone else does, either. I do know this: that what we speak of as homosexuality is profoundly individual. It is a point where many factors meet: self-determination, identity, psychology, philosophy, genetics. Any one of these things might be sufficient, in an individual heart, to add up to homosexuality; and any one of them might be radically insufficient in the heart of another. So what are we talking about, then, when we speak of a person "changing" from homosexual to heterosexual? We are speaking about a change of orientation: not the orientation of the sexual organs, or of the psychological matrix, but of the heart. We are speaking, in short, of what Christian theology has always called "repentance," a turning away from something in order to gaze, instead, at God.

CHAPTER 5

Statistics

I have long been a fan of that strange substrata of literature referred to as the "psychological case study." I find it fascinating to read about the psychoneurological avenues open to the human mind, and to see what can (or can't) be done for people who have gone down the various byways of experience. Aside from my reading, I have been a participant in the universal human project of serving as psychotherapist to one's acquaintances — a process generally called "friendship." Starting from this limited backdrop, I developed several crackpot theories about the field of psychology, and the process of psychotherapy.* It was tremendously gratifying when I sat down to listen to a series of recorded lectures by Carl Jung and found that the great man himself had come to many of the same conclusions that I had, dragging behind him a much more impressive string of evidence.

What are these conclusions? Nothing that obscure; Jung's observations traipse across the spectrum of the human soul, from the purely mundane and commonsensical to the quite occult and esoteric. The point which I wish to harp on today is that in psychotherapy, you cannot have a *method*. Every human being is different and unique, and every case has to be entered from an individual access point. The therapist has to get inside the experiential and symbolic realities confronting the patient, has to understand them, and has to help the patient to understand and accept them.[30] At the heart of psychotherapy is not a theory — Freudian, Pavlovian, or even Jungian — but a human relationship. What is profoundly effective with one patient may have no impact on another. Some psychotherapists may be able to relate easily to some patients but may be powerless to help others. The human heart is, as Dmitri Karamazov once observed, "too broad," and the major-

---

* I should note that my ideas were formed almost entirely in conversation with my husband — before I met him, I was still living in an intellectual's la-la land where the entirety of human experience could be described solely in terms of philosophical categories.

ity of psychoanalytic methods would narrow it. After all, if your job is to traipse around in the hinterlands of the psyche, it is much easier and safer if you can make for yourself a psychospiritual "golf course," where the only difficulty is to sink the ball of affirmation into the hole of self-loathing, than to enter a battlefield where God and the devil are at war.[31]

The Number Almighty

The primary tool that research psychologists and social scientists employ to navigate the jungles of the human psyche is the statistic. In the study of homosexuality, there is a deluge of statistics of every variety:

- how "sissy" homosexual boys are in childhood
- how likely tomboys are to grow up into lesbians
- the birth order of homosexuals
- the likelihood of homosexuality in pairs of twins
- the size of different pieces of the homosexual brain
- the environment surrounding the unborn homosexual fetus in the womb
- the amount of stress that a pregnant mother experiences while gestating her unborn lesbian girl
- the number of lesbians who are left-handed
- the ability of homosexual men to throw a baseball
- the age at which gays and lesbians first have sex with a same-sex partners
- the age at which they first have sex with an opposite-sex partner
- the number of sexual variations that they have tried by age 18 — or 30
- their likelihood of proving HIV-positive
- their average number of partners

. . . and so on, and so on, and so on.

Everyone is familiar with Disraeli's famous quip that "There are three kinds of lies: lies, damned lies, and statistics." I could tire you with comparisons of statistical studies performed by gay and lesbian scientists versus those performed by "right-wing" Christian scientists. I could run you through the endless hairsplitting debates about whether or not this particular study showed this particular result, and show how numbers have been mangled, conclusions overlooked, and data cooked up into a number of strange sociological dishes. But I won't. Instead, I will tell you a story (everybody loves stories; only dusty academics like squabbling over stats).

It was a lazy Saturday afternoon, and I was mucking around on the Kinsey* Institute Web site, entertaining various amusing and paranoid fantasies about what might be contained in the secret documents that you can't access without a password (much the same pleasure gained, I imagine, by people who like to ruminate about the alien skulls that must — unquestionably — line the shelves at the Vatican Secret Archives. After all, if there were no alien skulls, why would it be secret?). I came across a sex survey that was being put forward to the general public to garner a deeper, more substantial understanding of the mysteries of human sexuality. I thought, "I wonder what is in one of these things?" I had taken several of those unprofessional, juvenile "sex quizzes" that all children toy with in high school, but I was an adult now, and I wanted to know what real sexologists — serious scholars with degrees in the field — were asking.

Now you should know that if you are doing a survey, I am a very bad subject. If the survey is on paper, you will find very few of the boxes ticked, and extensive criticisms of your badly worded questions scrawled in the margins. The poor students that get mired in the offices of tele-survey firms during the long, languid hours of blissful summer have an awful time with me. I never like the options given. I always supply my own. It makes my opinions and feelings extremely difficult to tabulate.

This one included a very confusing section about "your own sexuality." It asked me, for example, if I was comfortable with my own sexuality. If I was satisfied with it. I answered yes. Only three screens later did

---

* Kinsey's "landmark studies" of human sexuality, published in the '40s, provided the scientific basis for much of the sexual revolution. The Kinsey Institute remains the foremost sexological institute in America.

I realize that what they were asking about was not the complex interplay of gender-identity, integration of sexual belief and sexual practice, and interior attitudes about sex — they were asking about masturbation. Now that this was clear, I was asked a series of questions about masturbation: What sort of fantasies did I entertain while masturbating? Did I find it difficult to masturbate if I felt that someone might walk in on me? Did I prefer to masturbate with or without a device? Nowhere, in any of the questions, was there a box that I could tick for "I do not masturbate." It was taken as a given that I did.

I understand why this is done: Kinsey and company have a theory that you ought to assume that *everyone* does *everything*. You always ask, "When did you first have sex with your pet dog?" In theory, this makes it more likely that people will admit embarrassing personal details — though in my experience, leading questions make people more uptight, even to the point of inducing a certain kind of person to invent experiences because they think it will please the researcher.

I am not scandalized by the questions that Kinsey researchers asked about my nonexistent masturbatory habits — I was doing research into the nature of sex questionnaires; I didn't expect the questions to merit the Imprimatur. This does, however, demonstrate one of the problems that inevitably plagues the field of statistic gathering: the observer effect. The fact that anyone studying a phenomenon will influence the results simply by conducting the study. This is true even in the hard sciences like physics. It is true to a much more extreme degree in the study of sexuality.

Truly Gay?

The first problem facing any researcher of homosexually oriented persons is "Who is homosexual?" This was discussed at some length in the previous chapter. Jones and Yarhouse, in their book *Ex-Gays?*, note that no "valid, well-researched measures of sexual orientation" exist.[32]

How do you research a population if you have no way of telling who is in and who is out? Such confusions would be cleared up if only there was a test — a blood test, or any of the urban myths like the theory that a certain finger-joint is longer among lesbians — that would determine, once and for all, who was really gay, and who was merely messing around. Jones and Yarhouse point out:

> Further clouding the question of what constitutes sexual orientation is the confusing, complex and inconclusive evidence existing for genetic, prenatal hormonal, birth order, brain structure, parental, cultural and other experiential variables. No one variable or cluster of variables stands forth as possessing dominant explanatory power (P. 194).

This is particularly the case when we are trying to understand same-sex attractions amongst women. With men, there is a certain amount of evidence to suggest that sex-atypical gender expression, particularly during childhood, (i.e. boys who behave like girls) is a good indicator that same-sex attractions will emerge later in life, and that the more sex-atypical a boy is, the more exclusive and "incurable" his homoerotic attractions will be. Social psychologist Anne Peplau warns, however, that "efforts to present universal theories of sexual orientation that apply to both sexes have tended to take male experience as the norm, much to the detriment of our understanding of women."[33] Still, we may reasonably wonder whether these universal theories are even effective in understanding homosexuality amongst men. Savin-Williams found:

> Of the many [same-sex-attracted] young people I interviewed, only 2 percent of the young men, and none of the young women, adhered to the published sexual identity models.[34]

Some might suggest limiting such studies to people who are "exclusively homosexual," people who would rate a six on the Kinsey scale.* But this would eliminate most people who identify as gay, lesbian, or bisexual — especially in adolescence. According to Savin-Williams:

> In every study conducted to date that gives young people a choice, they describe various degrees of homoerotic *and* heteroerotic

---

* The Kinsey scale is a seven-point scale, invented by Kinsey and his fellow researchers, that is supposed to plot human sexuality on a continuum from exclusively heterosexual (0) to exclusively homosexual (6) with various bisexual gradations in between (Kinsey, et al.[1948], pp. 639, 656).

attractions. For them, being attracted to one sex or the other is not mutually exclusive, and being attracted to boys and to girls might well fall along separate continuums.[35]

What question you ask (whether, for example, you assume that homoerotic and heteroerotic feelings are mutually exclusive, or capable of existing concomitantly) radically changes the data, and may even change who would, and would not, be included in your study.

Does Schrödinger's Cat Know If It Is Dead or Alive?

A larger problem is that those who are seeking to understand same-sex sexuality are usually looking for support for a specific theory. Savin-Williams, who does a good job of critiquing other researchers' presuppositions and unconscious motivations, lets a little of his own bias show through when he brags that by "listening patiently [I] probably subtracted a year or two from the average age [of first same-sex feelings] I elicited from the young women and men I interviewed."[36] The example that he gives of the sort of evidence that he dug up by patient listening is a young women who eventually recalled that, in early childhood, "I always wanted to color the pretty girls in coloring books, and I'd color nothing else. I'd just leave the boys in black and white!"[37] Perhaps Savin-Williams, having never been a small girl, and never having raised small girls, is unaware that if a scientific analysis were to be made of girls' coloring books, it would be found that the majority of women have had this sort "same-sex attraction" at an early age. I know a lot of small girls, and I don't think I've ever met one who didn't leave the boys white and color only the pretty girls.

The same criticism is also true of Jones and Yarhouse's research on change of sexual orientation: the results, overall, are fairly ambiguous. Some people working through Exodus's program do clearly arrive at a fully heterosexual identification. You can find out easily enough, by reading this book, or Alan Chambers' book, or the books of any other homosexual converts who happen to have ended up happily married, that there are cases where a very deep change in sexual desires and habits does take place. On the other hand, the study produced in *Ex-Gays?* seems to be guilty of exaggerating "success" results by conflating those who achieve a primarily heterosexual erotic life with those who gain sufficient control over their homoerotic impulses to be able to successfully pursue a life of chastity.[38]

So does this mean, for example, that when Exodus claims that "we see such a similarity in personal backgrounds among the men and women who seek our help. There is a pretty uniform picture of poor family dynamics in general, a rift in the father-son or mother-daughter relationship growing up, feelings of being an outsider among one's peers during childhood and adolescence, and instances of sexual abuse/incest,"[39] they are lying, or self-deluding, or fixing the results?

I think not. But, before we jump to any conclusions, I also don't think that this necessarily means that the patterns which Exodus sees would be found in a large-scale survey of randomly selected people with same-sex attractions. The population that Exodus is dealing with is not representative of the homosexual population at large; specifically, they will only end up dealing with people who feel that they need a religiously motivated support group in order to overcome their sexual temptations. There is a tremendous uncounted population of people out there, like myself, who have experienced same-sex attractions, who have identified themselves as gay or lesbian, but who, if they wish to abandon their same-sex behaviors, are unlikely to seek out the help of a support group — either because they have good support from family and friends, or because their same-sex attractions are not so deeply-seated that they need professional or experienced help to put them aside. The people who approach Exodus, or other groups like it, will always be taken from a cross-section of individuals whose same-sex sexuality is a) relatively compulsive, b) deep-seated, c) a cause of significant emotional turmoil, and d) who feel ashamed or unable to get help from their friends and families. One doesn't need a degree in sociology or psychology to recognize that these conditions are going to have a powerful influence on the type of person who arrives on Exodus', or Courage's, or Homosexuals Anonymous', or JONAH's doorstep. In other words, Exodus' description of the psychological patterns that they see might well be a better description of the sort of people who participate in self-help groups, or who seek the help of professional reparative therapists, than of the causes and issues generally to be found amongst homosexual subpopulations.

Still, the experience of Exodus members is not to be discounted, because it does represent the experience of those who are most in need of external help if they wish to overcome unwanted same-sex desires. Perhaps in former ages, and even in former decades, the Exodus membership would have been much more typical of the homosexual population, at least in areas where homosexuality was particularly disapproved of. In a culture where it is seen as an atrocious vice, completely abominated by one's society and peers, only those with fairly deeply rooted, even compulsive, same-sex attractions are likely to pursue homoerotic liaisons. In the modern West, on the other hand —particularly in cities like Toronto, where the rainbow flag of diversity is flown from every pediment — the percentage of the homosexual community who conform to notions of "innate" or "immutable" homosexuality can reasonably be expected to shift and dwindle in comparison to those who have, in some sense, "chosen" a homoerotic lifestyle.

The Unreliable Specimen

As if the waters were not muddied enough, we may add that not only do psychologists and researchers bring along a set of presuppositions which they hope that their research will vindicate, but that those being researched may also deliberately or subconsciously streamline their experience to fit a particular model floating about in the public mindspace. A read-through of interviews with gay men in the '70s[40] seems to provide a wealth of information to support the Freudian notion that male homosexuality is caused by a distant and disapproving father, and a mother who is overbearing and emotionally needy. The gays of the '70s speak openly of their search for "Daddymen" — sexual partners who resemble their fathers — and make a great deal out of their wounded family dynamics. Wonderful! We've hit pay dirt. Freud got it right, first try.

Well . . . hold on.

A look at studies of homosexuals in the '90s confirms same-sex-attracted youth are fraught with emotional problems and suicidal thoughts, that they feel constantly oppressed and bullied by their heterosexual peers, and that they are, on the whole, disturbed victims in need of kindly maternal care from heterosexual social-worker nannies. Testimonies from gays and lesbians towards the end of the '90s clearly show that homosexuality is fixed and congenital, and that the same sexual-identity models that proved so unsatisfactory to Savin-Williams in his postmillennium interviews were, in fact, largely commensurate with the experience of gay people at that time. Indeed, at least one author was so enamored with theories of innate homosexuality that she rewrote her autobiography to include early indications of a homosexual identity.[41] The writings of Athenian pederasts affirm that the real genesis of homosexuality is a fascination with beautiful youths, combined with disdain for women and femininity. Decorated anthropologists regularly assure us that although they've had no difficulty uncovering homoerotic behavior amongst the tribes and cultures they study, modern Western notions of sexual orientation and identity simply don't apply to the lesbianism in Moroccan harems. No doubt a serious survey of people confessing homoerotic temptations during the Middle Ages would show, beyond any shadow of a doubt, that it is a spiritual problem brought about by the action of demonic forces; while men in ancient Rome would have told you that "passive" male homosexuality was a consequence of the inherent inferiority of slaves, and that their own, "active" homosexuality wasn't really homosexuality at all, but a means of asserting their Patrician dominance.

There are two possible explanations for this: either homosexuality as we know it is a narrow, endemic phenomenon that has arisen, like the half-hour sitcom or the TV dinner, out of the particular intersection of cultural realities that we call the modern West. Or, homosexuality is a real phenomenon, but one whose roots and nature are so ill-understood and culture-bound that the only meaningful definition is something simple, like "Some men have sexual experiences, thoughts, and feelings about other men. Ditto for women." If the former, it is a massive presumption of Western superiority to claim that the Western homosexual model has any objective validity; our notion of homosexuality becomes a cultural artifact, a "social construct," which society has the right to alter according to its needs and prejudices. If the latter, the facts provide us with no ethical guidance, and no more explanatory weight than "some women like the smell of jasmine" or "some men enjoy beating goats."

Interior Distances

The truth is that sexuality is fundamentally personal and subjective; it has to do with the heart of the individual much more than with any objective, measurable data. This is why "objective" studies will never be able to truly penetrate the subject.

Take, for example, the oft-cited "sissy-boy" studies, which show that boys who are "gender atypical" often grow up to be gay. Many of the boys studied did not prove to have a particularly strong interest in "girly" activities — they just weren't interested in team sports, or rough-housing.[42] Most of these boys probably did not *feel* particularly masculine growing up — but does that mean that they were not? I had absolutely no interest in playing wedding, shopping, or talking about boys, and, like many young girls who don't conform to gender-stereotype, I eventually joined the feminist pack and decided that all gender-distinctions were arbitrary social constructs. But, as my husband once pointed out to me, there are many ways in which I am decidedly feminine — I just don't have the kind of femininity that is promoted in this society. I suspect that it is the interior experience, the feeling that one is not like other little boys, or other little girls, that is more important than objectively measurable facts.

Or, consider the notion that lesbians, in particular, are more likely to have been hurt or abused by men, and are therefore more threatened by relationships with men. Social scientists will point to the fact that some lesbians have been abused — but some haven't, and many women who have been abused are not lesbians. We might, from this, arrive at the conclusion that this simply isn't a relevant factor. But then, a woman might be abused and learn to trust again, or a woman might not be abused and still be intimidated by men.

One of the great difficulties here is that interior matter cannot be reliably investigated through interview or through questionnaire. The heart of man does not yield easily to scientific probing. It does not even yield easily to the inner eye of introspection — the art of self-knowledge must be learned, and this learning is often a difficult and laborious process. How, then, if we do not even know ourselves, is a scientist supposed to be able to understand us by reducing the experience of a thousand people to a handful of numbers, and then applying that with a broad brush to the entirety of human society?

If you had asked me, when I was happily involved in a lesbian relationship and found it impossible to have an intimate relationship with a boy, I would have told you categorically, without any traces of a doubt, that I was not even remotely intimidated by men. I would have told you that I was equal to men, that I felt I could hold my own against them, and that I was perfectly confident in mixed-gender situations. I would have cited my numerous male friendships, and boasted that my marks were as good as any boy's in my classes, and referenced the million tooth-and-claw philosophical debates that I had engaged in with men, and this would have sufficed. I wouldn't have been trying to deceive you: one of the great confusions of my young life was that I thought a good romantic relationship was just an intellectual friendship with physical intimacy added on. It never occurred to me that I was completely emotionally unavailable, or that I found the prospect of vulnerability, particularly around men, abjectly terrifying.

Convoluted human realities cannot be picked up by a quiz on human sexuality. They are only accessible through self-knowledge and the process of communication: through relationship or through art, that miracle of human communion by which a person is able to reveal himself to a multitude of unknown others throughout the world, and throughout history. If you read (with an open heart) one honest, well-written autobiography of a male hustler, you will understand more about homosexuality than can be gained thumbing through the statistical tables in a journal of sexology. If you speak honestly and intimately with gay and lesbian friends, you will have a better knowledge of their hearts, lives, and struggles than you will ever get from Kinsey and his compeers.

This is why this book is written in the way that it is. Numbers can lie. Human beings can lie as well, but it is possible to see through a human lie, or to discover some truth lurking in its shadow. Statistics are like a poker mask without a face behind it. They have no depth — but human sexuality is deep.

CHAPTER 6

Theology

Why is there so much hullabaloo today about sex? This question routinely baffles mainstream Catholics — even as we rush to cobble together intimidating tomes about Elizabeth Anscombe's proof of the immorality of contraception, and spend our time in bars grumbling about the evils of rampant homosexuality. Sex, we are quick to affirm, bores us. Not the act, itself, but the discussion. Can't we talk about something interesting, like demons, or whether or not Leviathan is an actual creature and if so, whether it will be literally consumed by the faithful during the marriage supper of the Lamb? These are questions worth speaking about. It seems a terrible and opprobrious imposition that, on account of the relentless chicanery of *Cosmopolitan* and *Sex and the City*, we should be blackmailed into squandering our time on the fruitless quest for a "natural law" argument against oral sex that will be convincing to the readers of *Maxim*.

This is how we see it: Western society has leaped pell-mell onto the bandwagon of scientism — not science, which is a valid discipline for the study of physical reality, but the *worship* of science, the elevation of a telescope to the level of a philosopher's stone . . . a psychoanalytic dogma to the level of a papal bull . . . a cell phone to the level of a consecrated host. In the realm of sexuality, the cult of the scientific expert caused hordes of sensible individuals to accept the snake-oil salesmanship of the white-coated goons who sold us the sexual revolution. Fifty years ago, we swallowed the notion that sexual "freedom" would be a panacea for the ills that have plagued human life since it was driven from the Garden of Eden. Loneliness would be abolished, spousal abuse gone, starvation banished, fear of pregnancy allayed. Today, we are reaping the "benefits" of this social revolution: the dissolution of families at a rate of 50%, the wildfire spread of STDs, the underpopulation/aging society crisis, the rise of depression as a ubiquitous feature of mental life, and so on. The great social experiment of the sexual revolution — an experiment performed on an entire population, without controls, and without reasonable safety precautions — has been a horrible failure. If it were a hair-care product or an aerosol cheese spray, the FDA would have pulled it from the shelves, and the companies responsible for releasing it in the first place would be facing bankrupting class-action suits. And yet here we are, fifty years in, blithely swallowing the same mental sewage, calling it "freedom" and "love" and wondering why we're all dying of depression, stress, and loneliness.

Sex and sexuality, bah. Pass me another plate of sea-monster sirloin.

The Sexual Counterrevolution

I exaggerate — I fell in love with Romantic poetry and Dickens at a young age, and it has forever condemned me to revel in the art of hyperbole — but this is essentially true. The only Catholics who actually want to talk about sex are liberals. They want to talk because they want Church doctrine to change, usually for the rather disingenuous reason that they want the Vatican to ratify their own preferred bedroom activities.

Yet it really must be talked about. Reality has always been, in some sense, a corrective for the excesses of the Church. Catholics are still bitter about the Reformation, but there has been enough time for it to become clear that there were real evils brooding in the heart of the Renaissance Church; the sudden loss of half of Christendom triggered that deep examination of conscience that we call the Counter-Reformation.

The sexual revolution within the Church will not, hopefully, come to a head in another schism. Although the Anglican church is already fractured nearly to the point of breaking by it, and many of the Protestant sects have naturally balkanized themselves along sexual lines, the Catholic Church seems to be holding a more stable course. In any case, the sexual revolution must come to Catholicism; we need it, and have been growing to need it for a long time.

Catholics like to say, "The Church is not against sex. It is society that is against sex, because they deprive it of its meaning, break down the family that sex builds up, and reduce it to the level of a tennis game. If you treasure something, you do not squander it. The Church treasures sex; society sells it." This argument often works reasonably well against people who can't be bothered with dusty historical tomes. It is not, however, entirely accurate.

The Church has constantly been warring against an anti-corporeal tendency within herself — whether it has come under the guise of Manichaeism, or of Albigensianism, or of Jansenism, there have always been Christian thinkers who believe that sex really is base or unclean. Read through an old Medieval "Lives of the Saints" and you'll see what I mean: Elizabeth of Hungary, who truly loved her husband, only went to bed with him out of pious duty for the bearing of children; every married martyr of the early Church was forced to wed, and spent their wedding night on their knees taking a solemn oath of celibacy with their husband.[43] What ridiculous nonsense. Not the notion that these things might have been true — dear St. Elizabeth might really have felt that it would offend God if she enjoyed the conjugal embraces of her earthly spouse — but the notion that this is the ideal of Christian sexuality.

This is not to say that Church history lacks champions for the dignity of sexual love, or that absurd simplifications like "People used to think sex is dirty, now they are enlightened" are true. St. Thomas Aquinas no doubt scandalized a few of the more Platonist monks when he wrote that sexual enjoyment would have existed in the Garden of Eden. Ever the champion of reason, Aquinas saw that there was no purpose in creating man "male and female" if there was no intention that they would ever make use of their male and female parts.[44] Still, the old psychobabble about people having difficulties in their sex life because an old nun taught them that sex was dirty — when stripped of its more melodramatic accretions — is almost certainly true.

If the Church has come to treasure sex, it is not because she has always been clear and unambiguous in holding the physical aspects of conjugal love to be a glorious revelation of God's intentions for man, but because she has had to pull herself together in the light of the secular sexual revolution. The brewing storm of sexual ferment prompted the writing of *Humanae Vitae*; once the storm was howling in its full rage, John Paul II wrote, from the eye of the hurricane, the *Theology of the Body* — his *opus* on the meaning of sexuality and the body.

The starting point for John Paul II's reflections is a conjunction of Scripture and experience. He begins with the words of Christ to the Pharisees, when He was asked about the indissolubility of marriage, and then moves back into the first chapters of Genesis, and the creation of man — male and female — in the image and likeness of God. From here, the late Pope proceeded with a deep contemplation of the meaning of creation, obviously based both on his experiences of God as Creator, and his experiences of body, as a corporeal human being. All of this was stewed together in a mind strongly influenced by Kant and Scheler, written down in Polish, and then translated various times to arrive at the texts that are available to us English-speaking readers. Predictably, the result is not as revelatory and accessible as we might have hoped: there are no easy answers here that can be picked up with a quick reading on a lazy Sunday afternoon. *Theology of the Body* is, perhaps, the most demanding work that I have ever read: not because it is difficult and impenetrable — any German philosopher can out-obfuscate John Paul II, even on a slow day — but because it requires a clear and honest introspective gaze.

It is for this reason, I think, that it has been skipped over by so many of its critics, lambasted as being dense, slow-moving, and unrewarding. Like sexuality itself, it is not a work that easily yields its secrets; if it had been any other way, it would not likely have been as successful (in terms of fulfilling its goals) as it is. Sexuality is not a subject that can be easily understood on the fly: it connects man with the deepest mysteries of nature and being; it is the means by which we came into this world; and it is the means by which we most profoundly transcend the subjective prisons of self and come into true communication — a "one-flesh" union — with another human being.

John Paul II's approach to sexuality is through the dignity of the human person. It is an obvious starting point, but one that modernist and postmodernist notions of sexuality tend to miss. A certain fixation on the act itself, and on the pleasures that can be derived from various manifestations of it, obscure the fact that this is a fundamentally human act — that conjugal love between human beings is not simply the same thing that horses and tigers do.

The animal represents the lowest form of sexual relating, at least in a human sense, which is why human commentators often speak of "animal lust," and which is also why bestial, wild-man figures hold so much appeal in pornographic art and writing. When sex is reduced to an exchange of pleasures, the other person's personality becomes a burden. This is, almost without a doubt, the reason why anonymous sex is so popular in the various "sexual minority" subcommunities. It is also the reason why, as Eduard Roditi observed:

> There are certain types of male homosexual who are only capable of having sexual relationships with people whom they despise. I've also had conversations with women prostitutes who also complained to me of a high percentage of men who go with prostitutes for the pleasure of brutalizing them and insulting them and who are incapable of having a really loving relationship.[45]

Sexual orientation is beside the point: if the purpose of sexuality is mere pleasure, sooner or later the other person, with all of their personality and their own, separate desires, is going to become burdensome. The ideal, then, becomes "no names, just sex"; the partners use each other to gain a particular pleasure, trying, as much as possible, to remain totally separated in their own realms of subjective experience.

A Vagina Is a "Really Neat Toy"

The reduction of the role and importance of human "personhood" in understanding sex — the idea of the sexual act as part of a lowest-common-denominator utilitarianism — is the foundational principle underlying much of the modern study of sexuality. What is taught under the guise of sexual education is a nuts-and-bolts approach in which the human person is ignored or treated as an insignificant variable in the equation. I recall, for example, going to the "Sex with Sue" lecture offered to frosh when I arrived at university. I was, at that time, attempting to construct a sexual ethic based on beauty and interhuman communication, starting from Keats' aphorism that "Beauty is truth, truth beauty." I was still under the misapprehension that a university is a place of higher learning where young people go in order to be inducted into the "examined life" of which Socrates spoke so highly. So I went to see "Sex with Sue."

Sue Johansen was a leading sexological expert who had been invited to teach froshlings everything they needed to know about sex. The condoms at the door ought to have alerted me, but I politely declined them (lesbians don't need condoms) and took my seat. All around me were thousands of fellow students, recently released from the constraints of parental supervision, swimming in an atmosphere of easy liquor, sequestered in coed dormitories. It all rested on Sue to provide some sort of sanity to this fermenting slop of hormones and freedom. Did she? No. For some reason, the allegedly intelligent adults who decide these things felt that what the frosh really needed to know was how to find the G-Spot.

I listened very closely. The psychological, spiritual, emotional, personal, and ethical dimensions of sexuality got precisely one line: froshlings needed to consider their emotional needs and maturity before deciding, for example, whether to engage in dildo-play.

I was scandalized. Suddenly, the date-rape statistics that we had been taught to fear (most of them culled from university campuses) made sense. This was what caused them. Had somebody gone insane?

I was not scandalized because of prudery — I was a practicing lesbian; I thought incest between consenting adults ought to be decriminalized. I was scandalized because I thought someone who had spent her entire life thinking about and studying human sexuality would have something intelligent to say about the matter. Obviously, the frosh didn't want to hear something intelligent: they wanted to hear *it's fun, it's free, it's here, so get down to it!* But Sue wasn't invited or paid for by the frosh. She was called in as an expert. And I will admit, she knew things about the mechanics of sex that I did not know before I went to that talk. Still, it occurred to me that I was eighteen, thought about sex rarely, had not studied it at all, and usually didn't bother to include it in my curriculum of literary and philosophical reading — yet I seemed to have a more profound and well-considered philosophy of sex than this woman who was supposed to be teaching us about the subject.

What many sexologists seem to lack is a foundation on which to start building a philosophy of sex. They are as likely to say something meaningful about the subject as a child is likely to spontaneously develop a metaphysics of Barbie dolls. Sue's talk ran more like "Hey, look, guys! I got a great new toy called a vagina! Let me tell you about all the neat things it can do!" than like an adult discussion of a serious issue.

Full of Sound and Fury

Underneath the pop and fizzle of sexological enthusiasm lies a fundamental despair — not necessarily about life itself, but about the body. This seems counterintuitive: surely, the sexual revolution is about the celebration of the body over and against the pretense that love ends below the neck. Yet beneath all the pageantry of free sex and self-love, there is a fundamental belief that the body doesn't *mean* anything, that it is insignificant in a literal sense: signifying nothing. You can do anything that you like with it, you can pleasure it with a vacuum cleaner or get a drunken stranger in an alleyway to whip it, and you can give it away to anyone for any reason. It's just a sort of wet machine, a tool that you can use and exchange for whatever purpose suits your fancy.

In order to believe this, you must either accept a) that your body is not you, it is just a shell, or a juicy robot, that the real you — the disembodied ghost — controls, or b) that there is no such thing as human value or dignity; it's just a nice pretense that we make because we are terrified of this senseless and nihilistic universe. Ironically, Christianity, which has always been accused of putting God before man, stands alone amongst a host of modern philosophies declaring that man is a unified, complete being, composed of both a mind with a free will, and a body, all of which has dignity and meaning. Humanism, after the promise of its first flowering, has not managed to produce an integrated and holistic understanding of the human person. It has produced dualisms, disembodied rationalisms, and mindless (literally) materialisms. The alchemical formula by which the angel and the beast are made one is lost to modernism.

At the heart of the modern philosophical project is the attempt to understand human existence without reference to God. The attempt is abjectly futile. It is as though a fourth-century Visigoth had been handed a heap of parts, some of which did and some of which did not properly belong to an airplane, and had been given the instruction to build himself a Boeing 747. The project of realizing our humanity, formed, as it was in the beginning, in the image and likeness of God, is so profoundly difficult, even with the image of Christ — God made Man — set before us, that it is impossible — and, in the sense that Sartre would use the word, *absurd* — without even that image to begin from.

With regards to sexuality, sexology is able to describe the pieces with some accuracy, but it is powerless to form them into a coherent whole. Hence the "Balkanization of sexuality"— the tendency of sexual identities to fragment and divide, seemingly infinitely, as the purpose and meaning of sex becomes obscured. *Theology of the Body* is an attempt at an antidote to this problem; a means of placing sexuality in the context of the whole human person, and of human history since the beginning.

In the Beginning

It begins with Adam and Eve. Whether or not you accept the inspiration of Scripture or believe that there really was a literal Garden of Eden that was literally inhabited by a man made from mud and a woman made from his rib, you would have to be aesthetically and mythically illiterate not to understand that this is an important piece of prose. For my present purposes, it doesn't matter one jot whether it actually happened or not: all that matters is that it conveys a great deal of mythic or psychological truth.[*]

Adam and Eve are in the garden, they are naked together, and they feel no shame (cf. Gen. 2:25). One thinks of the innocence of infants: a one-year-old can cruise around the backyard with his bottom exposed and be, literally, shameless. Our first parents, like our youngest children, are without shame because they are innocent. There is nothing that Adam's gaze could see, looking on Eve, that she would want to hide, and nothing moving in Eve's heart as she looks at Adam that would compel her to avert her gaze.

---

[*] All, that is, that matters for the argument: I personally hold that the story is true.

Nudists, of course, try to pretend that it is possible to role back the angel with the flaming sword and enter again into a garden of earthly delights in which clothing and shame are things of the past. The difficulty is, it doesn't work. Perhaps there is a time, somewhere down the line of nudist colony life, where people get "used to" it — the conscience, and one's sense of shame, will eventually dull themselves. But to begin with? I remember when feminists in Toronto first claimed the right for women to walk around bare-chested. Naturally, the only people who made any use of the privilege were squeegee girls hoping to make an extra buck, and radical feminists, who did it out of duty, for the sake of the emerging gynarchy. I was one of these. I made my attempt — if it was hot, damn it, I was going to walk around topless just like men. I didn't believe in shame and guilt, particularly not sexual shame and guilt. The only question I had to ask, then, was why I felt it so fiercely, like a psychospiritual rash running down my back? In any case, I was intensely uncomfortable, and not because other people made me uncomfortable or looked at me strangely. That intense, nagging feeling — the desire to run out and find a fig leaf to cover myself with — came from within.

Why do we feel shame? Because nakedness is a revelation of the body, and as such, a revelation of the self. To be seen naked is to be laid bare; physical nakedness is a symbolic representation of the nakedness of the soul. A husband and wife may be naked with one another because at the heart of their relationships there is knowledge of the other person; not merely "carnal knowledge," but also self-communication and communion, which allows the spouses to know each other in a way that they do not know anyone else. Anyone involved in a reasonably functional marriage knows and understands this: a husband or wife is privy to secrets that are otherwise concealed from the world. Ideally, in marriage, there is a movement towards a more and more perfect communication/communion, such that, over time, the earthly marriage becomes a more perfect symbol of the union between Christ and His Church, and even of the internal unity that forms the intimate life of the Trinity.[46]

Man, according to Christian anthropology, is made in the "image and likeness" of God. Sexuality is not a departure from this image, but an extension of it. God is not endowed with a penis or a womb, as various pagan deities are, but these things are an image nonetheless because of their internal significations. For this, we return to "the beginning," to Adam in the garden, in the first hours of creation, when he is granting to all of the animals their names (cf. Gen. 2:19). He makes a complete survey of his domain, granting to everything a fitting name; a word, by which it will now be designated and by which it becomes a part of the intellectual inheritance of man. No longer is nature "dumb." Man is her voice, and he calls her by name.

And yet, in all of the beauty of the primeval world, Adam does not find what he is looking for. He comes, quickly or slowly, to a terrible and crushing realization: he is alone.[47] He has named the world, but there is no one with whom to share the names. God is present, as close as mind itself, but God is of a different kind, infinitely above him. God does not need to know that a crocodile is called a crocodile, because God is able to penetrate the deepest essence of the beast and understand all the elegant curvature of the genetic code, and deeper matters of which Adam is entirely ignorant. The first privation has entered the world — the first thing, in a long string of "good" and "very good" creatures, that God declares to be "not good." Adam is alone.

With the weight of this original solitude piercing his breast, Adam goes to sleep. It is a deep sleep — God has made sure of it — in which God takes from Adam a rib and fashions from it a new creature, of the same kind as Adam, so much so that it is a part of him. Adam, on waking, declares joyously, "This at last is flesh of my flesh, bone of my bone!" (Gen. 2:23). He recognizes the image of himself, the likeness to himself — but it goes beyond this. Before, Adam has not understood — in a sense, has not known — himself. He has named and known all of the other animals, all of the other species, but not Adam. Trapped in a web of human subjectivity, he has not been able to survey his own kind from the outside. In receiving Eve, he receives not only a helpmate in the work of tending and subduing the garden, but also in the work of becoming human, of realizing himself. She too, at the same time and the same moment, is receiving this same knowledge: looking on Adam, she knows and understands both Adam and herself.[48]

The Epistemological Dilemma of Romulus

If all of this seems very distant, mythical, and abstruse, consider the plight of children who are raised without the benefit of other human contact.

For one thing, there is reason to believe that a baby, housed in a purely mechanical environment, deprived of human contact and human touch, will simply die. But experiments have been done of isolating people from other people, of seeing what they become. The product is a creature that reminds us of an animal, devoid of speech and all of the distinctly human benefits that speech confers. If Romulus and Remus had actually been raised by wolves, they would have identified themselves as wolves, would have understood themselves in the image of wolf-kind. What other rubric would they have had? To a wolf, this is not a problem. The wolf is not saddled with the burdens of self-knowledge. Cows do not have existential crises. Mice do not fret about defining their sexual identities. Yet Romulus and Remus would not have been wolves, even if they had been wolf-identified. But what language would they have had to convey these impressions to themselves with?

There is something to be learned watching an infant, or meditating on the meaning of life in the womb. A baby is without speech. It has no names for anything. And yet it is still possessed of a human consciousness. What does the world look like in that state? What does it mean to be in the world, conscious, with a human consciousness, processing everything directly, unmediated by language and thoughts and categories? Allegedly there are certain psychotropic substances that, if taken in high enough doses, will give modern, jaded man a taste of this kind of experience, and there is some evidence to suggest that certain mental "aberrations" or neurological "disorders" are really just a matter of people living in this sort of relationship to the world.[49] Even then, however, the man on a psychedelic high may only approach the threshold: he cannot actually enter back into that state when things are unnamed, and language has not yet intruded between the object and the subject.

A baby's self-knowledge is in a primitive state. In the womb, how can the child distinguish between itself and its mother, between its being and its environment? Senses slowly emerge. Sounds, feelings. Consciousness begins to map its boundaries out; the growing body is its extension into the material world. But there can be no understanding of what this creature — this body — is, of what it means. Only at birth, when the child suddenly becomes aware that it is separated from its environment, that there is another — a mother — can the process of self-knowledge and self-identification really begin. For a newborn, this is "all at once." Adam had already named and known creation before he was introduced to the astonishing revelation of Eve. The newborn finds it all in one blinding moment of pain and air and light, and it is too much. The little human cries, and is startled, and then roots around desperately, with his deepest instincts, for contact with the mother that has been his only reality until now. From there on he is learning things so basic that we take them for granted. He is learning to see: his mind is creating the pathways from which random radiances of spectral light are transformed into meaningful and concrete objects. He is relearning to exercise his muscles: to understand that there is a point of contact between himself and this strangeness, that he is able to manipulate, to operate, to act, to will. Eventually — developmental psychologists tell us, with difficulty, and with that terrible angst we call "separation anxiety" — he comes to realize that mother is a different creature from himself. He enters into that fundamental experience of solitude which confronted Adam in the Garden. He comes into the inheritance of that subjectivity which has been his birthright from the start.

To Know and Not to Know

The child comes to know and to understand itself, and its humanity, in relationship with other human beings. From subjectivity, he reaches out toward the other. The slow cracking of the subjective shell leads him into ever-expanding spheres of interaction and communication. But the world is broken. Children do not merely learn to share and reveal themselves; they also learn to hide, to conceal, to lie, and dissemble, and protect. They learn to be defensive; to keep quiet when something they feel or believe will bring displeasure to others. They learn to know others, and to be known — and, at the same time, learn not to be known.

It does not matter what sort of environment you raise your child in — how permissive, encouraging, gentle, and noncritical you may be, or how much you coddle their "self-esteem." The fault lines of the human heart cannot be healed by soft words. The child, left uncorrected, will grow monstrous; then, all at once, they will learn that the world has limits, and they will be like a tiny thwarted beast who has just discovered its cage. Humanity has learned to conceal itself because it has learned that there really are dark places within that it dares not let anyone else look. If you open up your heart to another person and reveal your dark side, your weaknesses, you become very vulnerable. Marriage — real marriage, not this "Let's have a ceremony and see if it works out; I've already arranged the pre-nup with my lawyer" nonsense — is supposed to be a protected sanctuary in which one can afford this kind of nakedness. That is why spouses cannot be forced to testify against one another in court. Even the confessional, or the psychiatrist's couch, does not have this sort of protection: in the confessional, you are traditionally "unseen" in that the priest comes to know your sins, but (except in some unique circumstances) does not come to know *you*. As for psychology, every good psychologist that I have ever read is constantly wrestling with the problem of secretiveness, guardedness, retentiveness, slant, spin, and self-deception in their patients. Nakedness does not come easily to fallen man.

By the Light of the Original Fiat

This, of course, is all a reflection of reality after the fall — man in his unperfected state, as we are all familiar with him. Yet within this imperfection can be glimpsed a little of the light that originally shone on the face of Adam — just as a phosphorescent algae holds within it a little remnant of the sun, and thus the nature of light is revealed in the darkness. *Theology of the Body* is a looking backwards, past the accretions of sin and death in the world, to discover the meaning and significance of the body in its original innocence. To be crude, if you wish to know how a vacuum cleaner is supposed to work, you would be best to look at the factory model: what did it look like when it was first made and was functioning precisely to the engineers' specifications? Looking at the rusted old junk heap that has been patched together with duct tape, that has half its brushes replaced with old circular hair combs, and that is lucky if it is able to wheeze in a handful of light dust before clunking down into a disheveled pile of parts, is unlikely to yield an accurate picture of the purpose of the machine. If it works badly enough, it might be mistaken for a work of modern art, or a musical instrument from Zubenelgenubi.

Sexology* is the attempt to reconstruct a series of uses for the broken vacuum cleaner. It sits around and tinkers with the bits, and watches other people tinker with them, and then runs around studying the different uses that are made of the wreckage. "Hmm, a whale's tooth-brush. How interesting. Chalk it down." The presumption is that there is not an intention; there was no engineer, the parts were not originally assembled into something meaningful, and there is no correct way of reassembling it so that it "works." Sex becomes a "found object" into which every person reads their own meanings and intentions, like children finding dragons and toy boats in the clouds. Over time, people develop a "script" that works for them, a way of being and relating to sex that makes sense in their particular life context. It is not for any-one to declare that anyone else's preferences are "right" or "wrong," any more than my interpretation of a Jackson Pollock is more correct than yours.

All of this is very well if you are talking about broken vacuum cleaners, cloud-forms, or meaningless modern art. There is, however, nothing "deep" or "profound" about senselessness. If you think that you have discovered the true meaning of everything by discovering that there is no meaning, or that there is something intently clever about the idea of sticking together bits and bobs in a haphazard way to create "art" that doesn't say a thing, you're in for a bit of a shock. This isn't "new" or "cutting edge" or "avant-garde": it's just the philosophy that

---

* I mean, here, sexology as an approach to an understanding of sex, not sexology in its strictest sense, as the study of sex. There is nothing wrong with a sexologist who studies human sexuality from a scientific point of view in order to better understand its human dimensions. Unfortunately, the discipline tends towards that scientific reductionism which believes that because a thing has been described it has been understood.

cockroaches developed long before your ancestors dragged themselves out of the slime. Gussying it up in big words doesn't make it any more penetrating or original.

Sex is not a more or less irrelevant toy. It is a life-making technology; an intense form of interpersonal communication; a tool for joining together disparate human persons into one; a transcender of subjectivity. It is a work of art, full of symbol and purpose, created by the highest of all Artists, and then given to humanity as a gift, in order to allow us to participate in the transmission and creation of our own species. It is not a bit of biological flotsam to be disposed of how we will.

Many people — particularly the sex-experts — do not believe this. It doesn't matter. If you think that an atomic generator is a neat toy, and that all the people saying it requires proper "safety precautions" are just party-poopers, you can expect to die of radiation poisoning sooner or later. It doesn't matter if you can come up with a clever argument, or a really neat joke, or a radically new sexual position to express your feelings about the matter. Reality is hopelessly intractable; she will not bend herself out of shape to fit your paradigm or conform herself pleasantly to human delusions — even if it can be statistically proven that those delusions are shared by 90% of the American people.

This is why truth — particularly truth about humanity, sexuality, and the body — is necessary. These are things of which we are made, fundamental components of our human being. We ought to figure out what they are for. The alternative is to muck around until we are completely broken, and, for the sake of a quick thrill, reduce ourselves to rubble and human scrap.

PART III

Homosexuality and the Human Person

CHAPTER 7

Body

I am going to try to step down from my soapbox for a moment. I feel very strongly about all of these things — not because I want to enforce them from the top down, establish a theocratic dominion over sex, or rob people of their fun. Nor do I care because I'm worried that "those disgusting homos are going to seduce my children," or that the world is going end in fire and brimstone, or that the American Empire will fall into the hands of invading Islamogoths as punishment for our iniquities. I care because *I* was lied to. I tried for years to live in accordance with that lie, and it caused me and those around me a great deal of suffering on account. I'm not angry. It was my own decision, and there was never any malicious intent behind the half-truths: my gurus were confused, trying to work out truth as well as they could, just as I was confused, and the whole thing no doubt goes back to a certain decision to eat a particular apple many millennia ago. I am not a prophet thundering from my mountain; I'm Balaam's ass, saying "Uh, Master, I think maybe we ought not to go down that road. What's that? Oh, you don't see the angel with the flaming sword. Well, it plans to cut your head off. I thought you should know."

Theology of the Body

That said, it is time to stop criticizing the sexologists, gender theorists, and liberal media mavens, and try to give a serious account of the truth. After all, there's no good in me shouting, "Don't listen to them! It's all a lie! A lie, I tell you!" if I'm not going to offer any reasonable alternative. I promised to discuss the meaning of the body, so here we go.

At the heart of the *Theology of the Body* is the idea of the gift. The body is a gift, given to man by God. It is the means by which man receives all other gifts. It is a gift which man may give to another or receive from another. It is the gift which, when given, creates another body, another gift, and so on and so forth, through an entire anthropological economy built up on donation and self-giving love.

The first sense in which the body is a gift is not deniable. You received your body, on the first day, as a gift from your mother, who received it as a gift from your father, both of whom received their bodies as gifts from their parents, and so on and so forth, back to the dawn of creation — when, if you believe in any sort of Creator, the first man and the first woman received their bodies as gifts from God. There was no sense in which you could possibly be construed to have "earned" your body: you didn't even exist before it came into being. You couldn't even go and beg for a mortgage under contract to pay for it later. Your parents could have decided to withhold being from you; there's nothing you could have done to cajole, coerce, beg, plead, threaten, bully, or buy them out of that decision. The nonexistent cannot plead their rights.

The body is a gift, given to a child at the moment of its conception.

The Gift through Which All Gifts Are Given

It is more than that, though. Without the body, there is nothing else. I once tried, as a thought experiment in solipsism, to break down a train of thought, to come up with the ideas and inferences of a human creature devoid of senses or experience. Pure reason, functioning in a void. About twelve steps in, the entire project collapsed. It was impossible to come up with anything to think without reference to some sort of sensory or experiential category. A thought is composed of words, and speech begins with concrete things and then moves towards the abstract. There has never been a child whose first coherent word/thought is "ontology." It is always "mama" or "dada," "cat" or "shoes," something concrete to which the child attaches particular significance. But without those first concrete parts of vocabulary, the rest of speech literally cannot be conceived. And without speech, without words, there are no rational thoughts.

"Ah!" the crafty critic exclaims, "Human beings can think also in images! Words are not the *sine qua non* of human thought. We can imagine, create pictures, swirling visions . . ." True. Yet these, too, are composed from concrete things. It is not possible to create an image comprehensible to the human mind that is not made up of real impressions garnered from the world — even if the "objects" in the image are not "real," the qualities which those objects possess (squareness, roundness, fluidness, hardness, bumpiness, ugliness, crystallineness, redness, etc.) are culled from reality.

I am not throwing my hat in with the Empiricists. Mere experience is not sufficient in and of itself. A three-toed sloth has the same amount of contact with concrete reality as a human being does, but it lacks conscious reason. No matter how many particular instantiations of the color red it encounters, it will never make the categorical leap to the abstract notion of redness. It will never name the red, or see the connectedness between this bit of red and that bit of red under the single glorious revelation that red is a quality which inheres in a thousand places, and yet is always the same. No, experience without reason does not amount to knowledge. A coherent epistemology requires both: one cannot separate one's mental faculties and put them at war with one another. To ask which came first, and which ought to have philosophical primacy, is like asking whether a child came from its mother or from its father.

So it is, also, with the body and the mind. A human being without a body is not something that can actually be thought about in a meaningful way; human reason requires sensory facts, incoming data, in order to function at all.* Sensations, experiences, information about an external world, all come to man through the body.

Some New Agers and Gnostics believe that the body is a sort of clay prison or chrysalis through which humanity is passing on its way to a glorious disembodied life, floating around through the stars or the realms of the imagination, no longer tied down to physical reality. That is all very well — except that in all these pleasant daydreams, the body is not done away with: it is merely transformed. The star child may not have a body of flesh and blood, but it does have a body: its consciousness inheres in a particular globule of light; it moves through

---

* This does not mean that God and the angels must logically be in the same boat: we cannot reason from "It is thus for humanity" to "I must logically be thus for categorically different kinds of beings."

space and time in a particular way; it is here, and not there — this, and not that. It has senses of some sort, and it has some definite means of interacting with the rest of reality. A ghost has a spectral body, made up, perhaps, of latent energies, or drops of water lurking in the midnight air. An esoteric traveler in the Middle Plateau has an astral body. A dreamer dreams a body for herself. Even the famous "brain in a vat" of rationalist thought-experiments has some means of interacting, sensing, and rendering its will effective in the concrete world — a computer body, perhaps?

What all of these alternative bodies have in common is that they are lesser, not greater than, the body we actually have. On first glance it sounds wonderful to have an imaginary body that can be transformed into anything by the will, and which is free to explore, forever, the infinite realms of fantasy — but the reality is, it would quickly become boring. The real world, if you are inclined to look into it, is full of marvels and mysteries; you do not need to "sail beyond the sunset and the baths of all the Western stars" to get "beyond the utmost bounds of human thought." I'm a writer of speculative fiction, and I constantly find that ideas which I consider stunningly original, the highest delights of the imagination, are actually things that exist in the world — usually in a more interesting form than the one I came up with. A couple steps off the beaten path of modernity, you will find Behemoth and St. Michael, strange lights glimmering beneath the waters, and cultures so alien they make the Klingons look as American as apple pie. This is one of the wonders of the real body: it can take us into places that we have not been before. It can stumble on the unexpected, and it can confront us with facts and realities that we could not imagine. The body is directly effective in the real world, but not so much so that reality loses its form and coherence. It is expressive, and it directs itself through the world in a purposive and significant way. More profoundly, it is capable not merely of moving and seeing, but of receiving. The entire life of the body is built up around this reception, this taking in, this constant tangible evidence of the gift. Air is pulled into the lungs, food is found and given to the stomach, medicines come as a relief to pain, life itself is culled from a mingling of bodies and DNA. The entirety of the world, all lived experiences, all rational categories, everything that we have and that we are comes to us, is given to us, through the medium of the body. It is the gift through which all other gifts are given.

This is the second sense in which the body is gift.

Love Comes of Age

The third sense is that the body is a gift which we can give to another. It is not merely a received gift, but also an invitation to an act of self-donation, the "sincere gift of self" to which John Paul II constantly refers. It is on this level that sexuality enters the picture in the fullness of its meaning. No longer is sexual union merely the means by which this gift came to us; it becomes something in which we may participate. Here, at last, the will is fully manifest, and the activity of the will is love.

Love: not a rising tide of bodily fluids and hormones, a psycho-physical mess to be cleared up by YM questionnaires about "Is it the Real Thing?" Love: an act of the will, a gift given without reservation and, in a sense, irrationally. Philosophical gobbledygook about "rationally self-interested morality" holds no sway in the courts of love. Love is madness. It is not the stupid, drippy, half-imbecilic madness that oozes off the screen at a romantic comedy. That sort of madness is far too sane for love. No, love is the sort of madness that makes people declare that they are going to fly to the moon, or build massive coral castles for their "sweet sixteen." To declare that you love another human being is to drop yourself off the edge into the mythic stream of reality, to consent to be carried along through unmapped realms, smashed against the rocks, shipwrecked, cast up gasping on alien beaches, and then rushed off to float through halcyon seas under a sky as broad as heaven. Once you have done it, there is no returning. You can swim against the current, lug yourself up onto the beach, and wander off, bruised and disheveled, hoping that somewhere over the rainbow there is another, gentler river, but you will never make it back to that state of innocence from which you undertook the journey in the first place.

This is, I am certain, why when I was a rationalist, a solipsist, a nihilist, an atheist, an existentialist, etc. etc., I absolutely refused to say "I love you." The "l" word was quite literally banned. I did not tell my girlfriend that I loved her; I did not tell any of my boyfriends that I loved them. I had nothing but the utmost contempt for all the little girlie-girls running around my high-school swooning over their latest crush and yammering about how they were "in love." *No you're not*, I thought, *you're in heat, in hormones, in delusion, in fantasy, in lust, insane. That is not love. If it were, you wouldn't sleep with him this month, and break up with him next.* Eventually, I came to the conclusion that there was really not much more to "love" — at least romantic love — than all this nonsense, and I wrote the matter off. Love was redefined in my vocabulary as excluding the body and the person: one could love humanity, could love one's family, could love in a wholly abstract sense, "to will the good of another." Plato's love. Aristotle's love. Fine. But to be "in love," to say "I love you," instead of "One loves humanity"? No.

Love involves the whole person. Romantic or erotic love involves the whole person most of all — there are plenty of other kinds of love in which you make a sincere gift that comes out of yourself, but do not actually give your self entirely. We are speaking, though, of conjugal love, married love, sexual love. This is the sort of love in which you actually give your entire self, and the body is the means by which this is demonstrated. Two lovers, in one another's embrace, hold nothing back. The body is naked, its most precious recesses are shared, its highest capacity — the capacity to give substance to another life — is exercised. Two become one, and in becoming one, create a third. The gift is not temporary, it is absolute; it is made concrete in the conception of the child. Something new has come into being; the ontological structure of the person is changed.

Humor: a Reality Check

But that's not what sex is about at all, is it? Lighten up. Sex is fun, it's relaxing, it's ridiculous. The problem with all of us Catholics is that we have this airy-fairy, pie-in-the-sky *über*serious understanding of sexuality. For the rest of the world — and even for most of the sane Catholics — it's nothing like that at all. When was the last time that you made love to your husband, or wife, and thought "Oh! We are becoming one! We are the sacramental manifestation of Christ's love for His Church! We are the Image of the intimate life of the Holy Trinity!"? Never. What you're really thinking is, "The baby had better not wake up halfway through like last time. I wish he'd had a shower in the last week. Did I remember to turn the dishwasher on?" Right? So don't give me all of this nonsense about how sex is holy and must be kept in a shining tabernacle, protected from the blasphemy of condoms and fur-lined handcuffs. Get real, take yourselves less seriously, put your high horse in the stable, and have some fun like everybody else.

Sex is, indeed, ridiculous. Let us be honest about this: it's not like in those Hollywood movies where perfect bodies move against each other with choreographed perfection and airbrushed skin, under a soft light, to the sound of swelling strings. The reality is that you take two bodies — one is skinny, the other is going to fat; they have hair in all the wrong places; their toenails are jagged; their noses are blunt and stubby; and it's three in the morning, so they both have bright red cheeks and bags under the eyes. Somehow, these misshapen puzzle pieces have to be jammed together so as to produce a rough approximation of ecstasy. They turn red, make funny noises, jiggle the bedsprings too loudly, wake up the people in the next apartment. A farce. It is not without reason that sex, along with death and religion, forms the basis of most of mankind's humor. This is very funny stuff.

Humor, though, is not a basis on which to reject myth or morality. To take life so seriously that you cannot stand to see it joked about is an error, but to take the joke so seriously that you miss the meaning of life is just foolish. When Bill Cosby says that children "are brain-damaged people," or describes his wife looming over the dining room table demanding that he go upstairs and kill their son, we laugh. This wouldn't be funny — in fact, it would be horribly sinister — if you actually took Bill Cosby seriously. It is funny because we know that Bill Cosby loves his children, and that there is absolutely no threat that he is actually going to murder his offspring — and also, because we recognize our own families and our own frustrations, and are relieved to know that everyone else is living in the same ridiculous madhouse that we are.

If, however, you believed the joke was the whole truth — that children are brain-damaged, and that being a parent instantly transforms beautiful, rational human beings into ugly harpies contemplating the evisceration of their progeny — you have missed the point. The point is not "Don't have kids, they'll ruin your life." The joke is only part of the truth, not to be mistaken for the essence of parenthood.

So it is with sex. The ridiculous noises, the fact that genitalia are absurd looking organs, impotence, lack of lubrication, the aging of the body — none of this has anything to do with the meaning of sexuality, any more than the absurd and sometimes hilarious transformations that a word can undergo during a game of "telephone" have anything to do with the meaning of language. Sex itself may, in any given instance, be silly, beautiful, ecstatic, charming, rushed, half-conscious, beatific. Sometimes you come very near to the fountainhead from which it springs, and then it is transformed, and all the scales of the world seem to fall away, and what you find is something like a revelation. Or, on the other hand, it can be as ordinary as a boiled potato.

Unconscious Reality

How a person experiences sex — the individual, and in some sense unrepeatable, experience of making love on a particular day — is a different matter from what sex, as an element of human reality, means. It is this way with every aspect of the human body: whether you are thinking about it or not, the body retains its meaning and its purposes.

A meal will nourish you regardless of whether it tastes like lembas bread or microwave porridge. You might, as certain esoteric traditions suggest, make sure that you always consume your meals with the utmost engagement of your faculties, so that you taste every morsel and shade of flavor; so that you become conscious of the food going down into your body, of the processes of digestion, of the miracle by which a carrot becomes the motive energy by which you open and close your hand. You might contemplate, as you snack on a rice cake, all of the complex chemical interactions that allow the wafer in your hand to become the stuff of thought. What an absurd and profound reality. Or you might simply stuff your burger into your head and get on with your day.

Most people never bother to deeply contemplate the processes of the body, to search out their spiritual meanings, to discover their literary resonances, to delve in the science of respiration, or the symbolic traditions associated with drinking, but this does not mean that the superficial experience of air going in, air going out, of thirst and urination, is all that there is. Human beings are conscious. Horses may have to settle for choosing to drink or not to drink the water; human beings have the option of contemplating the water, of experiencing it artistically, of weighing and measuring it, of making jokes about it.

So we come back to the meaning of sex, and the gift of the body. The gift is often an amusing, mysterious, unknown, strange, and difficult gift. Sometimes it seems like a white elephant. Still, it is a gift. This is the meaning of sexuality, underneath all of the superficial hubbub. The body has its own language; the meaning of sexuality flows out of the nature of the gift, which proceeds from the fact that man is not a hodgepodge of faculties and organs, but a unified whole. To give the body is to give the self.

Interlopers in the Marriage Bed

In childhood, everyone learns that you cannot give a gift and then take it back again. When the gift is something as important, as integral, as the self, this sort of gifting, reclaiming, regifting, etc. is exceedingly dangerous. Every time that you give it, there is some part that you don't quite manage to get back, and the value of the whole is diminished.

I have spoken to women, now married, who have lamented sleeping with other men before climbing into the marriage bed. "You're never really alone together. Those others are always with you." This is absolutely true. I have never "been with" another man, apart from my husband (let's call it one of the occupational perks of identifying as lesbian), but I know that there are times when I am kissing my husband, or lying next to him, and the image or memory of some other person that I once kissed or held comes unbidden into my mind. It's exceedingly unpleasant — I love my husband, I want to think of him, and be with him, and the memory of some past failed relationship is the last thing that I want cluttering up my consciousness when I am trying to make love.

Think of what promiscuity does to a person's understanding of human love. You make a gift of yourself. Let's say that you do it casually, what are you saying? "I'm not worth much, but fortunately, neither are you, so let's have some fun." If you do it seriously, with something closer to the gravity due to your own dignity, it is, in many ways, worse: it means that when the gift is returned, damaged, it is a deeply hurtful rejection. So often, people who are "toying around" with sex, trying to "have fun" get themselves involved in relationships where one party is treating the other as an object, and the other party is heavily invested. This is gravely immoral on the part of the person who takes another's gift lightly, uses it for their own enjoyment, and then gives it back.

This was precisely how I behaved in high school. I was a rationalist about it, of course, and I didn't laugh with my friends about my conquests; that would have been tacky. But I did believe that you could have "open relationships," casual arrangements between two people who wanted some sort of physical intimacy but did not want all of the messy complications of being "in love" or even of "going out." More than once, this caused tremendous emotional damage to the other person, but I couldn't see that this defied my moral maxims. Certainly, they had gotten hurt, but it seemed that it was something like mountain climbing: you knew when you started out that there was a risk of falling, and it was ridiculous to blame the mountain. It took a very long time to realize that I *was* the mountain — and that unlike a mountain, I had moral free will.

Retreat from Personhood

Even when I was young, on some level I sensed that sex — "real" sex — was different. That was the frightening, undiscovered country, the deep waters where the map reads, "Here there be dragons." Let me frolic in the lesbian shallows, and play at making out with boys on the side. But woe to any boyfriend who thinks he's getting my pants off. This is my inner sanctum; ain't no man getting in here.

The inner sanctum. That is, really, what a woman's womb is. Alice von Hildebrand once noted that the hymen is a veil that covers the woman's reproductive organs until it is pushed aside in her first sexual encounter. In the mysterious inner language of the body, this is the place where the miracle, the transmutation of sperm and ova into the body and blood of a new human being, takes place. It is a symbol, on the human order, of the highest divine mysteries: what some writers have called a "natural sacrament." The body is given, as a gift, to another, who makes an equal and identical gift of himself, and from this the gift of a body is given to a new human being who has never before existed. This is the meaning of the body. This is the meaning of sexuality.

But it is a meaning that is only possible according to one of the various sexual formulae proposed by sexological experts. The fluid of life enters the sanctuary of the womb only during "normal" sex. Normal, here, is a very appropriate word: this is the norm. It is nature's norm, it is the norm of myth and archetype, it is the norm for which the body was designed, and it is the norm of morality. The depth of meaning expressed through conjugal love between a man and a woman simply is not possible in any other scenario. The mouth is not the body's "holy of holies" — it is the organ by which you consume and digest things. The anus is the organ by which you excrete waste. On purely symbolic, archetypal grounds, oral and anal sex are a mess — and the beauty of these acts, considered objectively, is quite elusive. This often baffles good Catholics, who genuinely wish to be understanding and compassionate. For half a second the shadow of what gay sex actually involves flits across their minds and they demand, with frank perplexity, "How can they *do* that?"

There are several answers. They are not particular to homosexuality: as many gay activists are quick to point out, the forms of "sexual expression" available to the homosexual community are practiced by heterosexuals as well as gays.

The simplest, and probably the most common solutions, involve a retreat from the fullness of human reality. Particularly amongst those who practice promiscuity, it is common to resort to materialistic reductionism; if man lowers his level of conscious activity and functionally ceases to be a rational creature, then physical pleasure can be enjoyed as an animal might enjoy it. This is often accomplished with the help of alcohol or other intoxicants. Composer Ned Rorem once observed, "A lot of my drinking had to do with being able to go to bed with people, being drunk enough to put myself in certain positions . . . If you're drunk you're not ashamed of playing a certain role."[50] This is a pattern that I have encountered several times speaking with young women who are unable to break a habit of promiscuity: they feel they must get drunk because they want to "get laid" but couldn't do it sober.

On the opposite end of the spectrum is the retreat out of the body into the mind: one pulls back into oneself, conjuring up a fantasy in which the pleasurable activity is situated. This may be a fantasy of genuine romantic involvement saturated in archetypally erotic over-tones — as, for example, when a person masturbating imagines that they are making love to an idealized princess/wife, or when a lesbian imagines that she is in the arms of the mother/goddess who will wing her to heights of ecstasy and protect her from all harm. On the other hand, it may be a fantasy that evokes strong emotions that, even if they are unpleasant, add sufficient "spice" to distract the mind from what the body is doing — this is the case, for example, in fantasies of rape or sadomasochistic scenarios. It may be a fantasy of intense animalis-tic, or even forbidden, bliss: the sort of impulse to which advertisers so skillfully appeal when they describe their products as "forbidden pleasures," or "sinfully delicious."

Both of these options remove the other person, as a person, from the equation. "Anonymity," according to Rorem, "can be so uninhibited, the sex so incredibly fulfilling, that it could never be repeated with the same person, precisely because the next time he would *be* a person . . . some of the best sex I ever had was precisely because of the anonymity: when you're no longer a rational being, but a gibbering idiot throttled by Eros."[51]

One of the difficulties is that although the ethical roots of sexuality inevitably affect us, we are not necessarily conscious of them. Conscious participation in the ethical dimensions of sex requires an act of the will. Generally, those who are not infected with philosophy call this act of will "love," and there are a great many people, much simpler and less needlessly complexified than myself, who have the experience of "knowing and being known" in the sexual act without being able to describe it in polysyllabics. Making love is not, as they say, rocket science, but neither is it a mere submission to animal impulse, the sort of thing that can be accomplished as easily by a monkey as by a man.

The problem for the modern world is that a great many people have become sufficiently indoctrinated with a superficial and inhuman sexuality that they are no longer able to enter into the more human dimensions of the sexual act. Many men will defend masturbation as a valid form of sexual expression on the basis that "It's no different from having sex." If this is true for you, you have never had sex. You've just masturbated with other people.

Most people who have dabbled in the art of "casual sex" without turning it into an idol or a lifestyle are able to recognize this on some level. I remember very distinctly engaging in one of the usual forms of not-quite-sex prescribed to teenagers as a "safe" alternative to the real thing. I was with the last of my attempted boyfriends, and I had the same feeling of deep misgiving and discomfort that I had always felt during physical intimacy with males. In this case it was much more intense, and it finally sharpened itself to the point where it could be named, "I am," I thought, with a sense of deep self-disgust, "using this other human person as a drug." For that brief interchange, I was able to see with absolute clarity that the way in which I was abusing my sexuality, and exploiting his, was utterly incommensurate with the dignity of human beings as "ends in themselves."

Of course this wasn't my experience, generally, of my relationship with Michelle. That was heavily steeped in fantasy, and so my conscience and consciousness were able to escape into a world of delusion that was freed from ordinary ethical constraints. There was one occasion on which she suggested that perhaps, since we had been together so long, and since we spoke as though we were a couple who 'loved' one another in the erotic sense, we should try to make love without the crutch of a mutually agreed upon fantasy. We made it as far as a kiss — what she felt or thought about the experience I'm not certain, but I know, for my part, that I was suddenly aware of having a deep sense of alienation, both from myself and from her. The experiment was, in any case, sufficiently unpleasant that it was not repeated.

The Second Beauty

There is a final possibility, of which I ought to speak. Broken humanity is capable of finding beauty in ugliness — this is really the impulse that is being explored by so much of modern art, particularly that which disgusts, sickens, and appalls the non-desensitized viewer. Degradation, sinfulness, brokenness, disease, all can be perceived as beautiful: this is the appeal to what Dostoyevsky called the "second beauty"[52] — the attraction of evil that lurks in the heart of every person. It is the reason why some women love to have a man "talk dirty" to them; why there is a certain romanticism to the idea of being bound, gagged, and humiliated sexually in front of a pornographer's video camera; why gothlings seek out vampiric dens where they can suck each other's blood; why the ritualization of sadomasochistic degradations holds out an appeal to those who frequent leather bars. It is a sort of cancer of the imagination, which causes the deformed and perverse to become appealing in their own right: the Baron Harkonnen stroking his diseases and bathing himself in filth so that he can become more cankerous and pestilential. Sex, when it becomes infected with this aesthetic plague, ceases to be about the intensely human beauty of love, and becomes about this inhuman second beauty. Rape, humiliation, degradation, and lust become "beautiful" in their own right; self-destructiveness, what Freud called *Thanatos*, or the death-urge, worms its way into the heart of sexuality, and the act by which man conveys life becomes an expression, instead, of the desire for self-annihilation.

Lest the Catholic reader turn up her lip in disgust, this second beauty is something with which we are all familiar. Perhaps you do not find it in sex, but it is there, somewhere: an intense ugliness that you find terribly appealing. Find the sirens singing from the rocks of your own heart, and you will understand. Yes, this is human. We are all ugly — that is why Christ had to come.

CHAPTER 8

Family

What is a family? This is a question that must, at some point or other, enter into any serious consideration of sexual ethics. The primary difficulty that confronts those trying to uphold ideals of heterosexual monogamy is the confusion and conflict that surrounds this word. For some — particularly in the feminist and socialist camps — family is a "retrograde institution," a throwback to prehistoric times when cave-daddies are presumed to have beaten cave-mommies over the head and dragged them off to the cave, much as they would have done with a freshly killed water buffalo. Others still recognize the value and importance of the idea of family, but try to curtail the heteronormative and patriarchal sting of the institution by stretching it beyond any definition that most people would recognize. A large proportion, if not a majority, of homosexuals fall into this camp — not because they want to stretch the definition of a family to include a gay man living with a gay man, but because they feel that their primary loyalties are to "families we choose": a notion which often includes a "family of friends" or even to the gay movement as a kind of extended homosexual "family."[53]

A Terrible Freedom

It seems strange to me, looking back, to realize that this was the form of thinking about family that I adopted when I identified as lesbian. It seems particularly strange not because I now have a family, under the traditional heterosexual man-woman-children formula, but because I was part of such a family then. Somehow I arrived at a condition where I didn't recognize or understand the value of my family — that I would cry at being forced to spend time with them when I wanted to go out and celebrate the important milestones of my life with the people who were really important to me: my friends. That I didn't feel that the people with whom I lived, and who were bound to me by bonds of blood or gratitude, had a right to primacy among my loyalties. That I perceived it as a kind of insane injustice that I should be forced to consider these people first merely because of an accident of the genes.

For many Americans, this sort of thinking is perfectly understand-able — many Americans have never been a part of a whole family in the first place. We can't blame Orlando and Madison for lacking a deep understanding of the value of the family when they came from a broken home. The spiritually orphaned cannot be blamed for trying to build up placebo families for themselves using whatever materials happen to be at hand.

But this excuse does not apply to me. It applies, at least to some degree, to my lesbian girlfriend; her parents were still living together, but it was clear for years that her mother was just waiting for the chil-dren to move out of the house before serving up the divorce papers. I, on the other hand, am the daughter of one woman and one man who recently celebrated their 25th anniversary and the birth of their eighth child. So where on earth did I get this idea that the family was a cheap cardboard construct designed to keep women in their place and fortify the bastions of male dominance?

The source is obvious: I grew up in the '80s, when every sitcom stretched, diluted, or twisted the definition of a family in a different way. I went to school, and I read the newspaper, and I was interested in politics and philosophy, and I was a member of the school feminist group; it is clear enough where this idea came from. The question is, how did I ever come to see it as anything more than a blatant lie?

It was not that I simply swallowed anything that came down the liberal/feminist pipes. I did not, for example, ever embrace the idea that stay-at-home mothering was somehow a mundane and degrading occupation unworthy of female dignity. I had a stay-at-home mom, and I could see that her presence in our lives as children had been extremely beneficial for us, and that she was not particularly oppressed or unhappy in comparison with other women of her age. So it wasn't the psycho-intellectual equivalent of involuntary reflux.

The answer is the most terrible and simple thing in the world: I believed it because I wanted to believe it. I was not a victim of unhappy circumstances, thrown into this world cold and alone, forced to make my way along by feeling, guideless, blind, witless, helpless. I was a human being, and thus possessed of that dreadful capacity we call free will. I came to believe that the family was an imposition by small but definite degrees: by choosing to spend time with my friends and to shut out my sisters, by deciding to sit in the car and read a book at family gatherings, by failing to speak openly about myself with the people that I lived with, by insisting that I needed my own room two floors away from the rest of my household, and by hiding out in that room with the door locked once I had attained it. There, on the floor above, enjoying all the foibles, failings, and joys of life, was an ever-expanding group of people who were willing to love me unconditionally. It was there for the taking. I had only to open the door. But like the door between heaven and hell, the door between me and my family was locked from the inside.

Having locked them out, or, rather, having locked myself in, I naturally came to see the claims of filial obligation as a burden. What right had these people to make demands on me? I had not chosen them, they were not a product of my autonomous will. They were, on the contrary, the evidence of a divine reckoning that was madness to my individualistic rationalism.

Unconditionality

This is the crux of the misunderstanding between those who call themselves "pro-family" and those who insist that anyone "pro-family" ought to support gay families, single-parent families, and a host of other alternative family options. At the heart of it is this distinction between family as something that we choose to meet our own needs and desires (for comfort, security, affection, etc.), and family as something that we are thrust into and that makes claims on our moral and integral humanity.

It is one of the great paradoxes of the world that the latter model is the one that works. "Families we choose" don't work because they preclude the possibility of the one fundamental and essential element that binds together the traditional family: unconditional love. This love does not proceed from a similarity of personality, from a compatibility of temperament, from any mutual convenience. Those things may produce affection, loyalty, friendship, but they rule out a love that is unconditional — as soon as the similarity, or compatibility, or convenience disappears, the love, accordingly, begins to dissipate. Friends may hope to stick together "through thick and thin," but in reality, friendships tend to dissolve quickly when bonds of mutual interest cease to hold them together — they may linger on in name, and occasion the odd greeting card at special holidays, but they cease to involve a genuine knowledge of and involvement with the other.

This is not to say that relationships begun with a personal choice cannot end with unconditional love. Parents may adopt a child of their choosing, and then, having done so, make the commitment in their hearts to love that child whatever may occur in the future. Lovers may choose one another, and then take vows of marriage by which they agree to remain steadfast and faithful no matter what storms may come to rock the love-boat. But it is only when the element of choice — in the sense of preference — is diminished that genuine love begins. I do not love my husband most when we are getting along, working feverishly together on our novel, calling each other "oaf" and laughing over a bottle of cheap port. I love my husband most when I want to pull his intestines out and use them to garrote him, but decide instead to bite my tongue in half and let him shamble off to bed before I've received a pound of flesh in recompense for the wrongs that I feel he's done me. Of course I *feel* like I love him more when he's my favorite-ever-monkey-mynch, but, as thousands of couples who one day discovered that they had "just fallen out of love" can attest, such feelings are infamously fickle. Fortunately, love does not depend on them.

It is far easier to appreciate this truth when it is applied to the love of children than when it is applied to the love of spouses. Even in an era of no-fault divorce, there are very few people who would argue that it is sometimes "natural" for parents to grow apart from their children, to stop liking their sons and daughters, to realize that there is no longer anything holding them together, and to strike out on their own life-journey, leaving their children behind. A mother who has deliberately broken off all contact with her son — even if that son is over the age of majority — still looms in our eyes as a sort of monster, a latter-day Medea sacrificing her children to her own desires and ambitions. It doesn't matter if the son has transformed from a beloved Adonis into a shambling Caliban. Everyone instinctively recognizes that it is the parent who goes on loving and caring for a recalcitrant and spiteful child — who does not give up, or turn away in disappointment and loathing — that has given the greatest love.

Exactly the same thing is true of spousal love. Wedding vows contain all sorts of rank nonsense, like the "for richer, for poorer; in sickness, in health; for better, for worse" clause, or the promise to "love and cherish" "until death." Such sentiments are unadulterated balderdash if they are meant to refer to that lovey-dovey, honeymooney, touchy-feely, sweet-sixteeny feeling that we refer to as being "in love." They make sense only if (and precisely because) they refer to the same sort of unconditional, sacrificial love that parents are expected to show for their children. This love — a Christlike love — is worth building a home on. Building a family on feelings is like building a castle on a swamp.

This does not mean that being a member of a family is like a perpetuity in a dental chair, with the drill constantly at hand, and teeth being pried from one's jaw at regular intervals. It is heartening to note how quickly and easily feelings of belonging, of love, of affection, and of joy return when hatred, unforgiveness, blame, and grudge-bearing are put away. The problem is that the source of marital distress can run very deep, and all too often couples are willing to patch things up with a superficial filling when what is needed is a root canal. The resulting inflammation is so painful, and seemingly so irresolvable, that it seems impossible to do anything but yank the whole thing out, and perhaps try to start over again.

The Opposite Polarities of Human Experience

I remember talking with my girlfriend about our relationship, wondering at the fact that we never fought, that there was rarely any real conflict, that it was easy, comfortable, and convenient to be together. There are some researchers who suggest that this is a great strength of gay and lesbian relationships: two people of the same sex will generally find it easier to get along and to understand the problems that arise with the other person. Certainly this is the experience of many late-in-life lesbians, who enter into a same-sex relationship only after they divorce their opposite-sex spouse. How nice to have someone who understands why you have turned into a screaming psychopath, who knows better than to say "Is it that time of the month again?" or, worse, "Pull yourself together and behave like a rational human being." Someone who can just say, "Shh, it's okay. I understand," and who isn't just mimicking this because the marriage counselor said that it would work. And yet it isn't enough. It is enough to sustain a friendship, certainly — and there is a certain amount of research to suggest that lesbian couples are more likely than straight couples to stay friends after they have broken up — but it is not enough to sustain the kind of love that lies in the heart of the covenant of marriage.

It is the union of opposites, the bringing together of unlike things, the making of unity out of disparity, that is the essence of the family. The family is the school of that radical love for all men which is so essential to Christianity. It is not a love such as Romans had for other Romans — because they were countrymen, and hence, of the same kind. It is a love that confronts the "other," — an other so extreme that the sexes have, on occasion, been likened to alien species — and that makes it a part of oneself, so much so that the two become "one flesh" and are forged into a single family.

This was something that I didn't understand in all of the time that I was together with Michelle. I dated boys, but always under the assumption that they would somehow turn out to be like the fantasy men that exist only in feminist rhetoric — men so utterly effeminate and nonthreatening that they would be beaten up for being "sissy" in a gay bar. Like so many modern women who find it practically impossible to interact intimately with members of the opposite sex, I believed in those absurd "wife-abuse" pie charts in which 90% of the distinctive characteristics of the masculine psyche are described as bone-chilling atrocities, and a "healthy" marriage seems to involve an emotionally crippled woman living in a psychological bubble with a castrated lamb. The last of my "open-relationship" boyfriends was absolutely right when he accused me of having no interest in interacting with men as men, with allowing my femininity to come into contact with their masculinity. The moment that there was any threat of this, I felt that I was being oppressed, dominated, abused, demeaned. I only wanted to interact with the safe, the familiar, with that in which I could see the reflection of myself.

It is because of, and not in spite of, the tensions between the sexes that marriage works. Masculinity and femininity each have their vices and their strengths. The difficulty when you have two women or two men together is that they understand each other too well, and are thus inclined more to excuse than to forgive. That frank bafflement which inevitably sets in, in any heterosexual relationship ("Why on earth would he do that? I just don't understand . . .") never set in throughout all of the years that my girlfriend and I were together — naturally enough. We were both women, and we chose each other because we seemed to be particularly compatible women. It was the sort of friendship where you hit it off immediately and are able to talk for hours and hours about anything in the world or nothing at all. I recall, in middle school, walking rings around a little patch of ground where we had been sent out to stand during one of our school's frequent student-triggered fire drills — an occasion that always involved at least an hour's disruption of class while the fire department faithfully scoured the building for evidence of a fire that wasn't there. I couldn't have been happier sauntering down a cobbled walk through a Victorian garden with my bosom friend. And yet I never learned, with her, the art of being vulnerable, or the humility of being corrected. We did not fight, certainly, but this was because she was generally happy to trail along a safe distance behind in all of my philosophical excesses — to become a soft socialist when I was a Communist, or to burn the odd stick of incense to reason when I had elevated it as my god and was offering up a sacrifice of human emotion on its altar — and I was generally willing to follow her in matters of taste; these were the only respects in which we were inclined to differ. Our fantasy lives — from the innocent desire to gambol in forests and build elven cities to the murkier depths which unrestricted sexuality is always inclined to explore — were similar and became, in the course of time, practically identical. We had begun the process of "melding" which is so often used to describe lesbian relationships — a process radically different from the reconciliation of opposites on which marriage is founded.

There are certain types of fruit trees that, if you plant them in your garden, even though there is no other of its kind in any neighboring garden — lurking, perhaps, behind a massive pine, across a meadow, through some occult line of mind that only the bees are aware of — will still blossom and bring forth fruit. Such a creature man is not. The blossoms of our relationship hovered, undisturbed, on a summer's breeze, then dropped to the ground, and that was all. There was never any cause for alarm, because the violence of the carpenter bee drilling its holes through the membranes of the soul was not required. And yet, in this soil, apart from any conflict, so many of my faults were free to spread out of their roots, to curl their vines languidly around the base of my spirit, and to fan their leaves, untroubled, in the air. Was I overinclined to moody melancholia? Well, in her own way, so was she, and in our shared fantasy life we were able to indulge that taste for the feminine side of the darker realm of faery. Was I secretive to a fault, and prone to lock other people out of the fortresses of self, to erect a wall behind which the more insane elements of my pride could organize their Luftwaffe against the forces of human emotion that haunted the edges of my world? Sure, but she could understand that fear of self-revelation; she was willing to wait, perhaps to have waited forever, for me to choose to emerge from that shell. She rarely imagined that underneath the carapace was not a shy unicorn that had to be slowly coaxed from the underbrush, but an insane harpy trying to mastermind its own destruction. The one time that she did guess this, and tried to ask why I had become pale, and withdrawn, and stopped eating, she was instantly repulsed. She didn't have the courage — nor would I have had it — to organize an army, to storm the communication towers and allow the inner recesses of my personality to finally reveal what it was really like to live under the iron fist of Melinda the Rational Agent. But how could I have blamed her? Or she me? We were of the same sort.

To excuse, to exculpate, to understand, and in understanding to sweep another's faults under the rug, to mutually exchange a kind of false absolution . . . this is not love. Love is terrible because it refuses to leave the beloved as she is. This nonsense, so often pandered in modern pop culture, that the lover is a delusional myopic who thinks that their beloved is "perfect, just the way you are," has nothing to do with love. Love is not a cult of mutual self-affirmation. Love is a fiery sword that sweeps through the heart, ferreting out its hosts of orcs and goblins and piling their corpses on the battlefield to be burnt. It is a plow that tears up all the acres of fallow wasteland and makes them ready to bring forth life again — and woe to all of the insects who have made their secret lairs in the quiet and the dark.

Hence the opposition of the sexes. To us, it is painful: Eve can no longer stand before Adam, nor Adam before Eve, completely naked, and be known utterly, without shame intervening, for there is no longer innocence shining out from the center of their souls. And yet this nakedness, this plane on which the verb "to have sexual congress" is the same as the verb "to know," is essential to the fulfillment of our sexuality. The communion of persons which is the goal and purpose, not only of human life but, in a special way, of sexual love, cannot be accomplished without this battle, without the tilling of the field which to us — because we are the field — feels like an act of violation or of war.

Of Gardens and Wilderness

This is the foundation of the family. A family is a garden, which brings forth a profusion of fruits. The spouses make this garden of themselves, and wander through it together, and only if they cease to weed it, to work it, to prune and plant and water, does it turn back into a wilderness. It is hard work, of course. Since the time that our first parents were cast out of that primeval garden, the soil has only brought forth its harvest with toil and sweat and suffering. Still, the soil does bring forth its crop, and we are able to eat.

The difficulty with the notion of "families we choose" is that these families are not families. They are an invitation to walk together through the disparate wildernesses of our separate souls. Perhaps on that walk we will speculate about the kind of garden that we would like to build, and perhaps we will even, from time to time, stumble across a pear tree or a bush full of berries in season, and we will be able to sit and make a snack of it. But there is no one in the world who has ever been in both a garden and meadow who cannot tell the difference between the one and the other. The meadow is not without its beauties, but to call it a garden is an abuse of language, and to expect it to bring forth the same sort of fruit as a garden is to court disappointment and hunger.

Perhaps, as much as anything, the confusion on this matter arises in the modern world because there are so many people who have never been in a garden, or who were born into one so ill-tended and over-grown that it was difficult to distinguish from the wild. And certainly a meadow is a more pleasant place than a garden gone to seed, with its crumbling but restrictive walls choked with dead and broken vines, and the shattered fountain in the center breeding toads and slimes of algae. It is because the families of a generation past were so often left untended that the families of this generation are not coming into being: no one wants to put their back to the hoe if they think the product is going to be a festering pile of sludge and rotten leaves.

This is, no doubt, the reason that my generation is so loathe to marry, so eager to seek alternatives to family life, so willing to divorce, so quick to embrace alternate sexual identities. We have escaped the broken garden wall and do not realize that we could build something better.

How did it come to this? I'm not certain. If I could hazard a guess, I would say that somewhere during the last century, women became convinced that they ought not to have to put up with masculinity, that they ought not to have to forgive, that a man's faults were somehow more despicable and grating than a woman's faults. We became the heroines of a Margaret Laurence novel, making hate instead of love — carrying around our own baggage, our own fantasies of a better husband, our own resentments, without ever really allowing ourselves to be seen naked, or to see the nakedness of the men that we love. For the most part, those of us who have not given in to the temptation to divorce seem to see ourselves as practicing heroic virtue, grinding out our long-suffering years yoked to a misshapen Caliban. Few of us seem to ever really stop steeping ourselves in self-generated martyrdom long enough to stop and see the hunchback in the mirror, much less to contemplate, with gratitude, that the monsters we groan about love these malformed crones.

From This Broken Tree . . .

I do not know if there was a time, somewhere along the history of our broken race, when people were actually more successful in the difficult project of family life. Many conservatives and traditionalists point to the idyllic days of the 1950s, but I have heard enough horror stories of the suburban dystopia to suspect that behind the white picket fences of the happy nuclear family, the weeds were already well established. May we go further back, then? To the days when husbands were as free to beat their wives as wives are now to abandon their husbands? Hmmm. Perhaps not. No, I think it likely that human marriage has always, since the time of the Fall, been just as subject to neglect and mistreatment as it is now; that it is only a matter of how, and from which direction, the ax is being laid to the roots of the tree of life.

It is, none the less, a tree of life. The quest for individual immortality, the desire of kings and barons since the beginning of the world, has produced all of the great sterile monuments of man's inhumanity to man. The pyramids, with the blood of slaves poured out on their sandy sides, the immense tombs of the first Emperor of China in which living men and women were confined to die along with him in the shadow of a clay army, the mausoleums in which Lenin and Mao had their bodies preserved so that the men and women whom they had sent to suffer in Gulags would, if they survived, be able to come and look with wonder on the great men — these are the fruit of the desire, by human means, to escape the sting of death. And yet, while the immortality, in this world, of the individual person is impossible, participation in that great living monument, the family tree, with its roots in the ancient prehistory of man, remains one of the great possibilities offered to our species.

The Broken Contract

Marriage is a kind of insanity. It is the same sort of insanity that drives mountain-climbers to endure the seemingly unendurable in order to conquer the pristine peak of a sharp-toothed monster of rock and ice. You cannot do this if you believe in defeat. If while you are standing at the bottom of the mountain, you already have in your mind the conditions under which you are going to abandon the project and go home, you will, without a doubt, end up abandoning it.

The essence of the marriage is the covenant, and at the heart of the covenant is the free will of man, standing in its full splendor, and its full weakness, holding aloft the pillars of the sky from the earth. If you believe in biological determinism — the notion that your "sexual identity" is micromanaged by your genetic code; or in "free love" — the secret code word for "enslavement to lust"; or in "families we choose"; or in people falling in and out of love; or any of the other scenarios that comprise modernist ideas about marriage and sexuality, you haven't got a prayer. Sooner or later, you will be hit by the feeling that your marriage is a prison, or that you are biologically destined to seek out some other kind of partner, or that your spouse no longer loves and cares for you and that the bonds of matrimony have dissolved of their own accord.

This is the difference between partnership and marriage: one is a contract, the other is a covenant. A contract is a thing which, once broken, becomes worthless, an empty promise whose shattered remains are the fodder for disputes in courts of civil or family law. A covenant is a thing that, when it is broken, restores itself. A covenant is the liver of Prometheus, ever assaulted and ever renewed, groaning for the resurrection of the body into a universe devoid of pain.

The seal placed on the covenant of marriage is not the words "I do" but the act — this is why a marriage is deemed invalid, and subject to annulment, if it has never been consummated. The act, the becoming "one flesh," is a sign of the self-giving that is absolutely essential to the covenant. In it the spouses say, "I am no longer mine; I am yours."

Thus the sexual act, in its traditional form: one man, one woman, oriented toward one another so as to produce life. The tit-for-tat form of a contract — I will first pleasure you, and then you, in return, will pleasure me — has no place in a covenantal relationship.

The withholding of oneself, through contraception, has equally little place. You cannot demand the entirety of another person's self and say, "But not this part of me. This little corner, I am keeping back for myself. This, I will not risk." Sex as a form of self-expression, or a means of hoarding up pleasure for oneself, is abuse of the other person's gift. Sex as an act in which you give yourself entirely, without reservation, and allow the other to make of you a sacrificial offering on the altar of their own appetites is contrary to your human dignity. Only if sex is being used in a very superficial sense, if it is meant as an exchange not of selves, but of pleasures, can you engage in these acts and retain any sort of dignity — but then sex itself is stripped of its dignity and meaning.

One cannot play at making covenants — not without losing something in the process. The meaning of the act is the union of two persons, just as surely as the meaning of a punch in the face is anger. This meaning is absolute and incontrovertible. All of the other meanings that man has tried to heap on top of sex in order to justify his desires and appetites for something less terrible and splendid, something that he can treasure in the darkness for himself, these are all lies. The body can be made to lie, yes, just as surely as the tongue, but a lie is a poor foundation for a relationship.

This, I think, is the reason for the situation that I described above: the stewing antipathies that lie nestled in the heart of modern marriage like a worm against the pit of a cherry. There is not, I think, any coincidence in the fact that divorce rates skyrocketed in exact tandem with the use of artificial birth control. These two are death and life-in-death dancing together aboard a sinking ship, while in the hold, the deepest desires of the human heart slip slowly down into the sea. The body was made to lie, to bring that lie into the marriage bed, and even though the men and women of my parents' generation may think that they were liberated, may rejoice that they only had to suffer through the trials and difficulties of raising two children, their bodies know, and their hearts know. The canker, towards which their mind turns an obstinately blind eye, eats nonetheless at the foundations of their marriages.

This chance to sip at the cup of defeat is now on offer, in Canada, and increasingly in the United States as well, to the homosexually inclined. The sullied contract awaits your signature. We "heterosexuals" have crumpled it, abused it, robbed it of its power, castrated and mutilated it, used it up and murdered it, and now, now that the corpse is truly riddled with maggots, we offer it to you. Such is our charity.

Children

One of the things that simply makes no sense to the modern world is the idea that sex must be ordered towards procreation. "So you have to have a kid every time you do the jiggy?" they scoff, shaking their heads in disbelief. It is not merely that the situation has been oversimplified — the reaction will be the same even after you explain that it's not necessary to actually become pregnant, and that Natural Family Planning can be used in times of serious necessity, and that the "openness to life," not success in conception, is the important thing. In fact, after you've explained all of this, most people will be even more baffled. So you can intend not to have a child, provided you're willing to have one if there's an accident, and you don't put a bit of rubber on your thingy? Are you people serious? Do you actually believe that this makes sense?

Microsoft Ethics 3.1

Part of the difficulty goes back to dualism: modern thought about ethics generally tries to separate the act from the intention and the intention from the consequences. One is expected to line up roughly in one of these camps: either the intent is the important thing — in which case contraception and Natural Family Planning are the same thing; or the consequences are the important thing — in which case it's fine if no one gets hurt; or the act is the important thing, in which case this "openness to life" nonsense is just abstract flim-flam. Being a good intentionalist or good utilitarian is hard enough. The Catholic idea that a moral act must meet all *three* criteria — that it must be the right act, for the right reasons, in the right context — seems extreme and idealistic. No one could ever live like that.

Of course, they couldn't. But this does not mean that they should not strive to, or that this three-point moral analysis is not a good basis for examining and improving your moral decision-making.

There are really only two types of standards worth setting in life: a standard so easily met that it allows you to push something into the unimportant margins of life, and a standard that is impossible to meet, that guides your life's work. For me, laundry is in the first category. My standard for this task is: do not allow any article of clothing to sit on the laundry-room floor until it rots; do not allowed soiled bedsheets to fester to the point that they constitute a public health concern; and ensure that all members of the family have at least one outfit to wear every day — even if it combines a princess-pink tutu with a khaki and brown guerilla T-shirt. Sartorial beauty is not, obviously, one of my major life objectives. My writing, on the other hand (fiction, in particular), is a different matter. I want my novel to combine the world-building of Tolkien with the mythic inspiration of Tennyson, the word-smithery of Joyce with the psychological insights of Dostoyevsky, all wrapped up in a brand-new literary form that incorporates postmodernist experiments in mixed media, and is eminently accessible and enjoyable to read. Ha ha ha. It's completely impossible, and can't be pulled off, but it is worthy of being attempted — and it means that no matter how many years I live, and no matter how many novels I write, I will never hit those terrible soul-cramping doldrums in which I will be able to shrug and say, "Ah. It's good enough."

Man must always be working to improve himself: "to strive, to seek, to find, and not to yield," as Tennyson's Ulysses says. Otherwise there is nothing but "life piled on life," as though breathing and watching *Seinfeld* were sufficient justification for existence. In the domestic life — the world of vinegar and vim — there can be some justification for sacrificing the quality of the housekeeping in order to be free to pursue higher goals. But in the moral life? To what higher purpose are you going to sacrifice virtue and personal integrity? To sexual pleasure? Personal need-fulfillment? Are we really willing to accept a compromised, user-friendly ethical standard so that we can safely get on with the "more important" things in life?

Hence the insistence on a standard that is impossible to live up to, but worth living by.

Sex, when confronted with a three-point ethical analysis, requires openness to life, undertaken in a context of personal responsibility and sincere self-giving love. Why?

- Point 1: The act itself.

Sex *means* something. That meaning — the gift of self and transmission of the gift of human life — is "very good." Anything less is a privation, an attempt to cripple the sublime. Sex that is closed to procreation is not truly able to realize the unity of the partners, because that unity is expressed and consummated most perfectly *in procreation*, where the unity becomes manifest in a new human being. You cannot say "I want to be with you, completely, absolutely, always," while closing the door in someone's face.

- Point 2: The intention.

Sexual union must be undertaken in a spirit of genuine love and self-giving, with respect for the integrity and the good of the other person, and of the child that may be conceived. Marriage is a safeguard: you cannot intend the good of your family if you do not intend to remain faithful to it. If, in your heart of hearts, you intend to abandon the other person — and possibly your children as well — if loving them should become difficult, or someone else should come along to excite your affections, then your intent is not centered in the other person's good. The act, on some level, is selfish.

- Point 3: The consequences.

This is where Natural Family Planning (NFP) comes in. There are cases where it is not advisable to have a child, where it is not in the best interests of the family or of the spouses. Perhaps there are risks to the mother's health, or financial difficulties of such a degree that another child would jeopardize the well-being of those already born. In such cases, it is permissible — and perhaps even morally obligatory — to make use of the fact that the female body reserves certain times of the month for procreation, and the rest of the time is able to fully express itself in conjugal love without giving rise to pregnancy.

All of this is very abstract. In practical terms, the difference, however, is profound. Liberals who want to court the ethical line always insist that contraceptive sex is going to be undertaken by rational, loving, committed spouses who are contracepting for the same reasons that people use NFP — but this is actually almost never true. Contraception makes it *easy* to slip into sexual selfishness, or to refrain from having children when that refusal is *not* truly in the best interests of either the spouses or the family.

This is why the embrace of contraception led to a massive spike in divorces and extramarital sex: because it means that people have the right to be able to express their sexual needs when it is not in accord with reason that they do so. It means that pleasure, and that nagging, difficult impulse that we call "lust" or "libido," come to hold veto in ethical decision-making. It also means that the body is treated as a machine, to be improved and controlled through artificial means, rather than by interior acts of knowledge and will. Out of this comes a sort of commodification of bodies — an abstract point, again, but one whose practical implications are profound. If the body is a commodity, then it can be bought, and it can be sold, and it can be traded, tit-for-tat. We have already discussed the implications of this on the dignity of the individual person, but it goes deeper than that. If the body becomes a commodity, so does its most precious product: the new body . . . the child.

Caligula in Reverse

There is a scene (if I may digress ever so slightly) in *I Claudius* where Caligula (having declared himself Zeus) and his sister Drusilla (whom he has declared to be Hera) are standing in the temple of Capitoline Jove. They are laughing at Jupiter and Juno for being deities inferior to themselves. It all ends badly. Drusilla proclaims herself to be pregnant with the child of Zeus, and Caligula, fearing that his child will overpower him, chains his sister/wife to a floating bed, cuts the unborn child from her womb, and devours it. Only then does he realize that she was not a goddess.

Modern man is Caligula in reverse. We cut the unborn children from our wombs because we are terrified that they will not be greater than we are. We have made for ourselves a new god, a splendid god, all out of shining steel and invisible waves, of DNA sequences and chemical formulae. This god is a great improvement over the idols of the past. What is Zeus compared to such a god? This god is everywhere, in a thousand things; it is powerful — moves mountains, cures the sick, causes cities to be consumed by fire for their sins. It is fast becoming lord over the skies and over the hills, over the stars, and all that is under the stars. What greater god has the world ever seen and known than the mighty Technology?

But our new god demands progress, an eternal forward momentum which we are not capable of supplying. Confronted with this truth, we despair. We were supposed to be carrying the evolution of humanity in our wombs, to be the midwives of the Age of Aquarius, and yet everything is going on the same . . . the same. The steel god tramples the world beneath his feet, and it does not rise again. Why should we have children, in such a world as this?

Modernity has only a flimsy hope, a distant, science-fiction future — a future in which it does not entirely believe. Mankind will be saved by rocket ships and androids. Or will it? Perhaps it will be destroyed by aliens. Civilization may fall again, and everything return to a post-nuclear darkness. It may go on, and on, a Brave New World, a cyberpunk nightmare, getting more and more congested, more and more corrupt, more and more polluted and ugly. There are no certainties in the future. We have seen Technology turn against us in the past. We saw Hiroshima. We saw the Nazi experiment. We saw the world devoured by concrete. We saw television melting our children's minds. Our faith is very uncertain. Technology, it seems, cannot save us from the fault of being human.

Hope Made Present

Parents must have hope if they are to have children, and true hope is difficult. Some days, we are kept aloft by pleasant daydreams of the wonders that our children will one day be. On others, we simply want to send the child to the dark side of the moon to be looked after by Martians. Occasionally, we plunge into despair over the whole project and swear that we are never going to put ourselves through this again. The rest of the time we love, we forgive, we take joy in our children, we play, we teach, we believe. Somewhere in the heart, enough hope for humanity is dredged up out of the depths to sustain life. It is a question of balance: when everything is added up, and the dross is purified away, how much of the precious ore do we actually have?

To a certain extent, I think that the decision to contracept the family away is the result of a more pressing and immediate loss of hope: not despair of humanity and the universe, but something small, petty. Despair that there will not be enough money for every child to have brand-new Nike shoes at every stage of development. Fear that more children will bankrupt Mom and Dad come college time. Anxieties about one's own parenting — there is that question that never ceases to trouble a mother: "Am I doing a good enough job?" Stress. Dullness. Perhaps dullness, most of all.

This is the practical reality: the face of the lost hope in the world. Intellectual hope — a theoretic construct of glass and robotics, a Gnostic dream of ghosts upon the blue, or the vague, sappy notion that we are all inevitably drifting toward a better world — this does not help when you are a parent. Even the intellectual hope in the New Jerusalem is radically insufficient. Hope needs to be a daily act, a seeing through and into things, so that the thing hoped for is, in some sense, made present. This is at the heart of the Eucharist, in which the body, blood, soul, and divinity of Christ, of His redemption on the Cross, and of His coming again at the end of time, is made present and real now, here, on this particular altar. Hope for the family means seeing into its nature; apprehending, even without articulation, that these little creatures are new human beings, new humanity, and that in their miniature breasts there are all the breadths and depths and heights, all the curious byways and fantastic possibilities, that lurk beneath the surface of every human being. To hope is to see and desire that.

Without this hope, parenthood becomes dull. I have read numerous "mommy bloggers" talking about how, "scandalously," they have become bored with their children. How terrible. What bad mothers!

Of course, we're being facetious here. Of course, I feel the same way. All mothers do: that is why the feminist revolution happened. Being a mother involves a thousand meaningless, menial tasks. Dirty diapers, dishes, laundry, sick kids, homework, alphabet practice, pointless stories and meandering conversations, another game of dolls, a spilled fishbowl, dead guinea pigs, more laundry. Mothers envy Sisyphus his rock. We envy Atlas the weight of the sky. Just give us one day to lie around on Prometheus's rock and have our livers gnawed on by crows. It would be easier and more relaxing than trying to get my daughters to keep their room clean.

Usually if I happen to be talking to another woman — an ordinary woman who has a nice, neat family of precisely two children — the subject of family size comes up. It's natural: the train of three kids running pell-mell in front of me with a baby gurgling in the stroller is an unusual sight. Are they all mine? Yes. She only has two, but that's enough. With two, she never has time for herself, never gets the gardening done, is constantly in the car driving them here or there. She can't imagine how I manage with four. I say, "Oh, four is nothing. My mom has eight."

If I know the woman a little better, the conversation deepens. Underneath the worries and anxieties, the feelings of parental inadequacies, the frustrations of the life that one has put aside, there is a longing. "The baby is so cute. It makes me want another one. . . . I don't know. Sometimes I think maybe I'll adopt one. But then —" the money, the time, the energy, the work. The vast gray specter of eighteen more years of the dullness and drudgery. "Maybe it's better just to look. Eventually, I'll have grandkids. Can I hold him for a minute?"

The Far-off Light of Victory

Why, some wise philosopher once asked, does man find tragedy more beautiful than comedy? Why is beauty always mingled with sorrow? Why do we cry, with a terrible longing in our hearts, when our souls are raised to the highest apex of earthly joy? Why weep at weddings? Why give birth in pain? What is this mystery?

Redemption. At the heart of humanity, the contradiction of sin and salvation.

This is why Christians, particularly those who have a genuine, life-giving faith, have large families. It is why Muslims who really believe that Allah is all-powerful and will bless those who follow him with everlasting joy, have a trail of children following after them. It is the reason, also, why people in the Third World are more inclined to give birth: they know about suffering. They know about redemption, and resurrection. They know that at the end of the winter, when everything seems to be in darkness and the shadow of death is lurking over the starving children, there is spring. Oh there is death, yes, there is that, but it doesn't rob life of its meaning. There is sin, certainly, but it does not make humanity worthless. There is the same cycle, over and over, but it is a cycle rich in mythic significance, in purpose, in dignity. It is the cycle of life. The means by which we all were begotten, and by which, in an act of faith, we beget the continuation of the same old thing. Because it is a wondrous old thing: cracked, broken, sullied, torn, but beautiful. So beautiful.

Little gleams of hope in one's children inevitably come through — except, perhaps, into the darkest and most overgrown families. It is one's own vices, however, that rise up like the maple trees on my front lawn, blocking out the sun and gobbling up all of the nutrients and water from the soil. They have to be kept tended and pruned back, and their roots have to be dug up and ripped out of the ground. Otherwise, all the flowers and grass die. It requires hours of labor, and the battle must be rejoined every summer. But if it is fought, I can have a garden.

If you constantly fight against your own vices and failings, then you inevitably will have hope for your children. You can see, slowly, over the long, drawn-out battle, that victory is possible. The act of hope involved in helping your children to understand and conquer their own faults becomes possible: it stops being merely a matter of yelling and losing your head and stomping your feet in frustration. Agnes wants to be an adult; she is constantly bossing Philomena, and doesn't want to take correction or to be told that she has to do that math problem again, and insists that she is not grumpy, even though her face is fixed in the expression of a cave troll that thinks it is the Snow Queen. Looking in the mirror, I recognize myself. Yes, that is precisely how I am. I understand. I have been struggling with this all my life; it isn't fair to expect that she is going to overcome it all at once just because I lose my temper and scream at her to go to her room because I can't stand to look at her. I'd better sit down with her, teach her how to get over this. We'll work on it together, talk it through together, and we'll both learn to do better.

This is not delusion. It doesn't arise from the theory that my kids are going to be perfect and free of my faults, but from the realization that my own faults are conquerable, that the salvation of humanity does not lie in some distant star-spangled future. Salvation is possible here, now, for me. I am working it out, and I will work it out with my kids, and the more that we work on it, the more there will be gaps where the light of hope can come dazzling through the trees to transform family life from dullness to color.

The Balm of the Forsaken

The question is, why bother? Yes, yes, it appears that there is some reward for all this hard work, the flashing light of beauty dancing in a newborn baby's eye, and all that jazz. But let's say I'm happy to forgo that? Let's say that I find my beauty in a flashing thigh, or a crowded club? Let's say that I find my ecstasy in sex, and I don't see the need to set out on this arduous path that you have just described.

Most advocates of marriage and the family are ill-able to answer the question articulately. Those who get branded as "ignorant, right-wing, homophobic hicks" know that they are defending something valuable, but they cannot necessarily say why they know. They are fish who have never been out of the ocean, but they have seen the corpses come washing back in with the tide, and they know that if you go up there to play on beaches, sooner or later, you come back dead. They can't really say why the ocean is so wonderful, or why they need it, or why all the dazzling light and sound coming from the shore is a temptation that leads unto death. So they're reduced to hanging around beneath the low-tide mark saying, "Hey, you idiot fish. Get back down here. You gonna get yourselves real dead real fast up there on that beach." And, of course, all of the liberated fish are dancing around in the shallow pools, flopping their fins in the air, feeling the exhilarating rush of sunlight on their scales, and crying, "We are free, free of the ocean, free at last! The sun is ours. The open skies. You ignorant, backward fish, crawling around in the seaweed and the dark, how dare you tell us our pleasures are not to last?"

Family is the ocean. What is it for?

The great sorrow of humanity is loneliness. This single suffering is greater than all of the other possible sufferings that man has ever been forced to endure (except, perhaps, for meaninglessness). Tremendous waves of overwhelming pain can be borne willingly if you know that the result is going to be a new human being, a new remedy to this illness. Cancer is lightened by a circle of people who love and understand. People are able to overcome the most tremendous evils by pulling together, suffering together. Indeed, terrible trials can be made easy, even enjoyed, if they are undertaken in common. Watch *Roots* sometime, and ask yourself why all of these black slaves, living in terrible conditions, seem happy so much of the time. Why do they seem happier than you are? It's not because the story is a lie. It's because they are together. The greatest sufferings, the unbearable trials, and the scenes that rip your heart to pieces, are the ones where families are torn apart. Then all the rest becomes beyond endurance. The humiliations, the rapes, the deaths, the beatings. Without family? Forget it.

It is possible to be lonely surrounded by a crowd. This is the mystery of the modern city: in the country, where there are only a handful of people, there is community. In the city, where people are packed so close together that there ought to be constant opportunities for relationships to sprout, there is very little. People replace community with a crowded club and take drugs so that they can imagine that they are in some sort of deep interpersonal communion with the perfect strangers gyrating next to them. Loneliness is not simply a matter of being alone: it is matter of being unknown. The unshakable desire of the human heart is to know and to be known. Our subjectivity is our curse. This is the entire content of the last hundred or so years of philosophy: how do we get past the boundaries of self? How do we formulate an epistemology, a metaphysics, an ethical system, an ontology, without ultimately falling back against the bars of our own mind, our own experience, our own being?

Communion. This requires knowledge of another. We don't want to be loved by social workers who talk down to us from an ivory tower. I remember working at a homeless shelter, watching the well-meaning

New-Agey women with social work degrees talking to the kids in the shelter about the potentials that the universe was opening up for them, and how they needed to seize these opportunities, spread their wings, and fly out into the light. The kids' eyes glazed over. This had nothing whatever to do with their experience of reality, hemmed in by obstacles, delineated by false hopes and disappointments, dulled by marijuana and crack cocaine. *The universe is there to nurture me? No way.*

We want to be known. We desperately want for someone to look into the dark recesses of our soul and love us anyway. We want, also, to know. There is a tremendous comfort in realizing that we are part of the same humanity, saddled with the same diseases, the same lusts, the same crosses. To know, and to be known, to be understood, and to understand ourselves in the light of another person. To see the boundaries of subjectivity and know that there is something out there, beyond the self, something more than just a void. Another person. "Flesh of my flesh, bone of my bone."

If You Cannot Love Your Family, Whom You See, You Cannot Love the Burmese Child Soldier, Whom You Don't

Family is the most perfect natural means of accomplishing this. It is very difficult for someone like me to get into the mind of a child warrior in Burma. As soon as I try, I'm constantly running up against categories and presuppositions and prejudices that simply have nothing to do with that child's experience. What I end up with is a sort of cartoon, a pity-poster that looks about as realistic as SpongeBob Squarepants.

It is possible to get a more realistic picture of life on the other side of the globe, but it takes time and effort. When I first started reading Dostoyevsky and watching Tarkovsky films, I felt like I was looking at another dimension. Apart from certain beautiful and appealing images, I couldn't understand or penetrate it at all. Last week, I sat down to watch *Andrei Rubliev* again for the first time in ten years, and I was astonished. I remembered it being a dense, impenetrably murky work in which snatches of meaning and beauty occasionally flashed out, like Leviathan's tail fluttering in the deep. But upon this watching, it is surprisingly clear and, if not easy, manageable. Why? Because I have now watched enough Eisenstein, listened to enough Shostakovich, read enough Solzhenitsyn to understand, or at least to come to some approximation of, a common language through which I can have a meaningful dialog with the film. Slowly, I've come to understand something of modern Russia — at least enough to appreciate her art.

This is the problem with all that nonsense that they spent so many hours indoctrinating us about in school: the absurd notion of a "small world" and a "global village." Perhaps this makes sense if you live in Celebration, the Disney theme-park community where everyone keeps their grass a regulation length, the roads in are guarded, and there is no difference between a French belle, a Persian princess, and a mermaid girl from the kingdoms beneath the sea. In that la-la land, the idea of one big human family seems reasonable. After all, the token black people on the street are just like my family. No difference. And somehow, all of this was presented to us as an antidote to racism. "If we pretend that all humanity are just nice, normal, Anglo-Germanic white people in a variety of different cool shades, then we can all get along and love one another." What a beautiful vision.

It is a vision that rises up inevitably, because the same people who so ardently peddle the "human family" also, at the same time, are trying to break down the family of blood and similarity. They think that if they can break this primary, insular loyalty to kin, they will end up with a flourishing love for everykind. But it doesn't work. How on earth are you going to teach a man to love and appreciate the nuances of a Van Gogh if you teach him in childhood that only the backward, ignorant, repressed, and psychologically crippled need to rely on the use of their eyes to see? The family is where you learn to love. Sure, some people never get beyond that. But the situation is not improved by uprooting those people and making sure, for the sake of preventing an exclusive love, that they never learn to love at all. What you end up with, at the end, is not a panophile, pouring out the wellsprings of his heart indiscriminately on the multicolored flowers of the world . . . but Narcissus, bending in smitten adoration over a pool, unable to recognize the image as himself.

Baby Steps toward the Love of Humankind

The problem of man's alienation from man is too big to be solved by teaching school children to hold hands in a circle and sing songs about psychedelic frogs with all the references to sex and alcohol tastefully removed. You can't teach people to understand and value the Southeast Asian experience by reading one chapter of a Rohinton Mistry novel in your "Voices" unit in Grade 10 English. Escaping from the subjective caverns of the self requires a much subtler instrument: the family.

The ideal, most effective form is two parents, in contact with an extended family of grandparents, aunts, uncles, cousins, great-grand-mothers, and so forth, with children who are their natural offspring.

Why? Human beings beget human beings who are similar to themselves. My sisters frequently tease me, asking, "What does it feel like to be raising yourself?" My eldest daughter is exactly like I was at her age. She is, in many ways, exactly like I am today. It means that I understand her, in a way that I do not understand other people's children.

This likeness is not accidental, nor is it simply a matter of nurture. A friend of mine — a late-in-life lesbian who came to her sexual identity after a ten-year-long, childless marriage — was recently reunited with a daughter that she gave up for adoption when she was 20. She had not seen the girl, now 18, since she was a tiny baby, and had never had any part in her life. She was struck to discover how many things they had in common, how similar to her birth mother this child had grown up to be. The same experience, or a variant on it, is absolutely commonplace among blood relatives separated at birth. They find each other, and, incredibly, they are so much alike. Suddenly, things about themselves that never made sense are clarified, mysteries resolved. "This at last is flesh of my flesh, bone of my bone."

I said that it is important that both parents be involved. This is because both parents are involved in engendering the child. Agnes is not only exactly like me; she is also exactly like her father. In the birth of a child, both of the spouses receive an image of themselves, but they also receive, again, and in a new way, their spouse. This is why children are so able to keep a marriage tied together through times of difficulty and trial; it is not just that spouses grit their teeth and stick it out "for the sake of the kids," it is that they are able to find the man or woman they once loved in the faces, gestures, words, and personality of their child. The child is a constant rediscovery of the mystery of spousal love, and each child that is born expresses this in a different way, revealing an entirely separate, living dimension of the marriage.

There are things about myself that I would not understand if my mother had kicked my father to the curb when I was four years old. Most of the ways in which I resemble Mom didn't come to the forefront until I had children of my own: then I started to understand why it is that she does absurd, self-defeating things — like screaming and yelling that no one ever helps with the dishes, and then hurrying up from the table to start scouring the pots before anyone else has had a chance to finish eating. Until I married and had kids, this particular fault lay latent in me, and it was incomprehensible in a woman who was, otherwise, generally sane, rational, and — to my scattered, cloud-befuddled brain — insanely competent. My father, on the other hand . . . ah, how I hated to be compared to my dad when I was growing up. "You're exactly like him," my mother would say — and she meant, "Everything that drives me crazy about your father drives me crazy about you as well."

My dad and I are, in fact, exactly alike. Too cerebral, too private and reticent about our interior lives, too easily frustrated, too inclined to anxiety and despair. We are also both intelligent and creative, have powerful imaginations, and share a love of South American camelids. We both sing ridiculous nonsense songs to our children, quote Monty Python at each other, and can recite *Jabberwocky* in tandem. I have learned, and understood, a great deal about myself by observing and loving my father — even if we rarely talk about anything more relevant than squirrels and science fiction. It is simply a matter of knowing him: he is my father, and in knowing him, I discover myself.

This happens, also, with my children. Raising them, observing them, talking to them, I find myself again, from a different angle. It is not that I am thrust back into the subjective cave, but that I find handholds — familiar territory, solid ground on which to launch an expedition out into the other. The image is not quite a mirror image; this is a completely separate, different person, but like me, enough like me that I can begin to understand.

There is more than this. A child whose parents love each other can be confident that there is someone in the world who will never think that their differences amount to insanity. Someone will understand them, and will cherish them. There will be someone who will know them, as they really are, and still be willing to say, "You are my daughter," or "You are my son . . . I love you."

Deliberate Orphans

This is why being orphaned is such a tragedy. Adoptive parents may love their adopted child with all their human capacities, and they may manage to make up for a great deal out of the treasury of their hearts, but there is always a sense in which a barrier exists. I have noticed this, without exception, in every adopted child that I have known: they know that they are loved, but they do not know, not in the same way, that they are loved for "who they are," that they are known and understood. Of course, when parents die, there is no way around this. And when a teenage girl becomes pregnant and isn't capable of caring for the child, this is also the best option: it is better to live, and to discover love, and to be known as well as you can be known, than it is to be torn limb from limb and thrown into a medical waste disposal unit. It is not, however, something that should be thrust on a child deliberately.

A prosthesis is fine if a baby is born without an arm, or loses his leg in an accident. But if a parent deliberately cuts their child's leg off, that is a different matter. A mother, or a father, is a deeper, more essential, more human thing than an arm or a leg. To lose a parent is a greater suffering than to lose a limb: which of us would not sacrifice her left hand to ransom a parent from certain death? If we would not take a child and deliberately deprive it of the use of both its legs, how on earth can we justify the deliberate creation of orphans? Only on selfish grounds: I want a kid, I want it to be my kid, and I don't care how I get it. I have a right to have a child, just like everyone else!

Surrogate motherhood, sperm donation, and the deliberate decision to become pregnant with the intention of raising the child yourself (single motherhood by choice, or, lesbian motherhood in which the baby is conceived "naturally") all involve purposely creating a child who will never know at least one of its natural parents. This is not, and cannot be, in the best interest of the child — only in the best interest of the parent. But parenthood cannot proceed from those principles. Every parent knows that you can't be successful in raising a child if you only give birth to fulfill yourself.* The child turns out to be disappointing, it doesn't fit the bill, it is more demanding than you suspected, and so the child is turned away, rejected, in the heart of the family — where it ought to have found acceptance and unconditional love.

Of course, a child conceived for the stupidest and pettiest of reasons can grow up to be truly loved; human beings are capable of repentance, of growing beyond themselves. But it is sheer lunacy for a society to sanction and condone the practice of putting parental desires ahead of the needs of children in the vague hope that everything will be okay in the end.

So, if the sexual revolution takes place in the bedrooms of America, and we are all jumping on the sexuo-electric joy train, who loses? The answer has been in front of us since the beginning, since the first victims of the first no-fault divorce watched their daddy walk out of their lives, since some little boy first heard his mother hiss, "You're exactly like your father" and knew that Mommy hated Daddy and made Daddy go away. Ever since the first of the contraceptive generation woke up to find that they had no brothers and sisters to play with. Since the first little girl realized that Daddy and Mommy were so thrilled to have her that they decided to cut all the other little boys and girls out of Mommy's womb. Since the first child understood what it meant that they were "an accident." We've been hurting them a long time, our children. All in the name of sexual liberation, "self-care," and "personal fulfillment." All in the name of "me first." We sacrificed procreation for the sake of sexual pleasure — but we had hoped to confine this little evil, to keep it locked up between the bedcovers where no one would get hurt. Unfortunately for us, it has gotten out. We ought always to have known it would.

---

* Yes, heterosexuals can do this as well, even within the bonds of legal and sacramental marriage. The fact that an abuse is possible to one group of people does not mean that, by logic of equality, it must be made equally accessible to another.

PART IV

Homosexuality and God

CHAPTER 10

Faith

I have said a great deal here about the sinfulness and ugliness of humanity, and how this actually hurts people, particularly the innocent people whom we love the most. I am not speaking out of an ivory tower. My first child was born out of wedlock; I was certain that Chris was the one man with whom I would spend the rest of my life, that my love for him was categorically different from anything that I had seen before, and that eventually we would make solemn promises to remain faithful to one another. But we had not yet made those promises, and I had only my intuitions to go on. I could have been wrong, as thousands of women have been before me. My intent was not to have a half-orphaned child, but that would have been the effect if I had been mistaken.

One of the great difficulties in speaking about these issues is the immense emotional and personal baggage that each person carries into the discussion. There is an intensely human desire to defend oneself, to say that mistakes made in the past were not mistakes, or that errors made out of ignorance were done with the best of intentions. These things must be talked about, though, because otherwise there are no signposts warning others not to go off in the same direction.

This is obvious when we are speaking about physical obstacles: as soon as one person has driven off the road over the cliff and ended up in a wheelchair, a block is put up to prevent other vehicles from doing the same, and someone installs a bright yellow sign warning drivers of the dangerous conditions ahead.

Just so, I do not want to look back at my own history, to look at all the factors that led me to decide to start having sex before I was married to Chris, and I don't want to have to paint our premarital lovemaking — much of which was genuinely beautiful and conveyed very serious feelings of love — with the broad brush of sin. I don't want to have to describe the conception of my first daughter as an "accident" . . . but this is what it was. At some point I have to look realistically at the facts, to recognize that because I wasn't married, I was risking her future as well as my own, that one day she is going to know enough to understand why it is that she is in my wedding pictures, and she is going to wonder — as I have often wondered about my own parents — whether my husband and I only suffered the yoke of marriage on her account.

A Bright Yellow Sign

There are two ways that we can approach our sins. One is to exculpate, to excuse, to insist that we are not at fault. This is very difficult to overcome, especially when we are confronted with the fact that they have caused real suffering that cannot be undone. When I am sitting, looking across the room at my husband, and I realize that I have said something that has hurt him deeply — that I have taken a fit and torn him to shreds in front of our children, or threatened to walk out and abandon him — I desperately want for there to be someone else to blame. Surely it is his fault, because he didn't give me the emotional support that I was owed, or it was because of some faulty line in my genetic code, or some surge of premenstrual hormones, or because God in this moment of need abandoned me to suffering beyond my endurance. It was someone else's fault, not mine. The pain in the eyes of one I love could not have been caused by me.

But if it is not my fault, it cannot be healed. How many times have I sat wrestling in some spiritual darkness, trying to forgive something that my husband, my father, my sister, or my best friend has not apologized for? Bitterness rises up again and again. Perhaps there is a long and terrible silence, in which no real communication or communion becomes possible — the famous image of two married people sitting across from one another at the breakfast table where, by some trick of the interior light, the loaf of bread becomes a mountain, the butter an oil-slick, the toaster a defensive blockade, and the marmalade a cosmic divide that separates them. Or there may be arguments, flaring up over and over, each one more frustrating than the last, because the other person refuses to take responsibility. Unrepentance and unforgiveness meet and are wed, and the very fabric of human communion is torn apart.

But what if the sin is "victimless"? When my husband and I started to sleep together, who, precisely, was being hurt? I look back and see the first time that we made love: I know my interior state, that I was terribly in love, and that I wanted to express something soul-shatteringly beautiful. The experience was certainly not a disappointment. There was no interior divide: my faith was still an ill-catechized and fledgling faith. I knew, vaguely, that premarital sex was against the teachings of the Church, but it seemed to me that it was somehow in a different category from homosexuality — perhaps because it was not one of the issues on the front lines of the culture wars. I had neatly compartmentalized my sexuality under the aegis of the recently formed "Ministry of Beauty," a subsection of my own psyche that was responsible for making decisions about my creative and expressive life. At that time, I was able to see quite clearly that there was a lack of symmetry, of harmony, of elegance in what Michelle and I did together in bed, and so the dictates of Beauty and the dictates of Religion were at one. With Chris, it was different: all of the mythic and aesthetic resonances inherent in the idea of "making love" were there, so why should this be condemned?

Eventually, I understood. A year later, when my faith had become sufficiently formed that I understood the reasons why premarital sex was condemned, I wanted to revisit this decision, to turn back and live in accordance with the dictates of reason and morality. I found that I couldn't. It was impossible, or at least it seemed impossible. We tried, and we went to confession whenever we failed, but it was a losing battle. We were living together — the idea that living together outside of marriage was a foolproof method of losing the war for sexual purity had not yet penetrated our worldview — and I had discovered that I was pregnant. How could we possibly separate now?

The entire matter was very confusing. Morally, I made 1,001 mistakes. And I paid for them as well: if I had waited for marriage, I would never have had to struggle with the specter of abortion looming over the child in my womb, the terrible conflict in which a mother's heart must reconcile a terrifying unwanted pregnancy with an unseen beloved child. I would not have seen our sexual love devolve from something beautiful and intensely meaningful into a dark and bitter struggle, and I would not have entered marriage plagued with doubts about whether our lovemaking was a genuinely human act or just a concession to animal weakness. These things took years, and a great deal of suffering, to work through: I am therefore putting up a road sign. It's not intended to condemn those who have taken this route in the past; they have to labor under the burdens of their mistakes just as I have had to labor under the burdens of mine. (I sincerely pray that those burdens will be light and will lead up into glory and not down into despair.) It is intended for those who are contemplating the road ahead and have not yet committed to it. Go not this way: here, there is a steep precipice, difficult to spot until you have already stumbled over the edge, and the rocks at the bottom are sharp.

The Ecstasy of Ignorance

I know, I know — all of this could have been avoided if I had simply thrown myself into the arms of sexual desire, allowed myself to be washed along its currents, and never bothered with all of these neurotic religious self-doubts. The real cause of our sufferings was the misguided attempt *not* to have sex with one another, not our natural and self-fulfilling decision to take each other into our arms. Everybody knows that — the sexual experts have told us so. Beneath it all is that simpering, sickening, Christian moral feeling that sex is "dirty." Get rid of that, and all will be well.

I think this is untrue, and I have good reason for thinking it. My thinking about my relationship with my husband was influenced, obviously, by Catholic sexual morality; it was not, however, *limited* to Catholic sexual morality. I had had the experience in the past of being an object of someone else's sexual desire, and of seeing another person as an object of my own sexual desire. I knew how ugly and inhuman *that* was long before the Church came on the scene. I knew, also, that the beauty of the sexual act depended on its human integrity: on its being undertaken by the whole person, as a gift that was genuinely given, complete with its moral and spiritual dimensions as well as its physical and psychological ones.

A person can have HIV for years without getting tested: the lack of a test does not render them negative. A couple can have sex that is appetitive and compulsive for years without ever making the test of trying to practice chastity. This does not mean that their lovemaking is completely human and disordered; it just means that they haven't bothered to find out. Still, the fruits are there. A woman resents having to make love to her husband because she senses on some level that she is being used as an object of selfish desire; a man is jealous of his wife because he knows how easily he broke down her resistance and wonders whether she would prove just as easily overcome if another man made the attempt. Children come and are resented, or children are aborted, and this is resented even more. Couples are unable to find enough love burning in their marriage to keep the flames of sexuality alive, and yet lust is still there: they turn to pornography, or try to "spice up" their sex life by imagining that they are really making love to someone else. Men become nervous and lose confidence in their desirability. Women starve themselves thin for fear that their husbands will be unfaithful.

Integrity and Integration

Chastity is the means by which it is possible to negotiate a way through all of these problems. It is not a set of negative rules: "Thou shalt not have sex outside of marriage. Thou shalt not have homosexual sex. Thou shalt not masturbate. Thou shalt not look at pornographic images. Thou shalt not contracept," etc., etc. Chastity is positive: "Thou shalt be in possession of thine own sexuality." John Paul II frequently makes reference to the idea of "the integrity of the gift." The word "integrity" here is not used in a loose sense, to mean "reasonably reliable," or "vaguely upright." It has, as its root, the concept of integration. The integrity of the gift of self in the sexual act comes out of the integration of sexuality into the wholeness of the person. In this way, it ceases to be lust — lust, which drives the reason and the will kicking and screaming into the pits of sexual excess, or bludgeons the conscience into unconsciousness so that the genitals can get on with their fun. The practice of chastity demonstrates that one actually possesses what one promises to give.

To refrain from sex before marriage is a very concrete, difficult, and therefore valuable, proof that the other person is not merely an object of lust, that sexuality has been subordinated to the will.

But how do we get there? I said myself that all my own and my husband's best efforts to revert to chastity, after taking the step off the edge of the metaphoric cliff, were in vain. Many other people, both heterosexual and homosexual, have made the attempt and failed. In many cases, the oft-repeated claim of gay activists that for them, homosexual sex is natural, normal, and necessary for mental health, are founded on an experience of being unable to place sexual conduct under the aegis of will. The image of St. Jerome out in the desert, beating his own flesh with a rock in order to subdue his sexual demons, may have been appealing to the Middle Ages — and is still appealing to certain hardcore devotees of chastity — but it is a terrifying and inhuman picture to the vast majority of modern people.

This is not to say that it hasn't its modern equivalents: people would look with horrified pity on a man with homosexual desires who beat himself in order to try to escape them, but we feel different when confronted with a pedophile who bathes his hand in acid as a means of quieting his compulsion to go out and rape small boys.[54] There is still the horror — and perhaps some element of pity — but the matter takes on a deeper, more somber tone. The modernist would have told the homosexual to let go of his internalized homophobia and guilt feelings, to be free, and live and love his sexuality. This alternative cannot be offered to the pedophile. And yet the pedophile insists, as strongly as the medieval monks whose war for purity left such terrible scars on their bodies, that this is the only way possible for him to escape the stranglehold that lust has on his soul.

What, then, is to be done? First, there must be a frank discussion about the struggle. Chastity is not easy. I once drove past a huge billboard in Florida that read, "Chastity is Fun!" What on earth were the people who put this thing up thinking? Chastity is *fun*?!? Chastity is beautiful; it respects the integrity of the human person; it is a grave moral responsibility; it is an invitation to union with the cross of Christ; but it is not *fun*. Like all virtues, the more completely you manage to attain it, the more joy it brings. But joy and fun are completely different things — and, as with all virtues, the joy is generally the fruit of long and difficult labor.

Secondly, there must be a discussion of what chastity actually means. It does not mean, for example, a staunchly Manichean refusal to acknowledge that sexuality exists. Benedict Groeschel, in *The Courage to Be Chaste*, observes that "repression is a dangerous form of sexual control, especially when it is used exclusively to manage one's sexuality. Ed [young seminarian who came to Father Groeschel after his battle for angelic purity ended in a series of out-of-control sexual encounters] explained to me that whenever he was aware of the slightest sexual attraction or fantasy, he energetically put it from his mind. He was never troubled by temptations to auto-eroticism or any other sexual expression. . . . The moral of this case history is that conscious control, with all the struggles that it implies, is a far better way to manage life than is repression, or forcing all impulses into the unconscious mind."[55]

There is a tremendous divide between the medieval writers on chastity and sexuality and modern writers like Groeschel and John Paul II. They are all men, and all sworn celibates, but the moderns have something that is notably lacking in those who advise tying up the loins with rosaries to prevent succubi from seducing the monk in his dreams: they are obviously comfortable with their sexuality. There was a certain amount of sniggering when *Theology of the Body* was published: what could an old celibate white man possibly have to say about sexuality? Yet both *TOB* and *Love and Responsibility* (published when the late pope was still Archbishop of Krakow) demonstrate a deeply mature, thoughtful, and often surprisingly frank understanding of sex.

For a celibate struggling to come to terms with a frustrated sexuality, this would be unthinkable. For a celibate who has integrated his sexuality into his celibacy, it is quite natural: the former tries to eradicate all sexual knowledge of himself and of others from his experience, and therefore knows little about it. The latter knows and understands his own sexuality, but has made it enough a part of himself that his calling to unmarried chastity is not a cause of interior division.

This is not experienced and accomplished all at once — neither is chastity within marriage. As David Morrison puts it, "Chastity is a 'long-haul' virtue."[56] It requires patience on the part of both the ones who seek it and friends who support them. A close friend of mine, dealing with intensely unwanted sexual temptations, said that a tremendous turning point in his struggle for chastity came with this realization. Instead of expecting that he would be chaste tomorrow — and becoming intensely frustrated every time he failed — he said, "Lord, if I have to fight and fail for twenty years, I accept that. I'm going to persevere."

We're in This Together

The great difficulty facing the Christian who tries to minister to others is the darkness in his own heart. There is a good reason why homosexual activists so often insist that the most virulent anti-gays are actually repressed homosexuals — many of them either have been, or know people who were, vitriolic homophobes before finally coming to understand and embrace their own same-sex desires. It is an oversimplification: there are many people who viciously denounce homosexuality because they lost a son to AIDS, or are angry at a mother who abandoned their family for a lesbian relationship, or were homosexually abused as children. Since their life stories are usually not penned in on the bottom of the "God Hates Fags" sign, it's generally best to pray for those who persecute you, and try not to judge.

In most cases, though, the hatred is muted to the point where it is not hatred at all, but merely disgust, or anger, or frustration. The authors of *After the Ball* explain this as a kind of primitive animal imprinting: they tell an uncharitable tale of little Billy Bigot sitting on the carpet ripping the wings off of flies while his parents grimace in disgust at a limp-wristed piano player on the television screen.[57] They are wrong. The real reason that straights, and particularly those trying to live as Christians, have such a strong reaction against homosexuality is that we are angry about our own sexual struggles; we feel about gays and lesbians much as soldiers feel about deserters.

For a long time after I converted to Catholicism, I was quite angry with the gay movement. It had lied to me, hoodwinked me, led me into a past that I was ashamed to admit, seduced me into tarnishing my soul, and now I was stuck struggling with all sorts of dark sexual byways in my own psyche that I would never otherwise have bothered to explore. For a long time, I struggled with the feeling that my husband was gravely imposing on me by desiring me when I did not want to be desired — a hangover from a radical feminist individualism. It was an unreasonable feeling, but one that caused me a great deal of suffering and marital grief. For years, the dark sexual fantasies that had made up the imaginative superstructure of my lesbian sex life continued to rise up in my imagination, often with such force that it was exceedingly difficult not to entertain them. There are still other matters to be resolved — particularly surrounding my femininity and the ability to communicate honestly about sexuality in my marriage. Complete chastity, the full integration of sexuality into oneself, is a lifetime project, and I can't pretend to have attained it.

Still, I am a lot closer than I once was, and I have noticed that as I come closer to the goal of an integrated sexuality, I have become much less angry. I no longer feel frustrated that I don't know how to bring my homosexual friends into the Church, and I no longer feel that there is a terrible and unreasonable urgency in forcing them to realization that what they are doing is sinful. That anger is not, I am certain, gone completely: there is still a great deal of sarcasm that emerges from the depths of my psyche. I am still harsh when I ought to be gentle. One day, perhaps, I will be able to write a second edition of this book where all of the lapses in charity, self-righteousness, and hypocrisy have been excised. I promise to work toward it. For the moment, I beg your forgiveness.

Obviously, my particular anger, and the reasons for it, are particular to people who have come into Catholicism out of homosexuality. But there is also a motive for frustration among those who have never been tempted with homosexuality. The ideal of marriage, one man and one woman living together in fidelity and fruitfulness, is a very difficult ideal to uphold: not just if you have same-sex attractions, but also if you have extramarital attractions, or pornographic attractions, or a fear of giving birth. Because it is difficult, those trying to live it out will, on a social level, always insist that everyone else should do the same.

The reason for this is that the moral life is much more difficult if you are pulling alone. Often, I want desperately to get out of the city and move up north where there's a good Catholic community. Why? Because I want to be able to talk with other women about the vicissitudes of my marriage without having them say, "You oughta leave the bastard." Because I hate being stared at as though I've committed some sort of social obscenity by having more than two children. Because I want to walk down the street without a host of paper-and-ink women staring at me with their creepy eyes and their naked bodies saying "Take me, I'm available, buy my jeans." In a society where most people think that chastity is an old-fashioned throwback, and that children are an inconvenient, easily avoidable consequence of sex play, it becomes more difficult to be fruitful and chaste.

Of course, we should expect this. Christ always said that Christians would be against the world. When you try to have a State in the world that is entirely consistent with Christianity, you don't end up with a paradise of virtue, you end up with a Calvinist theocracy where it is easy to hold your fellow man in contempt. Still, we will never, in this world, get away from this: so long as men are trying to be virtuous, they will get angry that those around them are slacking on the job.

This is because the vast majority of those who are struggling with virtue have not yet achieved that clarity and compassion that we call Christian charity. The spirit and the law are always at war in the soul of a virtuous man, and it so often seems that there is someone else opening the door to let the devil into one's own soul. Sin, in the life of someone who is trying to be good, is terribly painful. Worse than physical pain — which is why you find St. Jerome out in the desert beating his breast with a rock. To the world this is madness, but as soon as you come up against the specter of evil in your own soul, you want it out. Out, at any cost, in the same way that you would want a psychopath out of your daughter's bedroom. It takes a terrible and very difficult humility to admit, when you do sin, that it isn't someone else's fault. "If only my husband would . . ." "If only she hadn't . . ." "If only they had a law . . ." When we eat the forbidden fruits of this world, we quickly find ourselves back in the garden, playing point the finger with Adam, Eve, and the Serpent. Only slowly, through the constant encounter with my own sinfulness, does it become possible to insist on truth without grabbing a stick and beating it into our fellow man.

Beyond Heterosexuality

I do not want to see sodomy laws put back in place; I do not want to see fag-beatings instated as a national pastime; I don't want my gay and lesbian friends to schlep around the streets hoping that they won't be thrown in jail for vagrancy because no one will rent an apartment to a "homo." I don't want the restoration of an absurd form of machismo that ostracizes any man who would dare to have a talent for fashion design. I do not want a return to the world as it was: I am not a conservative, or a reactionary. There is no distant, glittering past that I look back to with wonder, saying "Oh, if only we could go back to the days when . . ." I don't even want to convince homosexuals that they ought to "become straight."

What I do want is to say that there is something better than this: something better than fleeting pleasures and sexual release. Sex is good, and beautiful, and replete with meaning, but it is not the *summum bonum* of human existence. To say "I must have sex with women who are not my wife" or "I must have sex with other men" is to admit the subsumption of the conscious, moral will to the desires of the appetitive flesh. It is disordered — out of order, placing higher things at the service of lower things. In the hierarchy of the person, the genitals ought not be given the highest rank. Their desires and activity should not form the basis of an identity: people, regardless of the nature of their sexual desires, owe themselves more dignity than that.

A young gay man once asked me how I had come to change from a homosexual into a heterosexual. I didn't know how to answer him, because the question seemed strange and remote. Heterosexuality had nothing to do with it. I went from being an atheist, struggling along in a godless and unforgiving world, desperately trying to cobble together meaning from the scraps of glory that my nihilistic worldview hadn't yet explained away, to being a Christian. I didn't find the secret path out of never-never land that leads to the straight world, or the fountain of heterosexuality; I found Christ. I said, "Lord, do with me whatever you will," and He gave me a husband and a family. I didn't go looking for those things, and I think that if I had gone to God as a means of becoming "straight," I probably never would have. Heterosexuality, like anything else in life, can become an idol; you can no more come to the Church as a kind of ironing board to get out your personal kinks than you can marry someone because you think they'll be able to sort out your finances. I mean, you can, but the reason for coming is not commensurate with the dignity of the destination.

There are Christians who come to Christ, initially, for relatively trivial reasons — because they wish to marry within the Church, or because it will make their parents happy — and who then, eventually, are converted. Presumably there are some who come seeking release from homosexual inclination that they neither sought nor want, and who end up finding Christ. But there are also many who come seeking heterosexuality, and who are disgusted with themselves, with God, and with Christianity when they do not attain it.

Fear and Trembling

Now, if the only goal is faith, then isn't homosexuality in? Surely there are good people, faithful Christians who really believe and love God, but who are gay.

The difficulty with this argument is that it does not know what faith is. Ordinarily I would not resort to a "God says so" argument, because I think that anything which God says can be proved by reason as well. Yet everyone, every faithful Christian, knows what God has said about "lying with a man as with a woman" (cf. Lev. 20:13), knows that it was reiterated by St. Paul, and that it has been the constant Tradition of the Church. The activists and theologians trying to expunge this teaching know it better than anyone else. A man may lie to himself very prettily, but he can never really escape from the knowledge that it is a lie. There is nothing obscure on this point, except for the clouds raised by those trying to obfuscate it.

So what of the Christian gays? I believe that many of them love God. It is perfectly possible to love God without having faith: it can feel almost impossible to both love God and have faith. To say, "My God, I love you — but I do not believe you. I do not trust that what you demand of me will be better than what I claim for myself. I do not believe that you will give me the strength and the humility to come alive and rejoicing through the valley of the shadow of death." Is there a man alive, since Abraham, who has not said this in his heart?

When I came to the point of contemplating Christianity, I had already glimpsed the mysterious marriage of faith and suffering. The fields of my heart had already been tilled by Kierkegaard, by Michaelangelo, by Handel, and by all of those beautiful Russians whom I read with such devotion and never understood at all. I had a firm foundation in the beauty of suffering and sacrifice, even if the official philosophy promulgated by my internal Ministry of Truth insisted that such ideals were contrary to the dignity of the rational autonomous human agent. I was, in other words, like the assembly of Soviet dignitaries who gathered one Easter morning to hear a sermon preached against the evils of religion. All of them somber, nodding their agreement, applauding the atheistic sentiments of the speaker — but it only took one man to cry out "Christ is risen," and the entire crowd resounded with the refrain: "Christ is risen indeed, alleluia."

So what is faith, and how does it come to dwell in the human heart? It is different for every person, but I suppose that we have been trundling along this entire time, with oblique references to my own story, and no real explanation of what happened. An explanation is necessary: a lesbian feminist atheist turning into a Catholic homeschool mother of four seems more improbable than the Himalayas deciding, one summer morning, to get their trunks on and go for a swim. It is improbable enough that lesbians, feminists, and atheists often refuse, simply out of dogmatic prejudice, to believe that I am telling the truth about myself; like fundamentalist Christians who believe that the dinosaur bones are just a scientific scam made up to turn people into atheists, they think that I am just a delusional Christian making up false stories about my own past in order to peddle my religion. So here is the story of how the impossible really did come to pass.

Philosophical "Ground Zero"

I was born in Montreal, but moved to Toronto when I was one year old. Raised as a "low church" Anglican, I became an atheist at thirteen — a decision based, as all serious rational decision-making processes are, on a muddle of factors that included intellectual confusion, lack of good catechesis, a desire to sleep in on Sundays, real questions about the existence of God, and the fact that the Anglican liturgy had abolished kneeling, so a small girl was expected to spend far too long on her feet with her fancy dress shoes pinching her heels. In my adolescence, I went through philosophical ideals like a teenager going through her wardrobe before a big date. I was desperately thirsty for truth.

Now, it is the summer of the last year of high school. I have been a declared lesbian, out of the closet, for about three months. My family is a little bit behind the times: I came out when I was till toying around with the bisexual label, and I haven't bothered to update them on the status of my sexual identity. None of that is really important to me right now: all questions of sexual ethics and labels have been eclipsed. Something much graver and more serious is lurking on the horizons of my life, darkening, or perhaps illuminating everything else — it is hard to tell. In the confusion of radical upheavals, the dimming of the light of faith in the hearts of mankind can come to be called an "Enlightenment," and the flourishing of Byzantine civilization a "dark ages," so you will excuse me that I don't know what to make of this whirlwind that is whipping across the plains of my interior self.

The castle of reason has fallen. It has taken a long time: Chris and I have been arguing about whether reason or something higher than reason — something which, just to make the debate more infuriating, he has no name for — is superior. I am the clear, logical, absolute rationalist; he is the intuitive, creative, dark dabbler in wisdom. A perfect archetypal struggle, but we are playing the wrong roles for our genders. It doesn't matter: I am very feminine in my philosophical legalism, and he is very masculine in his intuitions. We are at an impasse, and have been for some time, in spite of endless hours spent banging our heads against the problem in coffee shops and woodland clearings. It is a matter of the utmost importance: after all, we are trying to design a psychologically realistic role-playing system that will blow *Dungeons and Dragons* out of the stratosphere, and it cannot be completed until this philosophical ball of twine has been made straight. We are agreed that wonder is better than pleasure, and that disinterested love is superior to that smothering ownership that calls itself love, that faith is above proof, and that skin-deep beauty is worthless compared to authenticity. All of this has been argued and hammered out in a Herculean dialectic labor after the past couple of months. Only this question of Reason vs. ? remains.

Chris has done something unspeakably dirty: he has called in the cavalry. I had no idea — I thought that we were just going to spend a nice evening visiting a friend of his in Orangeville who, apparently, has access to a very nice liquor cabinet. Now we are sitting in David's living room, sipping some sort of sugary concoction and discussing the nature of truth. Dave is smoking a pipe, rhapsodizing in almost perfect Shakespearean meter about the smell of tobacco, and trying to blow smoke rings like Gandalf. Slowly, the conversation turns towards my beliefs. A very touchy subject. Chris has informed Dave that I'm an atheist: is that true? The look on David's face suggests that an atheist is a strange beast indeed, somewhat akin to a hippogriff, and he is prodding with a certain morbid curiosity to see if there is really one sitting here in his living room. I am uncomfortable with my role in the philosophic freak show and mumble, "Agnostic."

Is David a Christian, living in some secluded backwoods of Ontario such that he never would have met a nonbeliever? Not at all. David is a Druid sorcerer, one of the top apprentices of a master who has published several best-selling books and runs an exceedingly private retreat center to teach the Old Ways to young men in upstate New York. The freak show is, therefore, mutual. Apart from Chris, whom I have long accepted is half-crazy, I did not believe there were really people who still believed in magic (stupid, ignorant people, and teenage Wiccans, of course — but David is articulate and intelligent). David does not believe that there are people in the world who actually worship nothing, so he presses further: surely there has to be something, some high and glorious and noble ideal that holds at the center of my heart and around which everything circles as the planets circle Helios. I grasp at the only thing to which I have held consistent allegiance for more than a year running: Beauty. On the spot, I improvise a kind of romantic manifesto with beauty reigning resplendent over the cosmos. David accepts this, for the moment, and we move on to a discussion of the supremacy of reason as a means of unlocking Truth.

Here, we are speaking as two alien species might in the instant when they finally managed to work out the rudiments of one another's languages. David's guru has encouraged him to drink widely from the streams of religious thought, and while he still accounts himself a practitioner of Druidism, his current religious inamorata is a Zen Buddhist teacher by the name of Joshu. Joshu, apparently, has a stick with which he regularly beats his disciples when they give answers to his questions which reveal that they have not yet attained Enlightenment. Chris and David are both endlessly delighted with stories of would-be devotees of his path standing out in the cold for years and gnawing off their own limbs to prove that they really wish to learn. I am a consummate Euro-American snob, even though I think of myself as very multicultural, and I am merely perplexed. According to my categories, this man sounds like an abusive madman. Why on earth is he celebrated as wise?

I press for an example of wisdom, and David tells me a koan — a sort of Zen riddle that is supposed to trick the student into becoming Enlightened. Joshu says to the student: What color is the grass? The student replies: It is green. Joshu smacks the student upside the head with his stick and says: No, stupid, it's green. Thus endeth the lesson. Madness, right? But this articulate, if slightly bizarre human being, a man who has read more Shakespeare than I have, thinks that this is a perfectly apt expression of the point that he has been trying to make all night, and which Chris has been trying to make for the past three weeks.

Eventually the argument ends, as all good arguments inevitably do, in a cordial agreement to dispute the same question again the next time we meet. As I am walking out the door, however, David presses a book on me. Actually, he doesn't press: he specifically makes it clear, at least five separate times, that he is not pressing — I am to take the book only in the event that I truly desire to read it, and under no compulsion whatever, and only provided I will be in no means put out or insulted at having been offered such a tome. The book, oddly enough, is *Seven Storey Mountain* by Thomas Merton. Merton is a Catholic, a Cistercian monk, but David thinks that there is some sort of spiritual resemblance between us, based on my *ad hoc* "religion of beauty" speech. I thank him and take the book.

At home, the book sits on the shelf. That stupid Joshu koan completely consumes my thoughts: I look up other Zen koans to see if they will illuminate what is supposed to be clever about this seemingly meaningless anecdote. No such luck: more seemingly meaningless anecdotes. I run it through my head backwards and forwards, trying to come up with different possible ways of interpreting it. Does it mean that there is a difference in language categories between the teacher and the student? That green has a different subjective interpretation, in which the Master believes that his is more correct? It doesn't seem to fit the facts: the whole idea of the koan has something to do with the irrational, and a postmodernist philosophy of language doesn't quite seem up to the dignity of being termed "Enlightenment." For three days, this consumes my thoughts and my attention. When I am not at school, I am wandering around the streets of my neighborhood beating my reason against the rock of Zen irrationality. Finally, I'm exhausted. I sit down on a green electrical box by the side of the road and stare at a pine tree that someone has planted there. I stop thinking.

I will not claim anything as pretentious as Enlightenment: a moment of insight, though. The tree is there, and it, like the grass in Joshu's riddle, is green. I am looking at it without thinking about it, and this is key: if anyone has ever read Dostoyevsky's *Notes from Underground*, they will understand the disease of hyperrationalism. I am a hyperrationalist. Ordinarily, I would either not notice the tree at all, or I would notice it as a part of a philosophic category, or as an instantiation of a particular kind of symbolic truth, or as a realization of an archetypal fact, or as an interlocking system of cells and sap and DNA. Now, it's just there. I'm next to it. It's a tree — though even that is too abstracted. It is it, and I am me, and there's not much more to it. Into my head pops the thought, "No, stupid, it's a tree."

A tree. Apart from all my categories and thoughts and reasoning. I didn't make it. It is real, objective, fact, but not scientific fact. It is whole, indissectable, in a sense. Its being is not a matter for my microscopes, either physical or metaphysical. It has, in a very particular way, nothing to do with me. All of this, of course, doesn't express it: the actual experience is of the breaking of a rational cage, an escape from intellectual categories, something approximating an experience of the "thing in itself," apart from me, and, particularly, apart from my linguistic prejudices. It is reality shifting like a sandworm deep beneath the dusty foundations of the crystal tower of reason that I have been carefully building for myself all these years. The sand moves around its deep, unknowable body, and a gulf opens up in the earth. The tower crumbles, shatters, and is gone: an infinitely splintered mirror scattered across the desert, indistinguishable from the sand.

Now what? For about an hour, I'm buoyed up, exuberant, rejoicing that finally I don't have to torture myself in the labyrinth of consciousness, wrestling with this thing. But my philosophy is gone. I'm all alone in a world that isn't mine, and I don't have any rational categories to protect me. Help! All of a sudden, Sartre's creepy rantings about man's fundamental alienation from doorknobs make sense. How am I going to go to school? How can I think about university, and finish my philosophy paper on the *Metaphysic of Morals*, now? It's all over. I put on my best black existentialist turtleneck (I own several) and a pair of black jeans and go buy a coffee to console my shattered nerves.

When I come back, there is *Seven Storey Mountain* sitting on my bedside table. Well, at least Keats's maxim hasn't been demolished: Beauty is still Truth, Truth Beauty. Maybe he was right, and that is all we know on earth and all we need to know. According to David, Thomas Merton has some sort of insight into these questions and, in any case, all bets are off. Pure reason cannot make and contain the universe entire, nor provide all the needs of the heart of man. That means that truth is up for grabs, and it could be anything. It could even involve God. I pick up the book and start to read.

CHAPTER 11

Hope

At the bottom of any search for truth, there is necessarily an act of faith. It does not matter what object this movement of the will attaches itself to — the movement is the same. The rationality of reason cannot be demonstrated by reason alone. The evidentiary power of the senses cannot be proven without appeal to sensory categories. Science must fall back on science to demonstrate its triumphs. A morality founded on the dignity of man must appeal to the dignity of man in order to justify itself. You can't even demonstrate that existence exists without appealing to existence. The only philosophy which does not require an act of faith is absolute nihilism of the darkest variety: the sort of nihilism which is too nihilistic even to move the heart to suicide, for suicide itself is a kind of act of faith in the comforts of the Deep Dark.

Sooner or later the will, either intentionally or by accident, attaches itself to some mental object which then becomes the foundation for all other beliefs and assumptions about the world. In many people, this is a somewhat cloudy and murky affair. The will is committed only softly, and they are not really sure to what it is clinging. A philosopher is, in essence, someone who insists on having this question answered, clearly and distinctly — someone who wants to know precisely what the foundations of their faith are, and whether those foundations are secure.

There is always a trade-off of sorts between the relative certainty of one's faith and the degree to which it is a faith worth having. "Existence exists" is a formula in which anyone but a madman or an Eastern Mystic can rest secure, but it is not really such a fabulous revelation, in that it doesn't *get* you anywhere. It is a faith that underlies a thousand other faiths but it, in itself, is not enough to provide a man with hope.

The Philosophic Suicide

> If there were no eternal consciousness in a man, if at the founda-
> tion of all there lay only a wildly seething power which writh-
> ing with obscure passions produced everything that is great and
> everything that is insignificant, if a bottomless void never satiated
> lay hidden beneath all — what then would life be but despair? If
> such were the case, if there were no sacred bond which united
> mankind, if one generation arose after another like the leafage
> in the forest, if the one generation replaced the other like the
> song of birds in the forest, if the human race passed through the
> world as the ship goes through the sea, like the wind through the
> desert, a thoughtless and fruitless activity, if an eternal oblivion
> were always lurking hungrily for its prey and there was no power
> strong enough to wrest it from its maw — how empty then and
> comfortless life would be![58]

So says Kierkegaard, and I cannot disagree (nor, strangely enough,
could I disagree when I first read this in my atheistic youth). For hope,
there must not merely be sense, reason, existence: there must be something greater. There must be meaning.

Meaning, though, is dangerous. It always ends up insisting that
this is true, this is right, this is significant, and this is not. The author
really intended a particular thing when they wrote, "The cat sat on
the mat." They did not intend a dog eating the moon, no matter what
your subjective experience of the story might have been. Meaning is
either hegemonic in its claims or it is worthless, a plaything blown in
the wind, a snapped twig to which the child clings in the middle of
the maelstrom in order to reassure itself that it is still attached and
holding on to the world.

The most dangerous form of meaning is the Meaning of Life. This
is founded, inevitably, in morality. Without it, a man's philosophy will
ultimately lead him down the winding road to despair and suicide. This
is something that I know from very deep experience. My first brush
with Romantic Platonism brought me very near to suicide — to what I
saw as easeful death, in whose arms I would at last be set free from the

prisons of the body, able to roam at will through the infinite possibilities of the mind, to see, and to know, and to apprehend truth entire, without the scales of matter lidding the inner eye. In the aftermath of a suicide attempt that never quite got off the ground, I realized that philosophy was not something to be taken lightly — that the search for meaning was one in which the ship of self could run aground, or sink, or be consumed by sea monsters. Out of this terrible necessity, I formed a three-point checklist that any philosophy had to meet if I was going to suffer it in my consciousness.

It had to be internally coherent and consistent.

It had to be a system in which it was possible to live as though it were true. Philosophies like hard determinism, whose implications were completely impossible to realize, got thrown into the pit immediately: if they were true, then truth didn't matter.

It could not lead to suicide. A philosophy, after all, is the place in which you invest the stock of your soul; I was no longer willing to risk metaphysical bankruptcy. I insisted, at last, on having not only faith but also hope.

The Difficult Matter of Morality

The trouble with hope, and with meaning, is that they lead inevitably into morality. If you believe in some truth, and you are committed to living as though it is true, and it gives you hope in the world, you are going to have to end up with a moral system. There is no getting around it: you might try, but sooner or later you'll wake up and discover that your philosophy demands something of you. The most sophisticated systems of philosophy have these matters already worked out. They carry with them a prescription, not only to avoid ingesting certain moral poisons, but also to imbibe deeply of the "Good Life," which is to say the morally Good life, the life of virtue.

Everyone in the world agrees with Virtue when they are watching a movie about Gandhi or reading *The Lord of the Rings*, but we are generally skittish about accepting its implications in our own lives. We vastly prefer to substitute some placebo, a token gesture that doesn't require any real sweat or suffering. Just put a bit of loose change into a donation box and pin an appropriately colored ribbon to your breast, and suddenly you're fighting breast cancer, or AIDS, or violence against women, or environmental degradation. Religion, too, can provide its placebos: Ivan the Terrible was scrupulous about saying grace, would make the Sign of the Cross over every morsel of food, and went to Mass every morning before descending into his dungeons to see his political enemies tortured to death. On a more ordinary note, there are the wives who spend an hour every day in adoration "praying for their husband's soul" while trying to work out an excuse to get an annulment . . . or the faithful who scrupulously drop a dime into the poor box every week and then walk with tight-lipped contempt past the beggars on the Church doorstep.

Simply put, we are proud. Very few people really want to fall down on their knees and cry out to heaven, "Lord, I am a sinner, have mercy on me." Perhaps we can do so in the most terrible moments of darkness, when the pit is yawning beneath our souls and we look into the abyss of our own heart and see the face of hell laughing up at us from the depths. But even then, it is much easier to self-justify, or self-loathe, or self-pity than to self-abase. We want to have "self-esteem," to think well of ourselves; to wake up every morning, pat ourselves on the back, and say, "I am lovable and capable. I am a good person. I deserve a good life." It is a lie. Every single one of us, in our moments of honesty, knows that it is a lie. But it's a lie that we are very eager to swallow.

Ironically enough, the more eager we are to believe that we, ourselves, are in good standing — that we are nearly perfect masterpiece whose blemishes can be covered with a touch of white-out — the less likely we are to imagine that this is true of everyone else. Oh, I don't mean that the self-styled holy people and the purveyors of self-esteem believe, philosophically, that others are doing poorly. But a person may declare loudly from the rooftops, "I'm good, you're good, let's all love one another" and still sit around in the company of their friends talking about the intractable stupidity of the masses. The abstract love of humanity is often accompanied by a generalized contempt for actual specimens of the species. It is far easier to "love" a helpless Indian child who sends letters of gratitude to your North American mansion than it is to go downtown and try to love a strung-out, diseased, schizophrenic homeless man who wants you to hold his scabrous and pestilential hand, makes the sort of comments that might ordinarily induce you to call in the "sexual harassment" squad, and tries to ply money out of you with obviously fabricated sob stories. Confronted with such a person, people who "love" humanity will usually start talking about how you have to think about yourself as well, how you have to take precautions against disease, and how there are some people who can't be helped, all the while shaking their heads sorrowfully and saying, "That poor man. There ought to be a program . . ." By this, of course, they mean that men like that ought to be lovingly confined in "rest homes" for the mentally unstable, where gloved men in white coats can medicate them into an innocuous, drooling idiocy.

Accompanying this sort of contempt is an inability to fathom the sins of others. Maybe you've been fighting with your brother for twenty years because you didn't get the piece of furniture that you wanted out of your mother's inheritance. Maybe you turn into a screaming lunatic whenever you feel that your husband isn't "valuing you as an equal partner" in your marriage. These things, you can understand. You don't like them, try to pretend that they're something other than what they are, sweep them under the rug. But when you're confronted with them, you inevitably respond, "What right do you have to judge? You don't understand how hard it is. . . ." And yet you "just can't understand" how someone else could get violently angry at their children, or look at pornography, or squander all of their husband's pay at Walmart. It's inconceivable. Hardly human.

The Pitiable Tragedy of Same-Sex Desire

Fundamentally, this is the attitude that most "straight" people are inclined to take towards homosexuality. This is why the gay movement relies so heavily on the claim that same-sex attractions are innate and inescapable. That way, the unfathomable is made palatable, pitiable, even acceptable, by means of biological necessity. "People are born gay," the literature croons, "You can't make a gay person straight any more than someone would be able to make *you* gay." The appeal, of course, has at its core the straight person's assumption that nothing in the world could cause them to choose homosexuality. The idea that no one does, and that it's just a matter of a genetic crapshoot, insulates straight people against the fear that they might be tempted with homo-erotic associations, and provides an easy-to-understand excuse why people would engage in behavior that many heterosexual Americans find inconceivable.

The problem with the argument is that it rests on the notion that, of course, a straight person couldn't possibly choose to engage in, much less enjoy, gay sex. But this is patently ridiculous. Straight America might like to think that there is nothing in the world that could pos-sibly induce them to participate in same-sex relations, and presum-ably there are many for whom this is the case — but the reasons are ideological and aesthetic, not biological. A simple, honest glance at the testimony of prison populations and at the test case of ancient Greece should be enough to tell any reasonably self-knowledgeable person that the argument doesn't hold water. There is simply no such thing as a "straight" person, nor any such thing as a "gay" person. The categories are arbitrary, and they are nonsense. Politically convenient nonsense, but nonsense nonetheless.

Where the confusion arises is with the fact that there is a statisti-cally small — but, in a large population, substantial — group of people who are compulsively homosexual, who are unable to choose *not* to engage in homosexual sex even if they desperately want to stop. (Hence, the insistence that they are "born that way" and that chastity is impos-sible.) Sexual compulsion is not, of course, limited to homosexuals; any practicing psychiatrist or spiritual director has probably worked with people who have a habit of compulsive masturbation, an addiction to pornography, or an extramarital sexual fixation that they just don't seem to be able to get over. Like any compulsive behavior, or behavior that a person feels unable to control or influence, sexual compulsions make people feel humiliated, powerless, demeaned in their own eyes, anxiety-ridden about the judgments of others, and intensely frustrated. They lead to self-hatred and to anger at whatever causes them. Hence, stories like that of Robert Duncan, who was badly beaten by a deeply closeted homosexual man with whom he was having an anonymous encounter.[59] Such anger (homosexual activists call it "internalized homophobia") can turn into outward violence and "homo-bashing" in much the same way that a man's humiliating addiction to prostitutes can cause him to become violent toward the women whose favors he purchases. Finding himself unable to control his vice, and unable to bear the burden of his own feelings of guilt, he blames the source of the temptations.

The Ubiquitous Human Experience of Failure

This should not be unfamiliar to most of us. Although I have to admit that my own lesbianism was never of the compulsive variety, I have plenty of familiarity with the general principle. My own struggle has been mostly with depression, which has plagued me since I was a teenager. I know that it is sometimes possible to dispel feelings of profound misery with an act of will, a subtle trick of the psyche, or sufficient prayer. In consequence, I often feel that I *ought* to be able to control my feelings, that I should be able to get some perspective, that the rational arguments against feeling unhappy really are enough, and then I feel that there is something deeply wrong with me because I can't make myself get over myself. I sit in my living room, with the sun pouring in through the window and my beautiful children playing out in the backyard, bringing me flowers and showing me the ladybugs that they've found crawling around in the peonies, and I feel as though I am absorbed in utter darkness. How could this possibly make sense? Naturally, I cast around in the dustbins of my mind, looking for some bit of psychological detritus that will explain the whole thing, so that I will be able to throw it away and return to my senses, and as often as not my mind will supply some sort of excuse. It's because I haven't been getting enough sleep, enough affection, enough time to myself. So who is depriving me of these basic rights, without which I am sunk in the chasms of despair? Obviously, my husband and my children.

Never mind that I had this feeling just as often, and with precisely the same intensity before I was married, and before I was a mother. This fact fades like a phantom before the rationalization that, at its source, the problem is not with *me*. It isn't *my* responsibility; it's caused by *someone else*. And so, if the chain of events goes badly, I become incensed, stamp my feet, break coffee cups in the sink, yell and scream at my husband, pull the closet door off the hinges, and so forth. And then, when the storm is over, I sink into a collapsed heap of abject self-hatred, unable to bear the burden of being myself, and desperately wish that I was someone else.

Of course, there are a lot of places along the way where it is possible to jump off the reckless train to self-loathing. But jumping almost always looks absolutely terrifying, as though you would be badly injured and probably die in the attempt. Experience says that it isn't so — and over a long, slow buildup of minor successes, it becomes possible to see that more clearly and to succeed more often — but it still always looks impossible at the time.

Sexual temptations are exactly the same. They begin with something that feels unavoidable, a riptide grasping at the soul and pulling it out to sea, and ends with the shipwreck of the self.

There is an alternative to the struggle: you can give in. Like a soldier in war, you always have the choice of desertion. Someone struggling with depression can stop struggling and learn to love the feeling of misery, to cherish thoughts of suicide, and to lovingly cut holes in their own flesh to demonstrate the depths of their aching sorrow. They can style themselves as "lost souls" and wander around dressed as vampires, listening to goth metal on their iPods. Or they can steep themselves in the wild ravings of romantic poets, write rhapsodic odes to melancholy, and go mooning around near rivers, thinking how lovely it would be to become Ophelia.

Someone dealing with compulsive sexual temptations has precisely the same option, and this is what the gay community is selling. Stop struggling; stop the cycle of wasted effort, failure, humiliation, and self-hatred. Be gay, be proud, be happy.

These often seem to be the only options: die or give in. Of course, really, they are the two horns of a false dilemma. There is a third option, but it requires humility.

The difficulty with any sort of compulsive or semicompulsive vice is that it is tremendously embarrassing and even, in a sense, dehumanizing. To look at myself and have to say, "I can't stop doing this, even though I know that it's wrong," is profoundly unsettling. It strikes at the core of my self-image as a rational, self-determining individual; it is the internal evidence of the greatest tragedy in human history. This is the image of Original Sin graven in the recesses of the human heart. It is the evidence that we are all condemned to death, that we really do need to be ransomed by something as radical and terrible as the Cross. We are not "okay," and we cannot save ourselves. We don't like that. We want to be able to say that we are self-made men, that no one ever had to lift us up out of the pit, and that we aren't weak and pathetic like all those other poor beggars with their psychological scars and their pitiful cries and the open, ugly wounds in the palms of their hands.

The Scandal of Never Being Scandalous

It doesn't help that everyone else is trying to put forward the idea that they are not in the same boat. This is the problem that I have always had with a certain kind of Christianity, usually found in "gospel churches" and works of Midwestern horror, where everyone pretends that they are shiny, happy, pious people. The problem with the Pharisee standing in the middle of the market square in his properly tasseled garment, with his hands lifted up in prayer and supplication, the evidence of his fasting clearly marked on the polished, white, sepulcher-perfect contours of his face, is not only that he is drowning his own soul in pride but also that he is drowning the souls of everyone who sees him in despair. The image of a "whitened sarcophagus" is absolutely perfect: inside, the Pharisee is just as corrupt and worm-ridden as the people he looks down on. His outward perfection is of the sort that people only possess in funeral statuary and eulogies, an ideal that we can only aspire to when we are dead.

So when this ideal is put forth as a living reality, as "being a Christian," it is little wonder that people turn away and say, "No. Not for me. I can't do that." Or, more commonly, "I can't stand those sanctimonious prudes. Why would I want to be like them?" This is the problem with Pharisees — almost paradoxically, by never doing anything scandalous, they scandalize everyone around them.

Genuine holiness requires humility. To admit, with St. Paul:

> I do not understand my own actions. For I do not do what I want,
> but I do the very thing I hate. Now if I do what I do not want, I

agree that the law is good. So then it is no longer I that do it, but sin which dwells within me. For I know that nothing good dwells within me, that is, in my flesh. I can will what is right, but I cannot do it. For I do not do the good I want, but the evil I do not want is what I do. Now if I do what I do not want, it is no longer I that do it, but sin which dwells within me. So I find it to be a law that when I want to do right, evil lies close at hand. For I delight in the law of God, in my inmost self, but I see in my members another law at war with the law of my mind and making me captive to the law of sin which dwells in my members. Wretched man that I am! Who will deliver me from this body of death?

— Rom. 7:15-24

This is a very difficult passage of Scripture because it reveals that one of the greatest saints, a man who had seen Christ in a vision and suffered every kind of physical and spiritual trial in order to conform himself to the will of God, still bore within his heart the imprint of concupiscence. It tells us that no matter how long and hard we struggle, there will never come a day — at least not in this life — when we will wake up and say, "It is finished." Even Christ did not get to utter those words until the moment of His death.

So what is the third way, the way of humility, that is revealed by St. Paul and by Christ? It is the way of the Cross, the acceptance of the fact that we require saving, and that we can't do it all by ourselves. We have to remember those words, uttered by God in the beginning, that "it is not good that man should be alone." The great struggles of our lives generally cannot be undertaken alone, in our bedrooms, far from the prying eyes of a world that might condemn us.

This is almost certainly why "cures" for homosexuality may prove to be temperamental, why so many ex-ex-gays have resumed a gay or lesbian identity after discontinuing their involvement with a psychologist or spiritual support group. The reason this happens is not that the person reverts to a fundamentally homosexual orientation, but that their struggle with same-sex attractions is too great for them to be able to carry it by themselves. To call psychology or support a "treatment" is a fundamentally idiotic way of thinking about it; the outcome desired is not a heterosexual orientation, but a resumption of personal autonomy, the ability to be able to conform one's life to one's values, and the creation of a communion of persons — the ultimate calling of human life. The fact that so many people are able to find a genuine, compassionate, honest human relationship only while sitting on a couch across from a person that they are paying by the hour is a tragic testament to the epidemic of loneliness within our society, but it has absolutely nothing to say about the intractability of homosexuality, or about same-sex attraction as a basis for identity.

The "cure" consists not in the healing of father-wounds, nor even in the assumption of heterosexual relationships, but in humbling yourself enough to admit that a struggle is taking place and that you can't do it by yourself. This is why frequent confession and compassionate spiritual direction is effective, while testosterone-replacement therapies are not. This is why people who go to the Courage meetings — even when they have to report that they had anonymous sex with another man the night before — will ultimately succeed, while those who only go when they feel able to pat themselves on the back will not. This is also why there are some people who will never be "cured." Because for someone whose primary struggle is the struggle with same-sex attractions, being cured is tantamount to being saved. Regardless of what certain Protestant theologians would like us to believe, that is something not completed until, finally, you stand before the judgment throne of God, and He says, "Well done, good and faithful servant" (Matt. 25:21).

Three Ways

Does this mean that, for the duration of this life, we are condemned to a cycle of failure and self-hatred? Absolutely not. We have three choices. The first choice is to abandon the attempt to be virtuous, to accept an exculpatory ethic that excuses whatever vice has seeped most deeply into the marrow of the soul, and to march off down the wide boulevard to depravity. This creates a cycle of its own; evil is without content, and can only thrive by consuming whatever is good within a person. Once it gets a solid foothold, you can be certain that, like an ambitious usurper, it is going to seek to expand its territory. Thus you get a cycle of sin, followed by self-justification, followed by deeper sin, followed by greater self-justification. At the bottom is total nihilism, and an utter depravity of which the Emperor Caligula would be proud.

Most people will never get quite that far. We tend to "bottom out" — that is, to return to self-hatred and tears — long before we get to the point where Gulags and rapacious orgies twinkle like malformed stars in the corners of our eyes. The abandonment of virtue is very often nothing more than a complication in the cycle of failure and self-hatred; it is a reprieve offered to oneself before returning to the rack of proud self-condemnation. Nonetheless, utter depravity is an option that is open to the human soul, and it is not one that has gone untried. (Nor, I would caution, has it been limited to the short list of malevolent dictators who have feasted on the blood of their citizens and condemned millions to torture and slavery — a person who is not particularly possessed by ambition can easily sink himself into the abyss of vice without making it onto the pages of history.)

The second option we have already discussed at length: we may try to maintain the illusion that we are good, upstanding people, and then, whenever we falter and fall, condemn ourselves with weeping and gnashing of teeth.

The third option is to put aside the notion that we are already good and work at becoming so. Think back to the days of childhood, when you decided that you were going to be a soccer star, or a ballerina, or a champion pogo-stick jumper. I, personally, was going to be a world famous poet. You sit down at your desk, twiddle a little band of hair around your finger, stick the eraser of your pencil in your mouth, and imagine the triumphs, the successes. Gold medals, blue ribbons, book-signings. Ahh. Ecstasy. Then you talk your parents into enrolling you in classes, and getting all of the appropriate gear, and off you go. First day, you expect to be scoring goals, or spinning across a stage, or receiving a laurel crown, but no. You get there, play the "name game," and do drills. Terrible, wretched, mind-numbing drills. You kick a ball up and down a field about a hundred times, or make little pairs of words that rhyme all the way down your page . . . for hours. *All right,* you think, *this is just the first class. Next time, we'll be ready to get down to the real business of being a hero.* Of course, next time you discover, to your immense disgruntlement, that you do more drills.

Eventually, you either get over the disappointment and develop a more realistic attitude towards your imminent achievements, or you quit. I quit being an ice skater, and a majorette, and a lead female vocalist. That wasn't because I couldn't have accomplished these things if I had really put my mind to it but because I found that they were difficult — and I realized that I didn't have enough interest for a sustained effort. I didn't quit being a writer; only now, some twenty years after I began to pen my first grade-school masterpiece, have I started to have some small modicum of success in selling my work.

The moral life is exactly the same. Sure, there are some people who seem to wake up one morning, decide that they are going to become a saint, and henceforth commit no serious sins. They make the rest of us look bad, and they are very good for our humility — but subjectively, they are just as obnoxious and intolerable as the kid in drama class who seemed to get the lead role every time because, seemingly without effort, they could just do it. (It is worth noting that generally those who actually become "overnight saints" don't see themselves as having done so. Most people who think they have become perfect all at once have merely become deluded.)

Most of us will struggle, and we will fail. We will fail just as many times as we would fail if we decided to take up the hobby of catching flies with chopsticks. Even after we have succeeded once, we will probably fail next time. This is normal. The sooner that we make peace with this fact, and decide to get on with the work, the sooner we will become saints.

Only armed with the knowledge that we are going to stumble, and that our moral muscles are going to hurt in the morning, and that people around us are going to criticize us for failing to be perfect first time out, is it possible to pursue moral perfection without surrendering to self-loathing.

This is the option that groups like Courage extend to their membership. It is also the option that is absolutely essential to living a Christian life, regardless of whether your personal struggle is with homosexuality, rage, drug abuse, unforgiveness, self-pity, or any of a hundred other temptations to which the human flesh is heir. It is not a recipe for self-hatred and "internalized homophobia," but for genuine self-knowledge and heroic virtue.

More Than Words

There is a moral here. It is not for the same-sex-attracted, but for the Christians who wish to bring them to Christ. Membership in our community is not extended only to the pre-perfected. We are not en exclusive country club that allows in only the brightest and best. The Church is a hospital for sinners; when you go there, you should expect to encounter the broken, the defeated, the unholy, the lost. If you encounter only the stern and upright, with their tight lips and their virtues dangling like medals from their chests, you've gone to the wrong place. When homosexuals arrive on the doorstep, they have to be invited in. We have to offer hope — not of a quick fix, or of an instant conversion to heterosexuality. There are certain "change" organizations that offer week-long retreats, often costing hundreds or even thousands of dollars, to parents hoping to save their children from same-sex attractions, or to homosexuals desperate to become chaste all in one go. There are "Christian" therapists who will fix your father-wound, or recondition your sexual responses, at a rate of several hundred dollars per session. I would not put much stock in organizations with miracle cures for deep-seated homosexual attractions. We are not called to be snake-oil-salesmen-for-Christ; we are called to offer a genuine, realistic hope, a support to one another under the burdens of the Cross, and an image of the love of a God who has not abandoned His children, even in the valley of the shadow of death.

Too often I have been in circles of good, orthodox Catholics — intelligent, caring people who genuinely love God, and who are generally very likable — and have heard them complaining about the "fags." Usually the offending members of the Rainbow community have been petitioning the local school council, or running about the university campus sticking up positive space stickers. My God, you will never hear such Pharisaical opprobrium as is poured out on a self-confessed gay man with a degree in fashion design and a lisp. Of course the good

Catholics in question insist, at least in this part of the world, that they would never talk this way in front of *actual* "sodomites." But how do you know you haven't been? Even if everyone in the room with you is married or wearing a collar, you don't know. Tell me, what possible benefit are you gaining from maligning your fellow man that justifies the risk of scandalizing another human being and jeopardizing their immortal soul?

The problem is not with words. I am not joining up with the politically correct brigade in their crusade to castrate language. (I happen to think that "catamite" is an absolutely lovely epithet, and I am kept up nights trying to think of imaginative ways of weaving it into my fiction.) The problem is with *intent*.

You can use the words "fag" and "dyke," even "sodomite," to your heart's content if you have the right sort of mind set behind it, just as one black man can affectionately refer to another as "niggah." One of my dearest friends — at that time, only a recent acquaintance — came to my apartment early in our friendship to play an RPG.* He cast himself down on the couch, then looked up at the conspicuous pictures of Mary and the saints that formed the entirety of our modest interior decorating.

"Uh," he said, "I guess you guys are Catholic." It was clear that the question had been weighing on his mind since he had first started coming over, but now he had decided to bring it up. We affirmed his suspicions. "I think you should know," he said, stiffening his spine, "I'm gay."

I could see the visions of our revulsion dancing in front of his eyes, the image of himself, thrown out, head hanging low, shuffling back along the Peterborough streets, friendless and dispossessed, with no one to go to when he wanted a good, rousing session of *Dungeons and Dragons*. "That's cool," said my husband, "my wife used to be a dyke."

Did the use of the word "dyke" seal up a portal between Heaven and Hell, confining this young man's soul to the nether regions for all eternity? No. In fact, this was the beginning of a long and very fruitful

---

* For those less geeky than myself, RPG stands for Role Playing Game — *Dungeons and Dragons* is the most famous, but also, in my opinion, one of the poorest of the options available to those who wish to indulge a taste for dice-directed interactive storytelling.

discussion of sexuality, faith, and everything else under the sun that was to last well into the next day, and which was to continue over the next few months, ending in his decision to join the Church.

That said, there is no fudging the data with this one. You can't say "Oh, I'm just fooling around. Of course I mean the words 'filthy and execrable sodomites' with the utmost charity and affection," if you shiver with disgust every time a man in a pink shirt walks past you in the streets.

We cannot offer hope to anyone — not to fags, or dykes, or winos, or strumpets, or capitalist pig-dogs, or lily-livered poltroons — if we are trying to reach down from the parapet of an ivory tower. We have to begin on the ground and lower ourselves beneath another human being if we hope to give them a leg up.

This is particularly true of those whom society has tended to condemn, and especially of people who are ostracized and put down by the general congregation of humanity. I am going to stand up and confess, here, that I understand exactly what my homosexual brothers are feeling when they give up on the quest for chastity, leave the Church, and try to find hope and happiness in the gay lifestyle. I have felt it myself: there are times when I look up at my ceiling at night, and I don't see the face of God — I haven't seen Him, or felt Him, in months, and I can't understand the burdens that are piling up on me — and I want to say, "To hell with it." Literally. Let this entire project of the moral life collapse under its own weight; just let me get out of the building first.

There are times that I feel as though I am a weak and anemic Atlas, struggling under the weight of my own superego, and I wonder if there is any point in the exercise at all. I have made the attempt to be good, to be holy, to do what God requests of me. But instead of a glowing happiness and a fuzzy heart, I have found heartache, pain, and despair, all swarming around me like maggots in a dung heap. Really, is there anyone among us who would not have secretly understood if Job had gotten up off his mountain of woe, cursed God, and lain down in the dust to die? Would any of us shake our heads in revolted disgust if Sisyphus decided to get drunk one morning and let the boulder sink into the mud?

If for a single second, on the rack of despair, I could actually convince myself that God didn't exist, I would throw the whole thing over. I would run away from my family, or commit suicide, or become a raging alcoholic and curse everyone who came my way. I would be worse — a hundred times worse — than any of the people hanging around the bars down in the Village.

A Ruthless Goddess

Without hope, no one can make it anywhere in the moral life. Even Christ was given the consolation of an angel when He was kneeling in Gethsemane. Most of us require, as an absolute precondition of moral perseverance, some sort of tangible manifestation of hope, some small reminder that God is still there, and that He will give us the strength to get through the dark night of the soul. Christians are called to provide this to one another — and to those who have lost it and have turned to sin, in the hope that it will give some relief from the insufferable burdens of living.

It is not enough to provide statistics and arguments proving that homosexuality leads to increased suicidal thoughts, or greater drug dependency, or higher rates of alcoholism, or eating disorders. It will not do to demonstrate, beyond a shadow of a statistical doubt, that these problems do not go away when the whip of social disapproval is no longer plied to the back of the homosexual person. Prove to a lesbian woman that her feelings of inadequacy, her certainty that people are constantly judging her, her deep and self-destructive insecurities, are not a result of the homophobic bogeyman; you will not have done her any favor. Now where are the jaws of blame and resentment going to feast? If there is no one else to blame, who can her rage devour except herself?

Take a gay man who has tried to be normal from the time that he first noticed that he was "different" from the other little boys, and demonstrate to him that indulgence in homosexual sex only deepens his loneliness and confirms his outcast status. Show him that all the negative judgments that he feels when he looks in the mirror come not from society, but from the depths of his own heart. You can expect to find his suicide note on the table in the morning. What is he to do? He feels the choke hold of biological determinism tightening around his throat; he has prayed for this to go away, but God has abandoned him to homosexuality. He was made this way. He has tried to be "other," and has failed. What hope is there now?

Do you think that you know, better than someone who is trying the path of flesh, that its promises are void? That you know better that it is all heartache and failed romance? That you have a keen insight into its existential abysses, lacked by those actually drowning in the darkness?

We needn't squander too much time demonstrating that there is no hope for man in the satisfaction of his impulses and desires. Those who pursue Lady Pleasure as their mistress will find out, sooner or later, that she is a ruthless goddess, a consumer of hearts, who feasts on the carcasses of her faithful and leaves their bones to the dogs. Those who are involved in sexual excesses of any variety — heterosexual, homosexual, or other — will eventually discover that they are held hostage in the prisons of their own desires, and that what looks like freedom tastes like death. People who languish in the dungeons of sin know. They *know*. They are only trying to tell themselves otherwise as a means of keeping sane — much as a certain kind of prisoner, confined in chains and kept for years from the light of the sun, will slide into a deep and imperturbable fantasy in which the bedbugs do not bite and the whip does not crack. If you feel compelled to rattle someone into a realization that they are sauntering down the wide avenues to hell, concentrate on the complacent, the respectable, the self-satisfied. The sinners — the public, obvious sinners, the prostitutes, the tax collectors, and the men on Queen Street with the leather thongs — they know. Christ was always very tender with these people. He saved the epithets and violence for the Pharisees and the moneychangers in the Temple.

I once read Nietzsche's *Beyond Good and Evil*, and I remember being struck by the fact that he consistently promised to show how much better it was to live in the light, in the pure, crystalline, mountain heights of reality, where (according to Nietzsche) nihilistic philosophers are privileged to dwell. Yet the entire book was nothing but a sinking, seeping, mud-dripping, maggot-infested description of Christianity as Nietzsche saw it. Time and time again he would rhapsodize about the clean air, and time and time again, he would show only the murky, turbulent depths of a decidedly disturbed psyche.

Nietzsche may not have had any choice, because Nietzsche's mountain is, frankly, founded in one of mankind's ugliest and starkest philosophies. But Christians have no excuse for making the same mistake. No one is going to imagine that we are there to deliver them from darkness and despair if all we do is arrive in the prison and start cataloging the maggots and telling them that the infestations of their wounds are disgusting and abominable. You cannot carry a leper out of death and into life if you are not willing to touch lepers.

CHAPTER 12

Love

Every Christian, in his own way, holds a tiny shadow of the key of the gates of heaven. The nature of the key is love — not happy-clappy, campfire sing-along love, but the love that suffers and dies on the Cross. If we are able to open those gates, just a crack, and let the light which permeates all creation shine into the darkness of sin, then people will come, and they will follow us out.

Unfortunately, this is rarely what we show to the world. I have an image in my head of a latter-day, right wing Bible-thumping Christ standing before a man crippled from birth and shouting, "You filthy, degraded animal. Get up and walk before I thump the living bejeesus into you."

This is not realistic, but it is the way that many homosexuals perceive Christians. Partially, partially, we may blame other people for the misunderstanding: certainly the Western media has done everything within its power to misconstrue Catholic teaching and to showcase the ugliest side of pseudo-Christianity as though it was the Christian norm. We've all had occasion to cringe upon seeing the latest character in some pop-psychodrama convert from a normal human being into a creepy, weird, delusional "Christian" who behaves like the aliens in a "we come in peace — shoot to kill" movie. We know that news reports about papal activities are often bizarre and largely unrelated to reality. The media lies. Sure. But it might occur to us that if there was not a grain of truth in the malignment, they wouldn't get away with it. After all, if someone tells a blatant lie about a friend of yours, depending on whether it is insulting or merely outrageous, you will either take up arms to defend them or laugh your head off and make the slanderer look a fool. Everyone knows Christians. Why are they not, *en masse*, turning off their television sets and driving down the ratings every time that the networks portray us as hypocritical lunatics?

A friend of mine had just embarked on a quest to becoming a high-school teacher and was concerned that she was not a fit role model.

So she asked a Franciscan, a wise man of our acquaintance, what was she to do? How was she to present herself so that she would be a good example to the young minds that she was called to educate? The monk said, "Don't worry about being a good example. Be authentic."

Christians worry far too much about being a good example, about showing the right sort of stripes, and making sure that everyone knows that we are healthy, holy, happy people. But it is transparent. Everyone can see that we have shoes that squeak, just the same as their shoes, and that we have children who cry in supermarkets, and that we quarrel with our spouses, and that sometimes we want to curse God and die. Yet there is the façade of peace, the pretense that somehow we are managing to lug the Cross to the top of the hill without blood or agony. To many, and particularly those who are suffering, this comes across as painfully inauthentic. Thus, having known the shiny-happy people, they nod in recognition rather than laughing in disbelief when Todd in *Thursday-Night-High-School-Melodrama* starts wearing a Jesus T-shirt and behaving like he's had an alien brain transplant.

The Apologetic Snare

Even when we're not trying to show off to the world, too often, we embroil ourselves in pointless arguments with it. I was giving a talk recently to a group of Catholic girls, talking about my experiences with homosexuality and answering their questions. One girl wanted to know how she could convince people that she was arguing with in class of the truth about homosexuality. I had given several long, rambling answers about the necessity of addressing each individual person as an individual, understanding where they are coming from, and building up a unique proof that is mailed specifically to their address, but she continued to press, "How do you prove the Church's teaching to someone who just refuses to accept it?" She wanted one good, solid, clean technique that would knock 'em dead every time — the apologist's equivalent of the ultimate move in a 2-D fighting game.

Eventually, my husband cut in. "Do you have a relationship with these people?"

"No," she replied.

"Then you can't."

No one has ever abandoned a homosexual lifestyle and embraced Church teaching because of an argument from natural law. No one has ever been pulled into the loving embrace of Christ, the heavenly Spouse, because a Christian out-statisticked them in a debate about same-sex marriage. No one. Ever.

Christians are not called to preach the gospel of heterosexuality, much less the gospel of anti-sodomy laws. Occasionally, we might convince someone who has never struggled with homosexual temptations that homosexuality is morally illicit by appealing to Thomistic arguments — but then, what have we gained? I've had this experience and found it quite disappointing. A young man with whom I had argued about homosexuality more than once came to me and said that, after some thought, considering it in the light of Jean-Paul Sartre's doctrine of "bad faith," he felt that I was right about same-sex attractions. So there's another person on the planet who now believes that homosexuals can make choices about their sexuality, and that homosexual sex is not a morally valid option. Great. Now what?

Arguments are not to be entirely pooh-poohed — I am an intellectual, and a convert, and almost all of my friends are also intellectuals and converts. (Catholicism, or at least Christianity, spread through our social circle like the flu through a kindergarten class.) The arguments in favor of Christianity certainly had something to do with my conversion, and influenced the conversions of many of the people I know. But it was the context in which these arguments were brought forth, far more than the arguments themselves, that made the difference. The shrill denunciations of my atheistic principles by well-meaning high-school Christians in philosophy class didn't make a single smidge of difference. I didn't really know these people. I certainly didn't like them, and I wasn't interested in understanding the basis for their arguments, so I simply presumed that they were speaking from ignorant and irrational foundations and used it as an opportunity to whet the knife of my philosophic tongue.

On the other hand, when class was out, and my dear friend Kevin and I would wander down to the creekside to discuss the nature of God and the universe, I was ready to listen. Of course I argued tooth-

and-nail against him — I loved to argue — but I took the things that he said seriously. Even if he never (or almost never) actually got an open concession on any point, a great deal of what he said struck my heart and changed my mind. It never occurred to me to assume that Kevin's Christianity was stupid, or that it was wholly irrational, or that he was a blathering, hypocritical idiot. I could see very clearly that he was not — on the contrary, he was one of the most dazzlingly intelligent people that I knew, and the foundations of my atheistic soul trembled every time that he opened his mouth to refute the foundational principles of my belief. I knew, sooner or later, one of these days, he was going to show me that it was all built on sand. I knew that he was marching out in force, and that I was only trying to buttress the walls enough to withstand one more attack.

It was not the arguments, though, that affected me the most.

Spring Rolls: The Ransom of Souls

There was a very ugly time, when I was in high school, when I decided that I was going to seriously embrace the philosophy known as nihilism. It had come to my attention that, as an atheist, I had no real reason or foundation for believing in any kind of moral principle, and, in any case, I could see little evidence that there was anything deeper than self-interest underlying the decisions that people made — even the allegedly moral ones. It seemed to me that everyone was going about trying to fulfill certain moral obligations just so that they could look good to other people or to themselves, and the prospect of evil suddenly opened up before me as a serious possibility. One could be duplicitous, manipulative, knowingly selfish, deceitful, and callous, and there was nothing in all the godless heavens to oppose it. As always, I was eager to throw myself into the waters of this new philosophical stream, and very quickly I began forming a new layer to my psyche, one that plotted, and schemed, and made up things to say so that the plots would not be obvious to other people. Kevin, as a Christian, quickly fell victim to scorn under the new philosophic regime — but I didn't say so. Not to him. You see, Kevin also had the strange notion that even though he wasn't dating me, he ought to pick up the tab if we went out to dinner or had a coffee together (it's not old-fashioned male chauvinism — Kevin had more available funds than I did and was inclined to be generous). I have always been inclined toward the love of good food and had elevated coffee practically to the level of a deity (I did, actually, have several coffee-drinking rituals that I would perform with priestly gravity whenever I imbibed of the dark drink — which shows you that man will find a way to work worship into his life even when there is very little foundation on which to build an altar), so I quickly became more readily available to go out in the evening with Kevin. Admittedly, this was a rather petty goal for my newfound freedom from the shackles of morality, but I was hard pressed to think of anything that I really wanted to do now that I had devoted my heart to the dark side. Vaguely, I would have liked to have taken over a significant piece of the world, and to have ensconced myself in a dark tower with serfs that I could treat like toys, but it wasn't a dream that I was willing to pursue with any particular relish. I am an absentminded, poetic type, and the practical ruthlessness required for ambition was never mine.

So my nihilistic will to power was directed toward draining Kevin's bank account in order to fulfill my love of Chinese cooking. Eventually, however, the entire thing started to break down. I realized that if you were entirely amoral, people eventually started to clue in; that everything they said in Sunday-school cartoons about becoming entrapped and entangled in your own lies really is true; and that, in any case, the air at the top of the Nietzschean mountain was strangely dank and claustrophobic. I abandoned the project and started looking for a foundation on which to build some sort of morality in a godless world — because it was clear, at last, that man needed morality as much as he needed breakfast.

I started by making a confession. I asked if Kevin would take me hiking, and he drove me out to a little stretch of the Bruce Trail where we could talk and drink cheap red wine among the singing birds. We walked down to a mossy bridge that ran over some slender, trailing, nameless creek, and there, I sat down and told him everything that had been going on in my heart — or, at least, I told him that I had been deliberately taking advantage of his kindness — and I apologized. I believe that he smiled. I remember very clearly what he said: "Yes. I knew that."

He wasn't making it up or trying to salve his male ego. He had *known*. Kevin's intuition was almost as sharply polished as his reason, so there hadn't been a single moment, in all the time that I thought I was deceiving and manipulating him, that he hadn't known precisely what I was doing. I was floored. The entire palace of pride that I had built up for myself crumbled, like King Haggard's castle when the unicorns are freed from the sea. It was a thing beyond believing, something that could not be reconciled with life and morality as I knew it. He had known, and yet he hadn't upbraided me, or accused me, or even — and surely to God, this would have been permitted him — insisted that I pay for my own butter tarts.

So that was Christianity. Did I immediately fling myself headlong into the arms of Christ and declare my undying devotion to the calm eye in the center of the ethical maelstrom that I had just discovered? No, of course not. I glimpsed it, for a second, half recognized it for what it was . . . but my God, it was bright. Too bright. It felt more like a spear or an earthquake than like love, and I was afraid. Naturally, it was impossible to go back to anything as stupid and ugly and banal as nihilism. My notion that morality was based entirely on the fulfillment of selfish desires, even on a sort of rational self-interest, was annihilated. But I was not ready for Christianity.

If I had not known Kevin — had simply been sitting across from him in a philosophy class, say — and watched him pin my atheistic arguments to the wall with all the casual simplicity of an entomologist sticking pins in beetles, I wouldn't have understood him. He would have infuriated me, at best. At worst, I would simply have dismissed him as being a rather more intelligent specimen of the Christian type. He had an impact on my life because first and foremost, he was someone that I knew as a friend. He had earned the right to show me that my morals were a shambles. The Bishop of Digne ransomed Jean Valjean's soul with a pair of silver candlesticks. Kevin ransomed mine with spring rolls.

La Solitude

If you concentrate solely on refuting the homosexual act, or homosexual marriage, or even the notion that homosexuality exists, you are not offering people somewhere to go. In many cases, the people that you are condemning do not have the interior freedom necessary to adopt the position that you are putting forward. I could not, if Kevin had insisted on it (and occasionally he did suggest it), have become an instant convert to Christianity. I wasn't there — there was too much of myself that I had given over, that I did not own, and until I had reclaimed it, I was incapable of offering it to Christ.

Generally, if you ask me to speak about myself, I will describe my experiences, my struggles, and the obstacles to my conversion primarily as the movements on an intellectual battlefield. The conscious activity of the mind, not the strange currents of the emotions, much less the stolid reality of the body, form the stuff of my life-narrative. And yet the body is always there, and the emotions are always there, lumbering along through the back of every shot, like an ungainly monster, ubiquitous, invariably out of focus, difficult to make out. Restoring this part of the story is a work of psychological archeology, but it is possible — and, if I am going to be honest, it needs to be done.

I never thought of sex as particularly important. I suppose, on some level, I was much more of a Manichean then than I am now — I thought of the body as base, of the emotions as an irrelevant imposition on my *real* life, the life of the will and the mind. Yet sex was always there, providing something, accomplishing something, and it was not easy to give it up. Impossible, in fact. After I became Catholic, I couldn't go and visit my ex-girlfriend just as a friend without sliding back into our old habits. Masturbation I was able to give up by dint of sheer stubbornness — after all, provided there was another person involved in my sexual transgressions, they could be catalogued as acts of cowardice, which was a sufficiently intellectual sin that it was grudgingly allowed into my catalog of failings. The only solution was to stop visiting Michelle alone, to go over only when there were other people there so that there would be no opportunity for me to fail in my attempts to be chaste, and to talk to her on the phone when we needed to discuss something personal.

What was the result? Loneliness. Bitter, heartrending, unbearable loneliness. Generally, when I speak of my time in Kingston (as I did earlier), I describe myself as having few friends there. This is not quite true. I knew a tremendous number of people in the city: people I had known in high school, people I had met on coming to Queens. Many of the latter I have to admit I remember poorly — I could not even tell you their names — and yet they were there, and I think that they would have been willing to become my friends if I had wanted them. I didn't. Instead, I shaved my head and took to wearing loose, strange robes of a sort that I don't think have ever been fashionable outside of a convent or a coven, and I spent a great deal of my time wandering around the city at night, sitting on the banks of Lake Ontario and looking out across the immense emptiness over which hovered a distant moon.

I prayed, a great deal. I went to Mass nearly every day, even though I couldn't receive communion yet. But in Kingston, I was alone.

Why did I not start forming friendships? Because I didn't just want people with whom I could sit around at the Sleepless Goat drinking coffee. Michelle and I had provided, for one another, a certain emotional service: I have mentioned, earlier, that our sex life was absolutely steeped in fantasy. We did not make love to one another, but each consented to serve as a cipher for the other's archetypal ideals. Through sex, I was able to become a different, stylized, idealized self, and to become one, as it were, with a certain projection of my own psyche, a perfected "other" who had the capacity to fulfill my deepest longings. The mythological content of the soul expressed itself through this interplay, and now it was gone. Of course I couldn't express that to myself, but I tasted the fruit of it: I have never, in my entire life, been as lonely as I was at that time.

Brünhilde's Breastplate

Thus the constant desire to run away from Kingston and go to Waterloo, where everything was entirely different. In my memory of the two cities, in Kingston I am always alone. If I am outside, it is night. With difficulty, I can dredge up the hours that I spent in university lecture halls, but the film quality is very poor, the sound-track muffled, the images dull. Waterloo, on the other hand, appears in sparkling color, like something out of a Jean-Pierre Jeanet film. Even the Coffee Time, where Chris and I used to sit for hours on end, consuming inhuman quantities of caffeine, is glossy and bright, as though it were the beatific coffee shop and not a dingy donut joint on the corner of a dull suburban street.

For me, romantically, there were only two possibilities. There was fantasy, which required absolute safety and emotional security. I had tried it with men, but it had proved exceedingly dangerous. No, fantasy required another woman, someone whose soul contained the same sort of emotional and archetypal content as mine did. Someone who would know and understand without me having to express or spell out anything. Or there was conquest.

In Greek mythology, there is a story of a woman named Atalanta, raised by bears and more interested in masculine pursuits than those of the feminine world. It seems that she was somewhat in demand as a prospect for marriage, but she was terribly afraid that she was going to end up married to the wrong sort of man — someone unworthy of her. So she set up a condition: she would marry only a man who could best her in a footrace. Even when a man appears whom she loves, and whom she desperately wants to marry, she doesn't drop that condition, almost as if it is impossible for her to relinquish it now that she has set it in place. The same story, in a different form, appears in Wagner's version of the *Nibelung* cycle — the Valkyrie Brünhilde, when she is condemned to marriage, requests herself encircled in a ring of fire on a mountaintop so that only a man of unparalleled bravery will be able to remove the layers of armor from her breast.

There was I. I had spent years perfecting and maintaining an interior fortress against not only masculinity per se but against emotional invaders of any sort. People who wished to get inside had to observe the forms, and they were permitted only in select areas of the keep. To get to know me was rather like getting inside the emotional wall that Roger Waters describes in Pink Floyd's "The Final Cut." The shaved head and the loose robes were, in some sense, a challenge: they made me as forbidding to the world as I was in my heart. I was alone in Kingston because there was no one willing to assay the Wall.

In Waterloo, there was. In fact, he had already done so. I am a strange case, perhaps, because the romantic war had already been fought: I had fallen in love with, and allowed my heart to be captured by, someone who was not my boyfriend, while still thinking and behaving as a lesbian. The romance came first, entirely divorced from any physical relationship or any threat thereof. But after I had taken away the supporting crutch of a fantasy sex life, it quickly became apparent to me that what I insisted on thinking of as a strange, exceedingly close male-female friendship was actually a romance. It was a baobab tree that had somehow managed to convince me that it was a safe, friendly sprout of a rose, so I had not dug it up. Now it was there, grown tremendous, with roots that had spread throughout the soil of myself, and it was tearing the stone of my heart to pieces.

I am getting ahead of myself. The story of my romance, and of the conquest of my inner Mordor, is one for another chapter. For now, it suffices to speak of loneliness.

It Is Not Good that Man Should Be Alone

Fr. John Harvey, the director of Courage, notes that "people tend to confuse sexual addiction with pleasurable or frequent sexual activity. The difference is that ordinary people can learn to moderate their sexual behavior, while the addict cannot do so. He has lost the ability to say 'no' because his behavior is part of a cycle of thinking, feeling, and acting which he cannot control. Instead of enjoying sex as a self-affirming source of pleasure in marriage, the sex addict uses it as a relief from pain, or from stress, similar to the way an alcoholic relies on alcohol."[60]

If you have ever talked seriously with drug addicts — those who are not checked into rehabilitation clinics — what you will quickly discover is that there is no such thing as a "drug addict." No one is addicted. They are all completely in control of their habit. They do it because they enjoy it, they love it, it opens their minds, frees their souls, and brings them relief at the end of the day. They could stop if they wanted to, but why would they?

It is precisely the same with those who are addicted to sex — and particularly to masturbation, or pornography, or promiscuity. It doesn't matter whether you are talking to a homosexual or a heterosexual. They are sexually liberated, their love is "free," loosed from the bonds of conventional morality. Theirs are broader horizons that bring together people who would otherwise suffer from being apart. They are having fun, or enjoying their own bodies, or whatever. They are not addicted. Not, that is, until they try to stop.

Then the real situation becomes clear. "Casual" sex is not about fun, or liberation, or self-esteem, or self-love, or healing the world. It is not casual at all. It is meant to be a very serious panacea for the deeper problem of epidemic loneliness which pervades modern culture. Man, having divorced himself from nature and from the family, is left with the problem of an unpleasant solitude. The pornography empires and glory holes have been erected on foundations of terrible loneliness, which they attempt to assuage with the superficial imitation of intimacy.

This loneliness is the product of the reduction of the family to a contract of mutual convenience, an arrangement that can be dissolved the moment that one of the partners fails in his responsibility to meet the other's self-defined needs. It has lost its covenantal power to overcome the original solitude of Adam, the solitude of which God once said, "It is not good that man should be alone."

This was the first privation in the world, the first time that the words "not good" were applied amidst a string of creations that God saw were "good" or "very good." Woman was the answer to this dilemma, not simply because she would be a partner and a helper, but also because she alone was "flesh of my flesh, and bone of my bone," to the man who had discovered loneliness in the Garden of Eden. The family, by which a woman leaves her father and mother and becomes "one flesh" with her husband, was the remedy which God intended for man's loneliness. When it was abandoned, loneliness, not freedom, became the hallmark of human existence, and the sexual act became its remedy.

Promiscuous sexuality is, at its heart, an attempt to access something like the Communion of Saints — to be able to enter into the intimate life of a much larger range of humanity than you would ordinarily be able to access. Of course, the problem is that it doesn't actually accomplish this end at all. You are ultimately left with a profound frustration, because you are pushed back into yourself, into your own fantasies of what other people's interior lives are like, or of what it means to be in contact with another human being, and you meet only on an exceedingly superficial level. It's essentially a cheat. It looks like it's going to be able to get you out, beyond the confines of your own subjectivity — then, instead, only reinforces that profound experience of solitude.

This is why it is rejected, absolutely, by the teachings of Scripture and Tradition. It's rejected for the same reason that a jeweler rejects a cubic zirconium, or a piece of iron pyrite: it has the accidental properties of something tremendously valuable but is actually worthless and commonplace. The Church is not saying, "Sex is bad," but "Ecstasy can be counterfeited. Don't be duped."

If Gollum were to discover that the One Ring was made of fool's gold, he would not throw it into the fires of Mount Doom. The "precious" would remain precious, subjectively, even if objectively it is worthless. Only if something real, a genuine pearl of great price, is offered in place of the bauble will the owner relinquish his treasure. This is what Christianity is supposed to be about: you bring your worthless bread and wine — the most quotidian ancient substances — to the altar, and they are transubstantiated into the most precious matter in the universe, the Body and Blood of Christ.

A Less-Than-Ideal Convert

When I was in Kingston, there was a Catholic community there attached to the University Newman Center. They were theoretically very welcoming; they had a very modern liturgy where everyone in the congregation could shout out their personal needs during the prayers of the people, and they had a biweekly supper which I attended with some regularity. A chaplain and a chaplain's assistant were available to talk to me. They welcomed me into the community of the Church with all of the usual liberal *caveats* about not having to swallow hard doctrines about contraception and premarital sex. I joined up with the RCIA and attended meetings until one night in late January, when I walked through the snow in my sandals halfway across the city to learn about the teachings of Christ . . . only to find that the meeting had either been moved or canceled and I had not been informed.

Suddenly, I was once more in precisely the same situation in which I've often been in social settings: on the outside, a little too strange to be properly adopted, accepted, superficially, with reservations. I went to dinner, and I joined in the small talk, and I volunteered to cook my famous eggplant Parmesan for the people there, but it was very clear that this was not somewhere that I belonged. I wasn't hurt, or disappointed, or angry at God, or inclined to dismiss the Church as a bunch of hypocrites who pretended at love when in fact they were just as petty and sectarian as everyone else. That would have been silly. I wasn't openly judged or condemned — in fact, the old Catholic ladies made a heroic attempt to be understanding and friendly — but the bald girl with the strange clothes just didn't fit in with anyone's idea of a respectable Catholic young lady. I was fine with that. After all, I had *chosen* to be the bald girl with the strange clothes.

Nonetheless, if the Newman Center had been my only contact with Catholicism, I probably would have slipped back into a comfortable lesbian identity, toyed around for a while with a superficial Catholic faith, and then ultimately abandoned it, throwing Christianity onto the pile of discarded philosophical systems like another garment that didn't fit. Fortunately, I had friends — genuine friends, who actually liked me in spite of, or in many cases because of, my strangeness — who were either Catholic themselves or well on their way to joining the Church. For several years this resulted in a bizarre, heterodox Catholicism: my catechesis came primarily from a Druidic Sorcerer who had sort of been converted by the Gospel and St. Francis of Assisi, but who, for the moment, was heavily enamored with the Hindu guru Sri Rama Krishna. Still, if I was inclined towards syncretism in my doctrine, my practice was essentially Catholic, and my prayer life, bolstered by the growing faith of those around me, was directed toward God the Father, Son, and Holy Spirit, and toward Mary. Orthodoxy came later, slowly, by degrees as I actually learned about the reasons behind the Catholic faith. For that, all of the arguments, apologetics, and rational discourse was essential. But for the beginning, when I had first come to the Church in search of truth, what was essential was love.

This is a nail that cannot be hammered in too many times. Respect-ability, "normality," and conformity with social ideals are *not* valued by the gay community. When a lesbian or a gay man arrives on the doorstep of your church, prompted by some convoluted inner workings of the

Holy Spirit, there is a good chance that they will not look like your ideal of a good convert to Catholicism. They will not talk the talk, and they will not do as the Romans do. They will need to be loved, genuinely loved, and genuinely accepted, or they will turn around and go back to the Village, where they feel wanted for who they are.

PART V

Homosexuality and Identity

CHAPTER 13

Gender

I would be lying if I were to claim that I'm looking down from a summit high above the rest of humanity, having transcended the categories of gay and ex-gay, from a position of absolute freedom. It simply isn't true. One of the great claims that the gay movement almost invariably makes about "ex-gays" or "converts to Christianity from homosexuality" is that we are still just as gay as ever, just deluded about our sexuality. There is plenty of evidence to support the claim: it is very rare indeed that anyone leaves a gay lifestyle to enter into a perfect, glittering, same-sex-attraction-free heterosexuality. There is always something that remains, which, for most of us, it will take a lifetime to overcome.

So I'm still struggling with lesbian attractions? Is that right? Perhaps I have managed to find a husband who is particularly feminine? Or maybe I am simply living out a lie, surrounding myself with the accoutrements of a happy heterosexual marriage when, in fact, heterosexual sex brings me limited joy, and I am constantly at war within myself, struggling and straining to keep up the appearance of normalcy, driven insane from the inside out?

Token Ex-Lesbian

I have to pause for a moment to laugh: I was once asked to come and speak to a Catholic school board that was trying to decide whether to allow a young man to bring his same-sex partner to the school prom. It was the usual sad undertaking, with a molehill blown up to the size of Mt. Everest, and everyone chomping at the bit to tear each other to pieces while this poor young man was turned — perhaps willingly — into a gay-rights poster-child to be waved around, in tears and in triumph; just another piece of political currency. He played his part well: I don't blame him for it. Mark Hall was everything that the gay movement needed in that place, in that time, to challenge the Catholic schools. I was everything that the Catholic school board needed, in much the same way, to justify their opposition, and so we were paraded out into the ring and made to go through the whole circus: the courageous gay boy resisting the oppressive Church, the supportive parents cheerleading their son whatever he decided to be, the Catholic school trustees with their gently mothering tone softly refusing to condone same-sex relationships, and me, the token ex-lesbian, speaking out for the right of religious people to practice their faith in the public arena. Naturally, it was made into a "made-for-TV" movie, with a strong gay-rights bias, and the already shallow proceedings were made even sadder and more trite by the accretion of a thick layer of stereotype. I got a minor part — cast, obviously enough, as a neurotic delusional married to a wet towel, complete with facial tics and electroshock therapy. This, of course, was the one great benefit that I gained from the affair: it was my first and possibly only opportunity to become a one-dimensional caricature on television. Wahoo!

For the record, I have never had electroshock therapy. Or hormone replacements. Or "straight" drugs. Or father-wound surgery. Or heterosexual boot camp. Or an *ad hoc* exorcism in the local preacher's basement to expel the spirit of homosexuality. I doubt very much that any of those things are particularly effective, except, perhaps, accidentally. If a therapist who talks about father-wounds happens to establish a strong rapport with a male homosexual client and is able to help him work out some of the psychological factors that compel him towards compulsive homosexual activity, then that may be effective. Or if someone needs a placebo to trick themselves into believing that they are capable of overcoming their bio/psychological instincts, then perhaps drugs will work. For the most part, though, I think that the heart of homosexuality centers on two primary factors: the first we have discussed at great length, and this is relationship. The second is gender.

Femininity. What is it, and what does it mean? Does it, in fact, mean anything at all?

A Goddess of My Own

These were questions that I ended up coming up against immediately, but rather accidentally, when I converted to Catholicism. I did not begin with a desire to be Catholic. I began with the realization that I could no longer, with any intellectual honesty, hold on to an atheistic understanding of the universe. This realization had been building slowly for years: I was far too aware that the things that happened in my life seemed to have a fittingness, sometimes symbolic, sometimes just, that resembles the way that one scripts a narrative. I was not the cause of it (unless I wanted to buy into the notion, held by some psychologists, that everything is a manifestation of our own free will, and that if a woman is raped, it's really because her subconscious determination to be violated caused a rapist to come along). The simplistic explanation — that I was simply choosing significant symbols from my environment, the way that a gatherer chooses the herbs and plants useful to her — was one that I had entertained, but it was clearly not sufficient to fit the facts. In any case, I had come to the conclusion that there was a higher intelligence whose nature was not known to me, but who had at least the same level of interest in my existence as an author has in the characters in her book.

For a long time, I half-believed this and never went any further. But at last, in the middle of the tremendous intellectual crisis that I outlined earlier (following the crash of my rational kingdom), I finally realized that I could not, solely on the power of my reason alone, explain, understand, or make sense of my world. I decided that I would ask whoever had come up with the world in the first place.

I wanted, above all, two things: I wanted to know what my purpose was — where my plot was supposed to be going; and I wanted to say thank you, the way that I would say thank you to John Keats, if it were possible to meet him (an opportunity I hope someday to enjoy in the Communion of Saints). I didn't like the word *God*. *God* was a patriarchal word, wrapped up in all sorts of Sunday-school associations, plus the accretions of nearly a decade of atheistic venom that I had spit in His direction. So I didn't pray to God. I prayed to "Thou who art," because it was gender-neutral and catered to my love of archaic diction. Secretly, in the depths of my heart, I hoped that "Thou who art" would turn out to be female. I desperately wanted a goddess all of my own to worship. Ideally, it would be the moon, which sparkled in the firmament above the little university dormitory window. The moon which had a face like a virgin girl, and also like my grandmother (the only person I had ever really known who had gone on into that great unknown which we call death). But I was not going to lower my intellectual standards enough to go making up spurious gods just to fit in with my own romantic ideals. If there was a god out there, I wanted to know who it was, and what it wanted me to do about it. So I asked. "Thou who art, whoever thou art, reveal thyself to me that I might know you, and know how to worship you."

It looked, very briefly, as though I was going to get my goddess after all. A gentle presence, definitely feminine, beckoned me, encouraging me, came beside me as I prayed. For a moment, I was lulled into a sense of relieved security. But the more I prayed, the more it became clear that there was something wrong. The proper form of address consistently came into my head as "Virgin" or "Mother," both, interchangeably — and this was good, because all good goddesses are mothers and virgins — but she was always pointing beyond herself. Slowly, as a thundercloud builds before a storm, the image became clearer and I knew who it was. Not my goddess, but Mary.

Mary. The Blessed Virgin Mary. The antithesis of all my feminist ideals of femininity, the object of all my gender iconoclasm.

Had she not been so soul-transfixingly beautiful, I would have pounded my Amazonian breast. (I do not wish to imply that I had a vision — there are ideas, personalities, and presences that are beautiful in their own right, even when the eye has nothing but the moon to see.) It dawned on me then, that if this was the Virgin Mary, there was probably a Christ, and if there was a Christ . . . I stopped, sobered. A church. Perhaps *the* Church. It was a grave and dreadful possibility, but one that had to be seriously considered.

I sat down with the idea of God and started looking it — or rather, dare I say, Him — over. It was clear enough that if I was going to be told to become a Catholic, that would mean changing my life. It would mean that I could not carry on in a lesbian relationship. Reluctantly, I made the bargain. *All right, God. If You want me to give this up, You want me to give this up. I came to You asking who I was, and what I was made for, and if lesbianism isn't it . . . well, I guess I'm not anyone in particular to argue with the author of the universe.*

Still, I hoped — desperately hoped — it wasn't true.

A Shiningly Rational Being

To give up lesbianism, that I could have borne. In fact, I was not exceptionally perturbed at the thought of putting it aside. I have always been sort of a myopic delusional who believes that everything can and ought to be subordinated to ideology, and if my sexuality had to go, all the better; throw it on the fire. These doubts about the existence of God had arisen at a time in my life when sex had lost a great deal of its luster: "Sex with Sue" had left me in complete despair about the rational faculties of alleged sexual experts, my attempts at relationships with boys had convinced me that "straight sex" was a joy that I was simply incapable of sampling, and it was becoming clear that my girlfriend and I had reached the end of the sexual road that we had been on for nearly seven years. Coming up with new fantasies to keep things fresh and spicy had been increasingly more difficult; the thirst for novelty persisted, but the various byways of my sexual psychology had, for the most part, been explored. There were really only two possibilities: either we could drift into the doldrums of lesbian bed death (hardly an appealing option for a woman not yet twenty years old), or we could take everything to a new level, perhaps purchase a strap-on or a leather scourge. She seemed to be conquering the problem by exploring her bisexual-polyamorous side, and just as my lesbian identity was becoming more entrenched, her relationships with men-on-the-side were getting more intense.

The idea that I might be jealous was not one that I was willing to entertain: I was a shiningly rational being, immune to such human foibles as jealousy. I did not own her, she was free to do what she liked, and it was wholly absurd and selfish for me to object. So I didn't. Nonetheless, I generally didn't feel a particular desire to have a boyfriend except when she had one, and when she admitted to me that she had slept with one of our mutual male friends — actual, real sex! Terror of terrors — I felt a strange, sickening feeling that I couldn't force away with any amount of rational platitudes. Suddenly there was something there, a rift at the heart of our sexual relationship . . . a place where she had been and I was unwilling to go.

In his memoir of hustling, Rick Whitaker speaks about the effect of this sort of jealous desire to be a part of everything in the experience of one's lover.

My boyfriend, Tom, was leaving me, and I knew he had hustled in the past. I was in love with Tom and I wanted, I guess, to experience something intense that he had gone through, vaguely expecting that it would help me to understand him better and that it might even somehow bring us back together when he found out about it.[61]

Whitaker was willing to prostitute himself in an attempt to transcend the boundary, the barrier that had risen up in a relationship that he desperately wanted to save. I was not. She had been with a man and would probably be with others. I was intensely aware of this, and terribly jealous, even if I didn't call it that. But to follow after her was unthinkable.

It was the first time that I had any real contact with the idea — one that I have encountered so many times since — that sexuality can be a source of pain. My lesbian relationship had been exceedingly stable, and in my heterosexual relationships I had never let the sexual element get past the point of minor discomfort. Now I realized that something had been broken at the heart of the sexual relationship that I had always relied on, and so the whole thing had started to seem like a charade, something shallow and not entirely worth saving. Did God want it, this broken plaything? Well, He could have it. That was fine. God, after all, was stunningly beautiful, a movement in the depths of my soul, a symphony that could awake the dawn, a solid rock on which my identity could finally be erected. To give up my sexuality for that seemed like nothing.

The difficult thing was not lesbianism, but femininity. A male God. A patriarchal Church. And me, a woman. What was I going to do?

The War of Melinda against Melinda

I had always maintained that men were the enemy. Not the particular men that I knew — who had, through no fault of their own, become inheritors of the Y chromosome — but men as a general species. I was a believer in the great feminist myth that once upon a time, all had been in harmony and beauty, the world was watched over by the fat matriarchal fertility mothers that archaeologists are constantly digging up from ancient cultures, and then masculinity rose up and overran the Earth. Men had learned warfare, and had turned against one another, robbing, murdering, ravishing. Women become objects to be taken and owned, and the great civilizations of the earth were founded on the torn vestments and ceaseless tears of Tamar lamenting her rape. Thus, everything that was good or noble or beautiful about humanity was torn from female hands and planted on high, in realms of power inaccessible to women, and was called "masculinity." The sun, the spirit, the intellect, the arts, activity, power, accomplishment, the gods: all were "masculine." The moon, the body, the emotions, the crafts, passivity, obedience, self-giving, mere morality: these were "feminine." They had not been so from the beginning. They became so because the men, having usurped power over humankind, had seen womyn as a dung heap onto which all of the inferior elements of humanity could be thrown.

Suddenly, the myth had to be abandoned. No longer could I look at the Virgin Mary and see the antithesis of everything I wanted for myself. I could no longer deride her, or pity her, or nod in sage agreement with the sentiments of feminist poets who wished that she had just said "No!" instead of "Fiat." Men and masculinity could no longer be demonized or blamed. I was forced to look at femininity, and at myself, and to realize that all along, men had not been the foe.

Caligula, in the height of his insanity, was constantly at war with various external powers: he went to the forests of Teutoberg to fight the ever-problematic Germanic tribes. Not finding any Germans, he sent his German guards into the woods, had them captured, and marched them in triumph back to Rome. He made war with Britain by sending his soldiers to collect seashells on the coast of the Channel. Yet in spite of these bloodless wars, Caligula's is remembered as a particularly bloody reign: it is simply that the blood shed was usually Roman. But underneath the futile war against the world, and the terrible persecution of his own people, I think that there was almost certainly another war, the real war: the war of Caligula against Caligula. Certainly, my war against patriarchy was really a war against femininity and, beneath that, against myself.

This war was not started by ideology but by the fact that at the core of my personality, there is much that is "masculine." In Jungian terms,

I have a well-developed "animus" or masculine side, which, when it is poorly integrated into my personality, seems to be in direct conflict with my actual femininity. Psychologist Fr. Benedict Groeschel notes:

> A certain kind of passive aggression and self-rejection may develop in the overly gentle boy or the overly aggressive girl. They may be forced by others to dislike themselves. If this is compounded by an anxiety about homosexuality, then the person may become assertive in a self-destructive way. It seems to me that a great deal of posing and self-mocking — even the use of the word "gay" — are leftovers from a childhood or adolescence filled with self-hate.[62]

I don't know about being "forced by others" to dislike myself — though if I am honest, this may have something to do with my generalized delusion that everything comes down to a free act of my own will. Certainly I had in childhood — and have always had — a great deal of trouble forming friendships, especially friendships with girls. I waffle a great deal as to the reasons for this. I know that I have a general dislike of "girliness"; I have very little sympathy for feminine vanity, and less for histrionics. (This, of course, is absurd; there are cases where I am just as histrionic as any woman, as my husband can tell you.) I don't know what to think about it: it's very easy to write about things that I've figured out amid struggles that I worked through in the past — but this one is not in the past.

At the beginning of this chapter, I said that there are things which remain, things which it can take a lifetime to work through. Mine is not homosexual attraction: at some point, I figured out that there are a thousand and one things that happen in the psyche that can safely be acknowledged and put aside. Women are more beautiful than men, at least to me, but I've become able to separate that aesthetic appreciation from the realm of my sexuality. I will notice if a woman is beautiful, and I can sit around drinking beer with the boys and argue about the nature of feminine beauty in a way that most women probably cannot, but it has no sexual teeth; it does not feel like desire. That said, I would not say that I am "heterosexual" in the sense of having a "heterosexual orientation," whatever that means. I am not attracted to *men*. I am attracted to one man. My attraction for him is real, it is very intense, and it arises out of our relationship, not out of some sort of fundamental orientation or alignment of the genetic stars. I love him, and I am married to him, and that is the foundation of my sexuality. For me, there is no particular struggle, no interior war, to be found here.

But femininity — my God, femininity! What on earth does it mean? I don't mean to imply that I think it has no meaning, or even that I am blind to the differences between the sexes. There are those who claim to be unable to see the difference between masculinity and femininity — perhaps, just as some people are color-blind, others are gender-blind. For the most part, though, I think that this "gender-blindness" is much more a deliberate and studied gender obliviousness. Certainly, it was so in my own case. I didn't see differences because I refused to see them — because I didn't want them to be there.

Violists Are Not "Sissy"

So long as I still believed that men and women were really just the same, I was tremendously frustrated and ill at ease with being a woman. I spent years trying to excise all elements of traditional femininity from my psyche, under the presumption that these were weaknesses and failings ascribed to women by men. I tried with all of my might to imitate the interior and exterior accomplishments of my male peers. Thinking that there was no difference between a man and a woman, I tried desperately to become a man. Why shouldn't I have, if masculinity was really just the set of human traits that had always produced success?

This sort of gender confusion has a great deal to do with sexuality. Obviously, when I was trying to claim the benefits of masculinity, I did not mean that I literally wanted a penis, or that I desired the privilege of loving women — I was not a "political lesbian" who chose her sexuality to accord with her feminist principles. Still, most homosexuals, at least in my experience and in my reading, have some sort of difficulty identifying themselves with their own gender. They may insist that they are masculine, or that they are feminine, but beneath this there is generally some sort of desire to redefine, to tear up the groundwork of gender as it is perceived by everyone else, to rework it so that it is a more hospitable environment for their particular personality.

In some cases, this is absolutely valid. How many times have we read the traditional old gay-development profile: a young man, lacking typical masculine interests, is ostracized by his peers and accused of being sissy, and, finally, of being gay. Eventually he comes to recognize what others have seen all along: that he is different from other boys. This difference, he comes to understand, is the result of his homosexuality.

In most cases, these are young men who simply happen to lack ability or interest in sports, and who have some sort of talent that this society associates with womanliness. Having been told that their personality is not masculine, they are, understandably, confused — even if one has grown up, and become insightful, self-knowledgeable, and intelligent, childhood experiences can have a tremendous impact.

One of the common themes among converts who have left homosexuality and come to understand themselves, and to live, as heterosexuals, is the reclamation of their masculinity or femininity. But how is it to be done?

I have, in many cases, found that "reparative therapists" and well-meaning religious counselors trying to help gay men reclaim their masculine identities send them out to play baseball. Every time I hear of this, I cringe. Perhaps for some people this works — interests change over time, and someone who hated sports as a boy might find that he enjoys playing with an amateur league as a man. It might even prove an effective way of forming and strengthening nonsexual same-sex friendships, an element that most gay and lesbian identified people find absolutely essential if they are going to live in accordance with Church teachings. On the other hand, I suspect that there are cases where it simply backfires: I can imagine what my reaction would be if, on converting to Catholicism, I had decided to go to an "orientation change" counselor, and had been told that what I really needed to do was to make more time to go out bra shopping with the girls. I would have left the office very politely, paid my bill, and never gone back. The counselor would not have had the opportunity to ask me what went wrong.

When we were discussing gender-identity, one of my friends ruminated that he was exceedingly lucky that he had the support of a family who valued his distinct, socially atypical masculinity. He plays the viola (at the Masters level), is relatively soft-spoken, a pacifist vegetarian, and I don't think I have ever seen or heard about him playing a sport. His parents didn't panic, or send him to a psychologist, or insist that he take more of an interest in "little boy" things. They were both musical people, heavily involved in the arts, so it was never an issue. To them, and to him, playing the viola *is* a masculine thing to do. Why wouldn't it be?

A masculine identity is not about soccer, beer, and breasts. My husband does not know the name of a single sports player; he can't tell you who won the Super Bowl last year, and I have yet to catch him ogling another woman. He insists that he likes fat girls more than thin ones, and consistently shudders at the images of alleged feminine beauty portrayed on billboards. (He does like beer.) He is also utterly, absolutely, insistently, and often completely infuriatingly, masculine. There is no doubt about it. Sometimes, in fact, he goes beyond masculine all the way to patriarchal.

Archetypal Femininity

Unfortunately, in this age of alleged diversity, while there is a proliferation of alternate sexual identities, there seems to be a concomitant narrowing of "normal" masculinity and femininity. Walk into a kindergarten class on Halloween, and tell me how many little girls you see who are not dressed as either a princess or a witch. Ask a random sampling of women my age whether they were tomboyish growing up — the *majority* will say that they were. Does this mean that the majority of women have a strong masculine streak in their natures? Not in my experience. No. I think there is a much simpler explanation: women perceive themselves as having been tomboyish because they have a notion of femininity that is so narrow and constricting (not to mention superficial) that almost no one actually fits the bill.

Looking back at my childhood, I always thought of myself as tomboyish. But my role models were female, and they were feminine — they just weren't princessy. Anne of Green Gables and Nancy Drew are girls. Mooning around by the side of creeks whispering Tennyson's "Lady of

Shallot" is not tomboyish. No actual boy would be caught dead doing this in a million years; he might sit by the creek side and recite the poem, but he wouldn't moon. He wouldn't dress up and lie down in a boat to float down the stream imagining that he was looking on his "own mischance with a glassy countenance" as he floated down to Camelot.

The difficulty is that the difference between the sexes are archetypal — and there is more than one masculine, and more than one feminine, archetype. My eldest daughter has a tremendous interest in "boy" things: war, swords, dragon slayings. She does not, however, express this as a desire to be a boy, but as a desire to be a Valkyrie. She wants, specifically, to be Brünhilde from Wagner's Ring Cycle. This is one of the complications of archetypal reality: there is an entire category of female heroine (and she is absolutely, without a doubt, archetypally feminine) who is perceived as masculine. Brünhilde, Atalanta, Eowyn, Joan of Arc. These women are as far as anyone could possibly be from the stereotypical Princess, but they are women, and they are feminine. Their femininity is only elusive if we are trying to pin gender differences down in the realm of stereotype rather than allowing them to flourish in deeper archetypal soil.

Of course, the difficulty with archetype is that it is difficult to define strictly, and especially so in the modern world, where our understanding of mythic and archetypal reality is only now beginning to emerge from the battered obscurity that it has suffered under the monomaniacal tyranny of scientific "enlightenment." For a long time we have been skimming along on the strength of stereotypes: it is no surprise that they have gotten tired, that they are incapable of describing most of humanity, and that feminists and gender theorists are eager to see them abolished. It is no wonder that secular folks, confronted with the option either to accept the *Sex and the City* nymphets and the "Gilmore Girls" as models from which to understand their own femininity, or to reject the category of femininity altogether, are choosing the latter. These images of femininity are *actually* repressive, restrictive, confining, and demeaning.

What I realized, when I was praying for a goddess and found Mary instead, is that the image of the Mother of God is *not*. For a long time I had thought that the ideal of the virgin, of the mother, of the intercessor, of the bride, were all ideals of feminine oppression. Mary was framed as an archetype of weakness, on her knees, allowing herself to be overpowered by a rapacious, omnipotent masculinity. What I did not understand is that there is a tremendous amount of strength, and even courage, required to lay down one's life in service to a higher ideal; that there is a dignity in submission that is lacking in defiance. The woman who stands up and shouts, "My body, my rights, my life," is not stronger than the woman who bears children and mothers the world. Breaking down the bastions of patriarchy didn't require anything of me except for a paranoid fear of masculinity, an ingrained terror of fertility, and a reckless dedication to the cause of myself. Mary, on the other hand, was a woman who had made the foundations of the earth shake, whose submission had turned creation on its head and set in the sky a cross, a sign of contradiction, a new reality that threw open the gates of heaven and splintered the gates of hell. Her "fiat" is at once an act of obedience and an act of radical cooperation, an echo of the first divine utterance which created the world.

In the months that followed my encounter with this woman — this pillar at once of strength and of weakness, of beauty and of paradox, of power and of absolute humility — the beginnings of a transformation occurred. My understanding of myself as a woman, of what it meant to be feminine, started to shift. The fight to establish a little outpost for myself in the great and prosperous kingdom of masculinity was over: I realized that my own sex was not inferior, that its strengths throughout the ages had always been strengths, that its contributions to the world were not second-class or insignificant. It was here, in this, that the cracks opened enough that I could risk falling in love with a man. Suddenly, I was not an interloper on his territory, trying to seize his castles and make them my own. I had my own kingdom, my own square of land, my own integrity. I did not need to demand power: I had it. I did not need to take something of value away from him and hold it to ransom: I had valuable things of my own. At last, I understood something of who I was. Not lesbian. Not bisexual. Not gay. Not straight, either. But a woman, made in the image and likeness of God. In possession of myself, with the right and the ability to give the gift of myself to another, sincerely, in love.

CHAPTER 14

Vocation

One of the questions that often baffles religious folks is why homo-sexuals insist on identifying themselves as gay or lesbian. Peter Kreeft once pointed out that most sinners don't go around identifying themselves with their sin (it should be noted, although I hate to disagree with Dr. Kreeft, that this is not actually restricted to homosexuals), so why do gays and lesbians? Kreeft asked this question of a homosexual with whom he had been debating, the man answered by asking what Kreeft would think of someone who said that they loved Catholics but hated Catholicism; who would pour out sappy epigrams on the heads of worshipers but forbid them from going to Mass or receiving the Sacraments. From this, Kreeft drew the conclusion that homosexuals are so attached to their lifestyle because it is a religion — a conclusion that looks quite convincing on the surface, particularly to Christians, who are sometimes a little too eager to add the charge of idolatry to any other transgression against Christian morality.

The Worship of Ganymede

Are there homosexuals for whom homosexuality is a religion? Certainly.

- Self-styled "androphile" Jack Malebranche speaks of masculin-ity as the natural religion of man, and of homosexual inter-course as one of its rites.[63]
- Gay poet Robert Duncan speaks about the ritualism of homo-sexual life, and concludes that "we can identify a kind of reli-gion in the homosexual and the homoerotic."[64]
- Poet/author/filmmaker James Broughton once raved, "I am for sexualizing everything: education, religion, politics, institu-tions, science. I would like to see sexual love implicit in all acts of human interchange. . . . I want nothing less than to establish Holy Orders of Sexual Love throughout the world."[65]

- There are lesbian covens of witches, and there are certain cults, both primitive and modern, that use homosexual forms of intercourse as an element of worship.

So this strain certainly exists, but we cannot deduce from that fact that all gay men are worshipers of the phallus almighty, or that all lesbian women are devotees of Sappho's Aphrodite.

The fact is that a great many homosexual people do not cast a particularly religious or ecstatic light on their sexuality. Many of them are avowed atheists; some are Christians. Japanese poet and homosexual Mutsuo Takahashi spoke in the '70s about homosexuality as a religious experience, but his was an attempt to situate it within a specifically Catholic context, to develop an almost sacramental theology of homosexuality, although he recognized the tension that this involved:

> What shall I do about the discrepancy between my believing in Catholicism and my being homosexual? In the end, sooner or later, I think I'll have to settle this problem.[66]

Others, particularly those in more liberal Protestant denominations, may not perceive any particular tension between their religious beliefs and their sexual practices.

Certainly, I never imagined lesbianism as any sort of religion, or as a foundation for any sort of mystical or spiritual experience. What mystical inclinations I did have were of an exceedingly antiphysical type — I was suspicious enough of the body, of emotions, and of romantic love to begin with, and was much more inclined to go chasing after ideas of a Realm of Forms or of a purely rational/spiritual existence in which the body and all of its inconvenient appurtenances were utterly done away with. The notion that sex might be an ecstatic, almost religious experience never occurred to me, and if it had, I would quickly have dismissed it as base, pseudomystical mumbo-jumbo of the most banal possible variety.

A Foundation on Which to Build the Self

A much better approach, I think, is to compare homosexuality to its heterosexual equivalents rather than try to force a religious interpretation on it. Why are homosexuals so angered by the idea of "love the sinner, hate the sin"? Because you are asking them to leave their loved ones, to break apart their living arrangements, and to abandon the people that they have bound themselves to. Those who have "married," or entered into some sort of pact, or blood-brotherhood, or private vow, look on well-meaning Christians in much the same way that Christians look on well-meaning radical-socialist-feminists who want to destroy the idea of the family in order to liberate women from patriarchal oppression. If these women ever managed to achieve sufficient social clout to "lovingly" force me to leave my husband and my children so that I could be brought into the sisterhood of womynkind, I would not join them with gratitude. I would fight them with sticks.

The search to identify oneself within the context of same-sex relationships often has many of the characteristics of vocational discernment, which is why so many people are adamant that they cannot give it up. They are committed very seriously, often after a process as long and as involved as the process of discerning marriage or the priesthood. To change, to adopt a different identity, involves a radical upheaval not only in lifestyle but also in one's understanding of oneself.

Homosexuality is strongly linked to identity because it is *sexual* in nature, and therefore deals with the relational capacities of the human person. There is no one, or almost no one, in the world who actually identifies himself with his deep-seated desire to eat a box of greasy donuts every day, but there are equally few people who identify them*selves* with a solid diet of chickpeas and leafy greens. Our relationships to other human beings are, on the other hand, an essential element of our identity. Our calling to humanity, in the image and likeness of God, is a calling to a communion of persons. Whom we love is an integral component of who we are.

Homosexuals don't identify themselves with a desire to run around and have gay sex. They identify themselves with desire to form a permanent, satisfying relationship — a communion of persons — with someone, and to consummate that communion with sexual intercourse. The fact that many of them never actually achieve this end is, psychologically, beside the point. Homosexuality seems to be a component of identity, because the relationships that people form, or hope to form, are relationships in which an identity, a name, could reasonably be rooted.

Catastrophic Independence

This paradigm, however, is not quite true. It is one of several possibilities, probably the one that applies most to people who enthusiastically embrace a homosexual label. I was quite slow to accept a lesbian identity, even though there was really no impediment to my doing so. It wasn't fear of rejection; it was a reaction to my internal decision to try to be entirely individual, to found my identity on myself. Michelle wasn't a part of who I was, and I didn't want to be a part of who she was. Our relationship was too "open," too uncertain, to form the groundwork for anything as important as personal identity. It was a foundation of sand, and I wasn't willing to set up anything more solid than a tent on top of it.

Of course most people are not as coldly, rationally, obsessively individualistic as I was. I was the sort of girl who, whenever I got into a "relationship" of the formal high-school variety, would sit down and do a highly reasoned meditation on the likely future prospects of the fling. Since I absolutely refused to date anyone that I hadn't known for at least a year, I generally had a lot of data to go on; I would look at it as objectively as I could, try to imagine myself married to the young man who had had the misfortune to ask me out, and then soundly reassure myself that this was not going to be a permanent arrangement. With this certainty under my belt, I could proceed in safety. Their presence in my life was definitely not going to interfere with my catastrophic devotion to my own independence.

Is this what all homosexuals are like? I am not alone, that is certain. A particular kind of self-insular feminist will, I think, tend to drift into lesbianism on the basis that it doesn't seem to impinge on freedom and autonomy, because a relationship with someone who is *like* oneself naturally contains less threat of compromise. The same is true, I gather, of a certain subset of the gay male population. The fact that monogamy is valued much more rarely, and that individuality is valued much more highly, in the gay scene points towards the idea that there is something to this hypothesis, even among those who are less extreme and conscious in their desire to remain insulated and disentangled from other people.

There is, however, a flip side to this. While I was superciliously brushing off my lesbian girlfriend's desperate attempts to get me to talk with her about my depression, a friend of mine was drinking a cup of spit to prove his devotion to the boy that he had fallen for. For every lesbian marching around in a "A woman needs a man like a fish needs a bicycle" T-shirt, there's another who can't bear to be apart from her lesbian lover for a single day. For every gay man who says, "No names, just sex," there's another who is out trying to contract HIV so that he can have absolute solidarity with his seropositive lover. Kenward Elmslie spoke about a relationship between these opposites:

> I fell totally in love with him, asked him to marry me. Out of niceness, he said yes. He was twenty-three, and I was thirty-six. He cherished his independence, nights off, while I was after the whole works, not realistic on my part.[67]

People on both sides of the emotional fence will fight just as adamantly for the right to identify themselves with their homosexuality — but for absolutely opposite reasons. Those who are trying to build deep, loving relationships want to be able to identify themselves with those relationships just as strongly as heterosexuals identify themselves as husbands and wives, mothers and fathers. Those who want absolute autonomy want the right to define themselves as something opposed to the heteronormative — and hence complementary/relational — rubric laid down by centuries of human experience. One wants to *be* a member of a homosexual family, the other wants to *be* their own person, not defined by their relationships at all. Both want their form of identity to be absolutized, in some sense, and formally recognized by society just as strongly as most people want to be called by their names, or to be married in front of their family and friends.

The Cure for Lesbian Bed Death

The difficulty — and this is part of the reason why the Church consistently condemns homosexual sex, and insists that homosexuality is a "disordered inclination," not a fundamental "sexual orientation" — is that both of these possibilities are invitations to build the framework for one's own sense of self on deeply flawed foundations. As David Morrison points out in *Beyond Gay*, "An enduring relationship between gay men may look 'relatively normal' to neighbors, but is quite different from a monogamous marriage." Morrison quotes heavily from a study by David McWhirter and Andrew Mattison (one of many) that demonstrates the lack of fidelity and longevity in homosexual unions:

"My parents were faithful to each other, and I expected us to be the same," said one man, expressing the not-infrequent ideal. But such hopes, the authors document, are simply contrary to homosexual yearnings, and not a single couple reported sexual fidelity lasting longer than five years.[68]

Most homosexuals, and particularly homosexual men, are quite frank about this. They admit that their relationships are open; that although they consider themselves "married to" or "in love with" a single person, there are usually other people on the side. They state, simply, that they see no reason why heterosexual notions of monogamy and fidelity should be grafted unnaturally onto homosexual relationships. Some have thought quite deeply about this and are able to recognize a tension within themselves between the deep desire to have a relationship that is a foundation for identity (as opposed to an inclination towards a certain kind of relationship — identity, one might say, by proxy), and the reality of homosexual life. As gay writer Sam Steward put it:

Perhaps a basic component of the homosexual matrix is the butterfly syndrome — always looking for the Ideal Friend, always searching for new shepherds in our pastures. We're with one for five dirty minutes, and then we're on to the next, looking for the man of our dreams, and a permanent "arrangement."[69]

With lesbians, the difficulty is not so much the end of the relationship, but the end of the sexual relationship. The phenomenon of "lesbian bed death" has been written about, studied, and flogged to death by lesbian therapists and lesbian social scientists desperate to find some explanation for the baffling fact that so many lesbian relationships — stable, apparently healthy ones — seem to develop into sexless friendships. There are heterosexual couples who experience the same basic pattern: a comfortable living arrangement develops, and when the flames of desire have burnt themselves out, the couple simply goes on, washing each other's linens and sitting across from one another at breakfast. A quiet, unobtrusive, pastoral arrangement, closer to a house-mateship than a marriage.

There is a cure. The lesbian magazines, like the "straight" women's magazines, are full of handy tips and helpful advice for staving off sexual starvation. The fires may have gone out, but they can be rekindled, at least for a few seconds, if you throw on a couple sheets of pornographic reading. Or perhaps you would find sex more exciting if you got your partner to shackle you to the bed. If there's no emotional risk involved in your lovemaking, generate some by pretending that you're in a Gulag.

My girlfriend and I managed to keep things spicy and interesting by a sort of psychospiritual promiscuity. Bodily, we were always the same two people, together in the same bed; if I had not converted to Catholicism, I think that we could have gone on that way indefinitely. Mentally, though we were a parade of different people, different characters in different situations. Whenever something got old and ceased to be interesting, it became necessary to invent something new.

From what I have read in lesbian magazines and Internet forums, we were not alone. Fantasy seems to be the primary antidote to "lesbian bed death." You are comfortable together, you enjoy living together, but you want sexual variety — so instead of sleeping around, you read books that you find titillating and agree to become the characters in those stories for one another. A simple, satisfactory solution to the problem, and one that saves you the disappointment of a series of frustrating searches for an "ideal person" who doesn't exist. If they are ideal, they exist only in the realm of ideas — so why not go and find them there?

The Power of Imagination

The problem behind this playing with "ideals" is the disintegration of identity. John Keats once wrote, "A Poet is the most unpoetical of any thing in existence; because he has no Identity — he is continually. . .

filling some other Body."[70] This is certainly one of the occupational hazards of literature. It's difficult, I think, for people who only have a passing familiarity with the imagination to understand its capabilities, just as it is difficult for those of us who have never stood one-footed on a twenty-foot-high pole for days on end to understand the limits to which the will can stretch the body. Generally, we expose ourselves to a very small subsection of human reality and think that is all there is; occasionally, we catch a glimpse of something outside that, whether in "Ripley's Believe It or Not," in a book about "Unsolved Mysteries," or on one of the stranger late-night radio shows. But these things are limited to cranks and creeps, weirdos who believe in flying saucers and probably ought to be contained. Authors and artists . . . well, everyone knows that genius is closely allied to insanity, but since they paint such lovely images on their way to the loony bin, we'll sit back and watch the show.

A writer must, regularly, allow other personalities to emerge and take form inside the mind. These creative children sometimes have surprising capabilities, and the result of the process of creation is often one with very strange consequences. I have frequently had the experience of being completely unable to accomplish something — I am struggling up a hill with the youngest of my children in a backpack on my back, and I feel lightheaded, dizzy, practically unable to take another step. Then, it occurs to me that this is a great opportunity to do a meditation on one of my heroes — a military man who might, conceivably, have to climb a similar hill on a march. I call up the character, put myself in his mind-space, and five seconds later, the weight on my back is inconsiderable, the air is crisp and clean, the sky blue, and the hill an insignificant bump on the road.

When a thing is written, is communicated, it carries tremendous power. When my sister died, I spoke, obviously, with my family, but we were, in some sense, too much in the same place — all going through the same grief, with the same limited perspective. Sorrow had only just started to put down her roots, to break apart the soil of the soul, and with such pain . . . such pain. It is difficult to speak out of agony, and though there is something beautiful in the sharing of griefs, there is also something lacking, a wise voice that has contemplated and penetrated the mysteries of this suffering from a situation of calm. These are the birth pangs of the tree of mourning; what will its fruits taste like several seasons hence? I sat down and cast around on the Internet, read several pages written by pop psychologists and grief counselors, and found that the condoling, drippy-sweet tone did nothing but lend piquancy to the feeling that I was alone, that there was something profound here that I could not communicate and which others could not share with me. "They" told me that I would feel angry — at my sister for having died, or at people in my family for having failed to protect her, or at myself for having failed to reconcile with her first, or at God for having taken her from me. The only thing that I felt angry at, though, were the writings of grief counselors, with their pat answers and simplistic formulae for human suffering. Finally, in frustration, I turned to the ever-bubbling wellspring of consolation which I keep next to my computer in the basement: the *Norton Anthology of English Literature*. I flipped open to Tennyson's "In Memoriam" and here, at last, was a soul like my soul, a heart like my heart. I was no longer alone.

The imaginative realms have tremendous power because they are a part of the human inscape — the inner landscape that we all inhabit, where all of the really important things in our lives secretly take place. The great battlefield where God and the devil are at war, the Kingdom of Christ which lies within, the savage and awe-inspiring realm of myth and salvation . . . all this is inside the human person. There is a sense, a very real sense, in which the human heart is broader than the entire physical universe, with all of its quasars, black holes, and superstrings. The universe, for all its beauty, is not conscious. It is reducible to atoms and waves and subatomic particles. But the mind of man can hold so much of it within, and can create — on a much less operatic scale — entire new universes of its own. It is man, not material creation, who is in the image and likeness of an infinite and eternal God.

What happens in the realm of the imagination is not mere "fancy." The wings of poesy are dreadful and powerful, capable of bearing us "beyond the sunset and the baths of all the Western stars," or of blacking out the sun and plunging us into eternal darkness. Fantasy, like sex, can be silly, foolish, charming, and ridiculous, but it can also be dangerous — beyond the edges of what is permitted there are sea-monsters and yawning gulfs. You can frolic safely on the shore, and you may bring in a bountiful harvest from the shallows, but if you set out into the deep, you had better take along a sextant and a compass to make sure you can get back.

An artist creates characters, nourishes them within her mind, allows them a little breath of her own free will, and transcribes them in a flesh of words or paint. She does not marry them. She does not raise them to her own level, and try to form a union of soul and mind with them, much less attempt to imprint them over the top of the real personality of another human being so that she can have sex with them. There are artists who try to do this, certainly, and it comes across in their art. How many times have I sat down with a book by someone who is a genius with words, read the first few pages, become engrossed in the lives of the characters and the premises of the world, and then discovered, to my dismay, that after the first few chapters it devolves into a series of sexual fantasies that don't go anywhere? Presumably there are those who like engaging in this sort of mutual masturbation with their favorite authors, but literary pornography is still pornography; I don't want to come into another person's head to sit there and watch them pleasuring themselves with a blow-up space-warrioress.

The Atomic Self

As I said, the risk, whether with imaginary or physical promiscuity, is a fragmentation of personality. It is little wonder that the postmodernist, steeped in the psychology and philosophy of the sexual revolution, has come to think of man as a series of masks behind which there is no fixed substance. When Catholic theologians say that by engaging in sexual acts outside the realm of morality, a person is risking their immortal soul, they are not simply speaking about an arbitrary punishment sent down from on high at the end of mortal life. If you give yourself over and over again to people who will use you and squander your most precious gift; or you wed yourself to a host of your own creations, to the lesser fragments of your own psyche that populate your sexual fantasies, you lose the center and core of your being. It becomes like a pulverized mirror, returning a more and more shattered image until, at last, it is dust and reflects nothing at all.

I recall a recurrent image that arose in dreams and in waking daydreams during my adolescence; an archetypal reality that I frequently crept out of my house at night to go seeking. The thing that I was searching for was perfectly round, pale white, luminescent. It was in a grove of a nearby woods, a clearing that I had never uncovered, not in all of the childhood hours that I had spent exploring and seeking out places to build my faery forts. There was a sense of the inviolable about this goal; it was, in a very literal sense, atomic: even Oppenheimer's cadre had not conquered its indivisibility. I never found it, wandering around my small, enclosed, and sheltered suburban forest, but I knew what it was. It was myself.

Eventually, in one particular incident, it was uncovered.

I had been arguing with Chris for several days after he pulled a piece of hate-mail out of the garbage, one in which my most recent ex-boyfriend iterated a desire to murder me. For some strange reason, Chris insisted that I was obligated — *obligated!* — to have a moral and emotional reaction to it. At the time, I was of the philosophical conviction that guilt was one of the great evils which religious repression had foisted on the unthinking masses; so, although I felt that a person could learn from their mistakes, there was no good in recriminations, self-doubts, and guilt feelings. I had been considering the situation and came to the decision that I ought to simply label myself lesbian; this would be the most honest, most authentic course of action, and it would prevent this kind of misunderstanding from ever happening again. I had written a very cordial and rational letter to my ex-boyfriend, gently lamenting his desire to rip my intestines out of my stomach, and expressing my willingness to resume friendly relations at any time, now that the regrettable matter of our failed relationship was over. Oddly enough, this letter had been returned, burnt at the edges, with a scorched picture of me at my high-school prom, and violent profanities scrawled across the back. It was this piece of relational miscellany that Chris had fished out of the garbage after I had carefully considered it and decided that it wasn't worth keeping.

Chris confronted me with it, and I insisted that I wasn't obligated to feel guilty, and that I was not, in any case, to blame if other people decided to be utterly absurd and ridiculous about what had clearly, from the beginning, been an ordinary adolescent fling. Chris thought that I should go, get down on my knees, apologize, and tell the murderously-minded young man in question that he was free to kill me if he thought best. Chris was absolutely sure that this would not end in murder but in reconciliation; he read, in my opinion, too much Buddha and Gandhi. So we were arguing.

From the question of guilt and reconciliation, we had quickly gotten into an argument about whether he — a person who was not under the control of my autonomous will — had any right to get involved in these affairs. I accused him of being presumptuous and controlling; he accused me of being the emotional equivalent of an armored tank. Eventually, he hit a nerve. Not just *a* nerve, but *the* nerve that ran down the central spinal cord of my psychology. I was never going to be a writer, he said — not a good one, anyway — if I was completely incapable of emotional honesty. He added to this that he thought I had the capacity to be a very good, even brilliant writer, and passed me a note in class, when I was staring daggers at him, that said, "Shine on you crazy diamond." I didn't know Pink Floyd well enough at the time to get the reference.

I did know it well enough to get the reference when he started quoting lines from *The Wall* and slowly, over the course of this multiple-day psychological wrestling match, something arose inside of me — a resistance cell that did not want to live under the tyranny of my ruthless independence. There was something, Chris said, that I desperately wanted and needed to say, but I wasn't allowing myself to see what it was. Madness. I said that he was playing psychological chess and messing with my head, and that I wasn't going to have it. He said that was fine, there was no basis on which he could demand that I work it out. I was the one who wanted to be a poet, not him. If I thought he was wrong, I didn't have to bother. I insisted that he was wrong, but I bothered. Because I knew, infuriatingly, I knew . . . that he was *right*.

Finally, in an epic, eight-hour-long telephone conversation that went on into the smallest witching hours of the night, my fledgling, trembling, starved, and atrophied emotional self, encouraged by the reports that Chris had an army camped outside the city walls ready to rescue it from certain slaughter at the hands of my ego, crept out of its dungeon sinkhole and stole towards the city gates.

While this was going on, my conscious self — the overblown, ego-maniacal, self-concocted witch-queen that ruled over my psyche — sat in her tower and sent out her troops against Chris's army. It was a strange conversation: never had I been so deeply aware of the divisions in myself; never had the lines been so clearly drawn. I was quite conscious of two almost separate and warring personalities, and I was appalled to discover the nature of the one that I had been, for years now, cultivating and encouraging as my "self." She was ruthless, mad, willing to sacrifice anything — *anything* — to keep her secret treasure stashed away in the darkest pits of my internal keep. I was actually conscious of destroying myself emotionally, of deliberately pushing myself into fits of self-pity and rage so that I would strike out at Chris and, hopefully, convince him that the battle was hopeless — or, at the very least, not worth joining. There was a startling clarity and rationality to all of this, a part of myself that was perfectly calm, unruffled, actually enjoying the spectacle of the rest of my psyche being slaughtered and put to the torture for the sake of its aims.

She lost. Eventually, the resistance managed to get a hold of a radio and started sending messages out to Chris — between tearful-ness, wailing, gnashing of teeth, and deliberate attempts to smash his inner child — that this was worth it. That there was a real person somewhere in there who actually desperately wanted to be rescued. That, sooner or later, the gates would open and it would be possible to get inside and tear down the wall. There was a literal battle within myself for control of my tongue, and I probably sounded and seemed quite schizophrenic to an outside observer. At last, with great effort, I managed to get the gate open, just a crack — but it was enough. The truth, the terrible truth that had been gestating and hiding itself in my breast, and which I had not dared to show to myself much less speak aloud, rose and spoke its name. "I love you," I said. "Not romantically, but not just as some sort of philosophical abstraction. I don't know how to express it, but I love you."

CHAPTER 15

Beauty

At last, at the heart of my understanding of myself, I came up against a tension between my homosexuality, my desire for radical independence, my notions of myself as a woman, and my desire to be an artist. Obviously this is not important to every homosexual, but it is certainly essential to many. Often, homosexual writers, poets, playwrights, actors, and artists of every stripe insist that this is, in fact, part of the reason why they must be homosexual: they feel that their best work springs out of their relationships with other men (or women); that their artistic creations are the children of their same-sex love, the fruit of a tree which the world perceives as barren.

Platonic Love

Plato addressed the relationship between homosexuality and beauty in both his writings and (almost certainly) in his life as well. Louis Crompton, in his history *Homosexuality and Civilization*, summarizes Plato's conclusion to the *Symposium* as follows:

> When a temperate man finds beauty in a youth and tries to educate him, such an intellectual marriage, Socrates declares, is more intimate than the union of man and wife. But Socrates thinks men should ideally turn their attention for the beauty of individual boys to a beauty that is abstract and general. They should turn from intense love of one person to a love of all beautiful forms . . . step by step, the love of fair boys and youths leads ultimately to a love of divine beauty purged of the alluring beguilements of the material world.[71]

Socrates is quite clear that relationships between men ought to be chaste — this is the source of the idea of "Platonic love," a term which is often thrown about, nowadays, to discuss opposite-sex loves that are not sexually expressive — and the dialog ends with an episode in which Socrates's philosophy of sexual relations is shown through the arrival of a beautiful youth whose seductive advances Socrates has recently spurned.

Here, in Plato, is a man who was not immune to the charms of other men. Several poems generally ascribed to Plato describe his attractions towards certain, particular men,[72] and his philosophy of the movement from this sexually-loaded love of particular boys to the abstract love of the Beautiful has far too much of an experiential cast for it to be reasonably presumed that he arrived at this notion out of pure abstraction. He lived in a society that lauded, rather than condemned, homosexual relations, and yet he gives many of the same reasons for disbelieving in homosexual intercourse that would later appear in the works of Christian theologians. Thus he forms a convincing portrait of how someone with strong homoerotic desires would take those attractions and turn them outward, toward the service of the Good.

Adam versus Bacchus

There is a certain suggestion that this is precisely what was done by one of the Western world's greatest artists. Michaelangelo does not deny his attraction to the male body — and even if he did, one look at his masterworks would give us serious cause to doubt. Eve lingers in the background of the Creation of Man, a not particularly attractive woman, suffering from many of the same faults that plague the feminine form in Greek statuary. Adam, on the other hand, is as close as we could hope to come to seeing the Platonic Form of the male body; as a realization of Man, in his masculinity, as God first created him, Michaelangelo's representation is sublimely convincing. According to his student and biographer, Ascanio Condivi, who worked with Michaelangelo in writing his life:

> He has also loved the beauty of the human body as one who knows it extremely well, and loved it in such a way as to inspire certain carnal men, who are incapable of understanding the love of beauty except as something lascivious and indecent, to think and speak ill of him.[73]

Michaelangelo's poems are perhaps more damning, and they reveal something of a soul struggling between this ideal of beauty and the torment of sexual temptations. It is uncharitable and unjust to assume that this was a struggle that he generally lost, particularly as he, himself, consistently defended his chastity.

Michaelangelo is not alone amongst the Renaissance painters in having been attracted to men. His work, and the work of others who were producing at the same time, gives a revealing portrait of the effects of homoeroticism on art. The tension between the love of masculine beauty and the scars of concupiscence which turn that beauty into lust is written large across the frescoes, ceilings, and statues of Renaissance Italy. It appears in the works of Michaelangelo — if *David* struck my femininity like a lightning bolt, even at a time when I was actively trying to suppress it under the delusion that feminism precludes femininity, Michaelangelo's *Bacchus* completely shut me, as a woman, out. This is not to say that I can't appreciate the skill of craftsmanship, the accuracy of proportion, the efficacy of composition, and all of the other factors that art critics are fond of talking about; apart from all of its merits, there is a lack of communication. *Bacchus* is not *for* me, not for human-ity in the way that the Sistine Chapel or *David* are. The same is true, though even more extremely, with Caravaggio's painting by the same name. If Michaelangelo's *Bacchus* is merely alienating, Caravaggio's is perplexing. I was always a lover of Caravaggio's work, but had, I sup-pose, only ever seen the religious works — those fabulous, often violent, terrifying chiaroscuros of St. Peter's crucifixion or of Christ being laid in the tomb. When I saw *Bacchus*, I had to look, several times, at the name-plate — I couldn't believe that this drippingly indolent, fleshy, uninspiring pretty-boy, this creature that looked more like a bit of taste-less Italian overornamentation than a masterwork of Renaissance art, could possibly be by the same man. Crompton makes the point that "We do not have the kind of legal and literary evidence for Caravaggio that we have [for other Renaissance artists] . . . Yet modern art historians find a marked homoerotic element in his early paintings."[74] Usually I am inclined to break ranks with modern art historians when they read sexual overtones into the works of old masters — usually they come across as "carnal men . . . incapable of understanding the love of beauty except as something lascivious and indecent." The Caravaggio street youths, with their bouquets of fruit and flowers and their languidly feminine eyes, do not, however, demand a great stretch of the intellect and imagination to place them among the classics of homoerotic art. Whether or not this proceeded from an actual attraction on the part of Caravaggio or merely from that painter's contact with certain notorious pederasts of his time — and his general delight in scandal (this is a man who deliberately used a prostitute as a model for a painting of the Virgin) — is a fact lost to history.

I could multiply examples, but it would perhaps be better to point out that this effect is not confined to homoerotic works of art. Exactly the same thing is true of heteroerotic works — and it is just as easy to tell the difference. There is always a great debate over the line between pornography and art, with pornographers claiming that line is very thin indeed, and their opponents claiming that "I know it when I see it." There really isn't any confusion: a man who wants very much to believe that he is looking at "art photographs" may not be able to tell the difference, but show the pictures to a panel of five women, and, unless they are all prostitutes or modern art critics, they'll all be able to tell you whether they're looking at a beautiful portrayal of the female body, or a work or pornography garbed in gossamer-thin respectability.

Lust and Alienation

This is true because of the nature of art. Art is a means of communication: through it, the audience is invited to enter into the world and experience of the artist; to view things, again, as though for the first time, through another's eyes. It is a means of breaking down the barriers of subjectivity. Through it, we participate in a sort of foretaste of the Communion of Saints; we are allowed to know, deeply and intimately, a little part of another person's humanity. The fact that we necessarily bring our own experiences to bear on the pictures that we see, the poems that we read, and the films that we watch does not diminish this truth, but renders it more astonishing and wonderful. It means that every single work of art, if it is truly a work of art, has the capacity to forge millions of relationships, all of them two-sided, each involving an intensely personal meeting between the artist and the individual who receives the work of art.

Both the artist and the audience bring a responsibility to this task: they are required to be honest with one another, even over the distance of centuries or millennia, and they are required to be respectful of one another. The artist ought to communicate what is worthwhile, what is beautiful and true within himself (and this may, provided the whole truth is told about it, include things that are very dark — I am not advocating sappy, castrated, spray-cheese "Christian" art), and the audience is responsible for putting themselves aside, for actually listening in their heart so that they can receive whatever the artist is communicating, rather than allowing the clutter of their own vices or their own desire to appear clever, to interfere. With pornography, and with erotic art in general, this presents a serious difficulty. If homo-erotic art is alienating to me, to my femininity, male heteroerotic art is worse. Looking at homoerotic art is like going into my living room and finding a complete stranger sitting there — merely unsettling. Looking at erotic portrayals of women is like looking in a mirror and finding a complete stranger. The artist communicates, through his art, his experience of the person that he is painting. When that experience is colored by lust, the audience has to either meet it on the level of lust or else be locked out. Many such works are certainly well beloved — just as the homosexual community is impressed by homoerotic overtones in the works of the masters, so are heterosexual men often impressed by beautifully enticing female nudes.

Are females immune to this, then? Absolutely not. It is just that we are, for the most part, less able to enter into the subjective experience of lust for bodies, male or female, as experienced by men, unless we have gone to a certain length to mangle our perception of the world in accord with the precepts of the sexual revolution.* Of course the situation is different when we are faced with erotic works by other

---

* I am, to some degree, simplifying the situation. There are certainly cases in which women will find erotic, and even abusive, portrayals of women enticing. The mind set in play there is somewhat similar to that in masochism or rape fantasies: it is the desire to be mistreated, to be reduced to the level of an object or animal, and it is one of the darker byways of human sexuality. Presumably there is some sort of male opposite, but not being a male, I'm not sure what it is.

women. Here the feeling ceases to be one of alienation, and becomes one of complicity or titillation — presumably the same sort of feeling that men have when looking at the erotic masterpieces produced by their own gender. If one is committed to chastity, it is an unpleasant knock at the door of concupiscence. If one is not . . . well, then, it has all the charms usually afforded by temptation and vice.

This is a problem that I have run up against several times in discussions about pornography with lesbians and sexually revolutionized feminists. On the one hand, there is the experience of distaste in seeing women portrayed as objects of sexual fascination, divorced from their personalities. On the other, there is a need to excuse the fact that one enjoys such portrayals provided they are suited to one's own tastes and desires. Generally, I have found that lesbians and feminists (if they are not adamantly opposed to pornography in all forms) will claim that it is the masculinity in pornography that is threatening and unpleasant, and that the real problem is one of patriarchal dominance — a criticism which their own preferred erotica cannot fall prey to. This is absolute hypocrisy. A work in which every passing nymphet is readily available to be seduced by the nearest lesbian, or where men are reduced to their sexual qualities in order to ravish the minds of female readers, is just as exploitative and reductionistic as one in which the same thing is done to women. The capacity to reduce a human being to the level of an object for personal consumption is neither restricted to men nor justified among women.

The Sterility of Homoerotic Art

The point, arrived at by a rather long and convoluted path, is that homosexual artists often imagine that their best work is that which appeals to homoeroticism, when in fact, the opposite is true. Over the course of my life, I have repeatedly experienced the frustration of running up against a poet of obvious talent who doesn't have anything to say unless it is about boys and their beautiful thighs. As exciting as I'm sure these poets are to the gay community, they are a loss to the rest of humanity. These are men who were given the gifts of a wordsmith, who had the capacity to describe the world in an entirely new way, to communicate a new form of seeing — in short, they are people whose calling is obviously artistic. And yet there is nothing to see in their work except the male body, reduced to an object of lust for the enjoyment of other same-sex-attracted males. Having fixed their own hearts and minds on the sexual experience, they lose the capacity to speak meaningfully about the rest of human life.

There is a distinction to be made here: this criticism is not true of all homosexually attracted, or even homosexually practicing, artists. Oscar Wilde's *Dorian Grey* certainly has homoerotic elements, but it "tells the truth" about a life of sensuality and about the obsession with youthful beauty which ultimately destroys poor Dorian. It is a work that proceeds from a life caught up in sensual and sexual attractions but which has not completely relented, which is still capable of that self-knowledge, that reflexive capacity, which allows beautiful works of art to rise up out of the mire of human weakness. On the other hand, artists who are utterly convinced that their homosexual love affairs are the source of all of their best artwork are generally those whose work is inbred, only accessible to the gay community, and in some cases, completely unviewable unless you happen to be a homosexually attracted man. The same is equally true of lesbian artwork; the world has its share of Sapphics who spend all of their time toying with beautiful female bodies in various artistic media, or writing soap-operatic tales in which every character turns out either to be gay or transsexual. You have never heard of these works, because they are of no interest to anyone who is not either lesbian or taking a course in Queer Studies.

Beauty Will Save the World

The case for a link between homosexuality and artistic sensibility is not ironclad, but it is a recurrent theme, and one with sufficient support that it ought not be lightly dismissed. So many of history's alleged homosexuals — or at least those who have a strong connection with homoeroticism — were artists. Saying "I went to art school — so naturally, I met a lot of homosexuals" is such a cliché that everyone hearing it understands precisely what is meant; and frankly, most of the homosexuals I have ever met have a significant connection with the arts and the creative life. I'm sure that this, like every other stereotype, is not universally true, but in spite of what politically correct ideology would have us believe, the fact that stereotypes have exceptions does not prove that they are complete balderdash.

The implication for this, in terms of homosexuality, is that the arts matter. "Beauty," Dostoyevsky once wrote, "will save the world." The purpose of Church art is to bring people into the presence of God, to point toward a higher and more beautiful reality than the one that we tread through day upon day throughout our lives. When Catholics create beautiful works of art, hearts, minds, and imaginations are baptized. More than once I have encountered people whose conversion to Catholicism or to Christianity has been effected, at least in part, by the liturgical compositions of the great classical composers. On the other hand, I have never met anyone who was converted by the sort of happy-clappy nonsense that Jesuit composers produced during the '70s — the same unfortunate songs which still fill the pages of our hymnals today. How, one is inclined to wonder, can the awesome contemplation of the God who created heaven and earth produce such lame music? It is no wonder that so many, their minds filled with the image of a multitude of bored, winged angels strumming "Peace Is Flowing" on their harps for all eternity, slouch off to find something more exciting in the secular world.

Beauty had everything to do with my own conversion. It began a long time before I was even aware of what was happening, in the silence of one of New York's most beautiful churches, when I was only thirteen or fourteen years old. There, with the light filtering in through age-old stained glass windows, amid pews scented with centuries of incense and the sound of baptismal water bubbling in an ancient font, a small group of music students on holiday from Ontario encountered — for just a moment — the glory of God. Not one of us was Catholic, yet not one of us dared to utter a single syllable above an awestruck whisper as we walked down the aisle where the old women prayed. I had a moment of clear understanding, even above my newly blossoming atheism, that here I was confronted with a faith and a hope that had sustained generations of humanity, through sufferings, and through triumphs, and that all of this beauty was a monument to that tradition.

I shook it off within a few short hours, of course, upon returning to the streets of New York. But after I came home, that church remained as the thing I most remembered about New York City — and it stood out as a counterpoint of beauty in a city that had seemed, otherwise, to be choked with meaninglessness, devoid of sunlight or trees.

The encounter with beauty remained the guiding light in my long and tortuous journey towards Christ. Sitting one day beside a tree that had been randomly and violently cut down by a group of ruffians from my school, which now stretched its hacked limbs across the banks of a stream that I had claimed for my own private lunchtime sanctuary, I noticed how new branches had started to push themselves up out of the fallen trunk: evidence of life sprouting up out of death and defeat. The image was such a powerful symbol of hope and of rebirth that simply looking at it, I was convinced that there had to be a purpose and meaning behind the world — that such elegant symbolism had to be intentional, which meant that the world had an author. Not God. No, I was very afraid of the word "God." But an Author. Someone who guided the narrative of my life and provided the necessary archetypal material for it to have significance beyond that which I could impress on it myself.

A Dim Approximation of Heaven

I could compound example on example — the beautiful wooden statue of Mary in a Church in Montreal, the haunting polyphony of *Ave Verum Corpus*, Dostoyevsky's *The Brothers Karamazov*, the radiant holiness of a young woman who spoke of Christ with the same love that lived in Alyosha's eyes — but I think that this suffices. Beauty is not a largely irrelevant addendum to the life of the soul. It is through beauty that we come to understand the appeal of heaven. The atheist can't get excited about sitting around forever with the big man on the throne. The sexual sinner can't imagine an eternity without sex. Almost everyone, at least on some level, thinks that this world is more appealing than the world to come. It is because we do not spend enough time contemplating beauty, because we do not take into our hearts the realization that all of the wonders and marvels, all of the joys and triumphs, of this world are only a tiny spark thrown from the fire of Beauty that burns in the mind of God. The feeling that we have when the Ring is finally destroyed in the Fires of Mount Doom is only a distant harbinger of the dawn that awaits the soul at the end of the world, when the darkness that sin brings across the horizons of our lives is broken, when the forgotten tastes of childhood rise up again in all of their intensity and then are shown to be nothing, a shadow and a ghost, in comparison with the reality that lies ahead. The master's brushstroke is only an approximation of his sight, of the manner in which he contemplates and appreciates the world. The arrangement of chords that pierces the heart, that seems, in a second, to draw the soul out of herself and bring us up into a higher world where chaos and meaninglessness quickly fade and are forgotten — this is only a rough approximation of the glory that sounded in the mind of the man who composed it. All art is only an imperfect realization of a perfect inspiration. Every artist knows this. It is a kind of sorrow, and of suffering, to know that some sliver of Beauty has fallen like moonlight on the mind, and that what you have managed to gather up in your hands to offer to the world is nothing in comparison to that fleeting vision.

The same is true of every human love, of every human communication. A mother holds her child and understands that she loves imperfectly. She is often distracted; there are moments when she sees him only as a burden or a difficulty, when the realization that this is "bone of my bone, flesh of my flesh" is drowned out in a cacophony of dishwashers and diapers. Sexual intercourse is subject to the same vicissitudes of human attention and realization; the moments of crystalline ecstasy when the other in all the fullness of their humanity is revealed, when the veils of the temple of the self are pulled aside and the image of God is seen glittering in the tabernacle of the heart, are rare. Much more often the mind drifts, the flesh wilts, the clumsy fitting together of biological pieces becomes a comedy instead of a sublimity — sex becomes, as it has always been, the worthy fool whose comic parade provides the butt for most of mankind's jokes. Everything, everywhere, is grown gray, not with the breath of Christ, but with the breath of man. Everywhere man is enslaving or enslaved, everywhere we clump through life in steel-toed boots, senseless of the living world around us.

We are the lotus-eaters, enfogged, sipping at our momentary pleasures, forgetful of kin and home. I would say "especially in the modern world," but I don't think that is necessarily so. The claim that so many older people make to have seen, in their youth, a newer world, fresher with the dews of glory, is as likely as not the result of seeing the past through childhood eyes recently sprung from the womb of eternity.

Christianity is the promise of something better — that the aching sorrow that, in our moments of highest ecstasy, tugs like a violin on the strings of the heart and promises them a pain sweeter than pleasure, a joy more sublime than the highest Shakespearean tragedy, will one day be answered by the chorus of beauty in which the world was conceived and made. The Christian is willing to put aside the baubles and trinkets of this world because we have a hope in a higher one. Not in an eternity of golden pathways and pearly gates — an eternal field trip around the palaces of some King in the sky — but an eternal communion. A communion with all of the men who ever lived. With the geniuses. To know, as intimately as if they were our own, the thoughts that never made it to the page; to see the movies that were still forming in the minds of Kubrick and Tarkovski when they died; to hear the perfected stanzas of the plays that Shakespeare never had a chance to write; to hear the music that sounded in Beethoven's deaf skull and which he jotted down, imperfect, as man's most cherished symphonies. To know also the minds of the inarticulate; to see the beauty that dwelt in the soul of a child who never learned to speak; to see the wonders locked up in the hearts of the "neurologically disabled"; to understand the entire world afresh through the eyes of every saint who lived in it.

And all of this, even, is nothing, for at the heart of heaven there is God. God, from whose imagination every earthly glory springs. God, compared to whom man is just a chalk drawing on the wall of a cave. God, whose intentions for His beloved children are beyond anything that eye has seen or ear can hear, more than has ever entered into the heart of man. Heaven is the wedding of the human soul to the divine, to know and to be known by the Author of galaxies and goldfish. It is communion. And the magnetic force that binds all of the particular souls, that orders and aligns all those human stars burning together in the radiance of Beauty and Truth, is love.

This doesn't mean that we exchange the wonders of this world for the pie in the sky, for a desire and hope that may prove itself untrue. All atheists are under this delusion as they sit around the table of life, gambling away their existence penny by penny, on bets small enough that the most they can hope to win is the ability to stay in the game a few more rounds. All of these trifling wins and losses that add up to nothing, set against a backdrop in which there is no prize — what's the use or the beauty in that? There is no heroism in the easy, riskless life. No drama. No narrative. Even modern literature only makes the rise and fall of ordinary man a subject of interest by showing that the same mythic current that runs through the heart of Ulysses runs also through the life of Leopold Bloom. The call to heroic sanctity is a call to bathe in that current, to live one's life carried along like a feather on the breath of God, to become the hero of one's own story, instead of a background character in the tragic drudgery of history, or a cog in the insipid narrative of technological progress.

When this life is embraced, is lived, it transforms the rest of reality into a foretaste of heaven. The entire project of human living comes into its own, develops its meaning. The light of God shines through life as though through a photographic negative. At last, so much that seems like meaninglessness and chaos resolves into order, into significance. The trials and sufferings and pains of life cease to be an engine, stopped in the sky and become the chiaroscuro etchings of a portrait so beautiful it is almost impossible to believe that this is oneself, perfected — as one appeared in the beginning, in the mind of God, before all the broken chemistry of a fallen womb or the first breath of hospital-scented air.

It is for this that I gave up homosexuality. I could feel the light creeping under the doorways of my heart, and I understood that it might reveal a future without lesbianism — I understood it with all the terrible clarity of Christ looking at the cup of suffering offered to Him at Gethsemane. There were absolutely no illusions, no possibility of turning and twisting Scripture until it said what I wanted it to say. I had told God clearly what I wanted; then I had said, "Thy will be done."

So it was that I ended up kneeling in the chapel at Queen's University, some three months after I had first started praying to an unknown deity, a formless "Thou who art." I started to pray as I usually did, offering up a general thanksgiving, an informal expression of my own joy in the world that I had been invited to inhabit. It was not long before prayers from my childhood began rising up in my mind, and I voiced them, as naturally as I had then. "Our Father, who art in Heaven . . ." The Hail Mary was new to me, but I had learned it in some quiet moment at the library, when I had first recognized the Lady in the Moon as the Virgin Mother of God. I prayed it as well. Finally, when I had exhausted all of the more innocent prayers, and sung the Christian hymns that I remembered, I realized that I desperately wanted to pray something more. There was something further, unexpressed. Almost without realizing what I was doing I began to whisper, "I believe in God, the Father Almighty, creator of heaven and earth. And I believe in Jesus Christ, His only Son, Our Lord . . ."

The creed ended in silence. And in that silence, I could feel God there, waiting. A question hovered in the air between us: *What are you doing?* It was not reproachful, and I understood immediately what it meant: why was I saying that I believed these things and yet refusing to acknowledge them in my life, outside of this little space that I set aside for prayer? Why had I spoken with my lips what I had not professed in my heart? I could see, with absolute clarity, that I stood at a crossroads. That either I would reiterate that prayer of belief, and make it real, entirely, with the rest of my life, or else I would turn away and never pray again. I had asked to know God, and to know God's will, and now I did.

I went home, dialed the phone, and said, "Michelle, I'm becoming a Catholic. That means that we can't be together anymore — not as lovers." It was the end of a relationship that had lasted nearly seven years. It was the beginning of a life more beautiful than I could have asked for or imagined.

Notes

1. Kirk, Marshall, and Hunter Madsen. *After the Ball* (New York: Plume, 1990), back cover.

2. Ibid., p. 183.

3. Ibid., p. 184.

4. LeVay, Simon. *Queer Science: The Use and Abuse of Research into Homosexuality* (Cambridge, MA: The MIT Press, 1997), pp. 61-63.

5. Savin-Williams, Ritch. *The New Gay Teenager* (Cambridge, MA: Harvard University Press, 2006), pp. 18, 121.

6. Kirk and Madsen, p. 178.

7. Savin-Williams, p. 221.

8. Ibid., p. 180.

9. This debate exists not only between the left and the right, but is divisive for both camps: there are gay activists who would marshal gay suicide statistics to demonstrate the evils of homophobia, and others who decry gay suicide headlines because they want to demonstrate that gay teens are normal, well-adjusted people, no different from their straight peers. On the other hand, there are right-wing writers who want to use gay suicide rates to demonstrate that this is a fundamentally self-destructive and despair-inducing lifestyle, and others who want to deny gay suicide because they feel that it has been concocted by the gay movement in order to gain sympathy for same-sex-attracted youth. Naturally, the statistics are accommodatingly inconclusive.

10. Malebranche, Jack. *Androphilia (A Manifesto) Rejecting the Gay Identity, Reclaiming Masculinity* (Baltimore, MD: Scapegoat Publishing, 2007), p. 30.

11. Savin-Williams, p. 201.

12. Malebranche, pp. 33-34.

13. Savin-Williams, p. 17.

14. Crompton, Louis. *Homosexuality and Civilization* (Cambridge, MA: Belknap/Harvard, 2006), p. 244.

15. Savin-Williams, pp. 47-48.

16. Ibid., p. 78.

17. Ghandi, Mahatma. *Young India, 1919-1922* (Madras: S. Ganesan, 1922).

18. Savin-Williams, p. 51.

19. Crompton, p. 146

20. Ibid., pp. 192-196.

21. McNeill, John J. "Homosexuality: Challenging the Church to Grow." *The Christian Century* (Chicago: March 11, 1987), pp. 242-246.

22. Jones, Stanton L., and Mark A. Yarhouse. *Ex-Gays? A Longitudinal Study of Religiously Mediated Change in Sexual Orientation* (Downers Grove, IL: InterVarsity Press, 2007), p. 94.

23. Ibid., p. 87.

24. Cf. LeVay. Much of LeVay's work on the history of the scientific investigation of homosexuality is concerned with the various "cures" that were tried throughout the twentieth century.

25. Jones and Yarhouse, p. 102.

26. LeVay, p. 53.

27. Cochran, S. D. "Emerging issues in research on lesbians' and gay men's mental health: Does sexual orientation really matter?" (Washington, DC: *American Psychologist*, 11, 2001), quote from p. 932.

28. Jones and Yarhouse, p. 196.

29. Savin-Williams, p. 7.

30. Cf. C. G. Jung, *Memories, Dreams, Reflections*. Audio recording read by Michael York (Boston: Shambhala Lion Editions, 1991).

31. Cf. Garnett, Constance, trans. Fyodor Dostoyevsky. *The Brothers Karamazov*, in *Great Books of the Western World* collection (Chicago, London, Toronto: Encyclopaedia Brittanica Inc., 1952), "The Confession of a Passionate Heart in Verse," p. 54.

32. Jones and Yarhouse, p. 210.

33. Savin-Williams, p. 101.

34. Ibid., p. 81.

35. Ibid., p. 30.

36. Ibid., p. 126.

37. Ibid.

38. Jones and Yarhouse, chap. 8.

39. Ibid., p. 69.

40. Leyland, Winston. *Gay Sunshine Interviews, Vol. 2* (San Francisco: Gay Sunshine Press, 1982).

41. Malebranche, p. 37.

42. Cf. Savin-Williams, pp. 106-107.

43. Cf. Stace, Christopher, trans. *The Golden Legend*, Jacobus de Voragine c. 1260 (New York: Penguin Classics, 1998), "Life of St. Elizabeth." I love *The Golden Legend* — it's tremendous fun, full of wonderful and edifying stories — but as a historical document, it is not beyond criticism.

44. Cf. Hutchins, Robert Maynard, ed., St. Thomas Aquinas. *Summa Theologica*, First Part, Qu. 98. *Brittanica Great Books of The Western World* collection, Vol. 19 (Chicago, London, Toronto: Encyclopaedia Britannica, Inc., 1952).

45. Ibid., p. 190.

46. John Paul II, Pope, and Michael Waldstein, trans. *Man and Woman He Created Them: A Theology of the Body* (Boston: Pauline Books, 2006), pp. 163-164.

47. Ibid., pp. 146-153.

48. Ibid., p. 165.

49. Sacks, Oliver. *The Man Who Mistook His Wife for a Hat* (New York: Harper and Row, 1970), pp. 156-160.

50. *Gay Sunshine Interviews*, p. 214.

51. Ibid., 213.

52. The reference is to an idea that occurs in one of Dostoyevsky's notebooks — that for *The Idiot*, I think. My husband stumbled across it years ago while researching a paper, and it has informed both his and my own thinking about beauty ever since, but I haven't been able to hunt down the reference again since.

53. Cf. Weston, Kath. *Families We Choose — Lesbians Gays Kinship* (New York: Columbia University Press, 1991). In a participant observation and in-depth interview study, Weston found this idea of "families we choose" to be a recurring theme amongst the gays and lesbians whomshe was studying.

54. This was in a magazine article that I read about a pedophiliac halfway house some years ago — a man who desperately wanted to escape pedophiliac urges had found that intense physical pain was the only way to distract himself. I don't recall what publication it was in.

55. Groeschel, Fr. Benedict, O.F.M. *The Courage to Be Chaste* (Mahwah, NJ: Paulist Press, 1985), p. 45.

56. Morrison, David. *Beyond Gay* (Huntington, IN: Our Sunday Visitor, 1999), p. 141.

57. Kirk and Madsen, p. 124.

58. Søren Kierkegaard, trans. Walter Lowrie. *Fear and Trembling* (Princeton, NJ: Princeton University Press, 1941), Chapter 1, "A Panegyric on Abraham." Cited from http://www.religion-online.org/showchapter.asp?title=2068&C=1870.

59. *Gay Sunshine Interviews*, pp. 81-82.

60. Harvey, Fr. John. "The Pastoral Problem of Masturbation" (Courage Web site, 2000: http://www.couragerc.net/PIPMasturbation.html).

61. Whitaker, Rick. *Assuming the Position* (Cambridge, MA: DaCapo Press, 2001), p. 1.

62. Groeschel, pp. 41-42.

63. Malebranche, p. 65.

64. *Gay Sunshine Interviews*, p. 93.

65. Ibid., p. 32.

66. Ibid., pp. 256-257. More recent interviews suggest that this has been settled, at least for the moment, in favor of homosexuality.

67. Ibid., p. 104.

68. Morrison, p. 90.

69. *Gay Sunshine Interviews,* p. 241.

70. Keats, John. "To Richard Woodhouse [October 27, 1818]" from Keats's Letters. *Norton Anthology of English Literature*, Ed. 6, Vol. 2 (New York: W. W. Norton and Co., 1993), p. 836.

71. Crompton, p. 59.

72. Ibid., p. 55.

73. Ibid., p. 270.

74. Ibid., p. 288.

Our Sunday Visitor ...
Your Source for Discovering the Riches of the Catholic Faith

Our Sunday Visitor has an extensive line of materials for young children, teens, and adults. Our books, Bibles, pamphlets, CD-ROMs, audios, and videos are available in bookstores worldwide.

To receive a FREE full-line catalog or for more information, call **Our Sunday Visitor** at **1-800-348-2440, ext. 3**. Or write **Our Sunday Visitor** / 200 Noll Plaza / Huntington, IN 46750.

Please send me ____ A catalog
Please send me materials on:
____ Apologetics and catechetics
____ Prayer books
____ The family
____ Reference works
____ Heritage and the saints
____ The parish

Name _____
Address _____ Apt._____
City _____ State _____ Zip_____
Telephone (   ) _____

                                                      A91BBBBP

Please send a friend ____ A catalog
Please send a friend materials on:
____ Apologetics and catechetics
____ Prayer books
____ The family
____ Reference works
____ Heritage and the saints
____ The parish

Name _____
Address _____ Apt._____
City _____ State _____ Zip_____
Telephone (   ) _____

                                                      A91BBBBP

OurSundayVisitor
200 Noll Plaza, Huntington, IN 46750
Toll free: **1-800-348-2440**
Website: www.osv.com